Protection of Prisoners of War

Protection of Prisoners of War

The Third Geneva Convention and Prospective Issues

Dr U C Jha

Dr Sanghamitra Chowdhury

Vij Books India Pvt Ltd

New Delhi (India)

First Published in India in 2021

Published by

Vij Books India Pvt Ltd
(Publishers, Distributors & Importers)
2/19, Ansari Road
Delhi – 110 002
Phones: 91-11-43596460, 91-11-47340674
Mob: 98110 94883
e-mail: contact@vijpublishing.com
web : www.vijbooks.in

ISBN: 978-93-90917-65-5 (HB)

ISBN: 978-93-90917-66-2 (PB)

ISBN: 978-93-90917-71-6 (ebook)

Contents

Preface

A combatant who falls into the hands of an adverse party during an international armed conflict is a prisoner of war (POW). The history of POWs is as old as the history of warfare. In primitive times, captured warriors were either killed mercilessly or forced into slavery. During the Middle Ages, when the concept of ransom was developed, it became beneficial for warriors to capture wealthy soldiers. Soldiers of lower rank or wealth were killed to reduce the enemy's numbers. During the 17th and 18th centuries, the status of POWs gradually changed and they were afforded certain basic rights; but this was solely dependent upon the captors will. Humanitarian treatment of POWs was not emphasized until the second half of the nineteenth century. International rules of war and universal standards for the treatment of POWs were developed through the First Geneva Convention in 1864 and the Hague Conferences in 1899, 1907, and 1914. The Geneva Convention of 1929 provided that POWs must be treated humanely, the captive nations must provide information about the prisoners held and permit visits to prison camps by representatives of neutral states. However, these provisions were generally violated during the Second World War.

It may come as a surprise to many that during the Second World War, Nazi Germany engaged in a policy of deliberate maltreatment of Russian POWs. It is estimated that out of 5.7 million, at least 3.3 million Soviet POWs died in Nazi custody; the greatest number of deaths occurred between June 1941 and January 1942, when the Germans killed an estimated 2.8 million Soviet POWs primarily through deliberate starvation and summary execution. The deliberate starvation, despite food being available, led many desperate prisoners to resort to acts of cannibalism. After the Second World War, the Geneva Convention for the Treatment of Prisoners of War was revised in 1949 and further supplemented by the Additional Protocols of 1977. The rules relating to the protection and care of POWs have been honoured by a number of States in the last seven decades. However, a few States have failed to implement the provisions on the ground that the type of enemy they faced in the war on terror was not entitled any protection under the third Geneva Convention of 1949 (GC III).

The POW legal regime is facing a number of challenges with the changing means and methods of warfare. Thus, there is a need to re-examine these provisions to ensure that the widely-accepted Convention does not become obsolescent in protecting POWs. Today, traditional means and methods of warfare such as massed armies and artilleries are being replaced by remotely controlled weapons. Some States are also attempting to enhance traditional soldiers into "super-soldiers", a development that may pose several challenges to the implementation of the provisions of the Geneva Convention. Do we have to modify IHL to deal with enhanced soldiers? Are members of special operation forces following the practice of "no quarter" bound to respect the provisions of the GC III? What would be response of a robotic soldier when faced with a wounded soldier? This book tries to find answers to some of these questions.

The book has been divided into seven chapters. The first chapter explores the historical development of the legal regime protecting prisoners of war until the Second World War. The 1929 Geneva Convention for the Protection of POWs was found inadequate in protecting prisoners during the World War. It was updated in 1949 and further strengthened in 1977. The second chapter covers in detail the protection regime available to combatants who are taken prisoners in international armed conflicts. Certain groups of individuals involved in an armed conflict may be denied protection as prisoners of war. These groups viz., spies, saboteurs, deserters, mercenaries, unlawful combatants, personnel of private military and security companies (PMSC), and foreign fighters, have been discussed in the third chapter.

Throughout the history of war, children have been recruited as combatants. To cite a famous example, Carl Clausewitz began his career in 1972 as a 12-year-old lance corporal in the Habsburg army. Children may play a variety of roles in an armed conflict: infantrymen, raiders, sentries, spies, trench diggers, and porters. Child soldiers exist in all regions of the world and need to be protected. The protection regime relating to children in armed conflicts is covered in the fourth chapter.

The participation of women in armed conflicts has grown over the last two decades, both in terms of number and in terms of the variety of roles they have assumed on and off the battlefield. Women may face an increased risk of capture in an armed conflict. The protection available to women as POWs is discussed in the fifth chapter.

The sixth chapter covers in detail the role of the International Committee of the Red Cross, as an impartial, neutral and independent organization, in the protection of POWs. And the last chapter, "POWs in the 21st century", critically evaluates the challenges being faced by the legal regime in protecting POWs in the changing scenario of contemporary armed conflicts. This chapter also suggests certain measures which could supplement the provisions of the 1949 Convention.

The authors express their deepest gratitude to Ms Medha and Ms Chandana for editorial help and to M/S Vij Books for the publication of this book.

U. C. Jha

New Delhi — Sanghamitra Chowdhury

Chapter I

Protection of Prisoners of War: Historical Account

The modern laws of war are designed to limit violence and protect the rights of individuals in times of armed conflict. Finding documentary evidence on when and where the first such rules emerged would be a difficult task, and naming the creator of such laws would be even more difficult. In the early days of conflicts, there was no protection against the maltreatment of those who fought for their tribe or nation, or even of those who did not participate in the conflicts. Large numbers were killed or wounded and the survivors- men, women and children -were at the mercy of the enemy. Victors made little distinction between enemy combatants and enemy civilians, although they were more likely to spare women and children. Men were usually murdered and occasionally taken as slaves, depending upon the whims of their captors. The lives of captives depended upon factors such as their usefulness to their captor and the availability of food. If permitted to live, the prisoner was considered to be merely a chattel- the private property of his captor, who exercised the power of life or death over him. In wars fought over religion, putting nonbelievers to death was considered a virtue. The Old Testament is replete with accounts of the slaughter of soldiers and civilians captured in war.[1]

1 It is estimated that the chronology of the Old Testament covers more than 1500 years, from approximately 2000 BC to 400 BC. The setting of the Old Testament is the ancient Near East (or Middle East), extending from Mesopotamia in the northeast (modern-day Iraq) down to the Nile River in Egypt in the southwest. See Numbers 31 :7-8,17; Deuteronomy 3:6, 20:13-17; Joshua 6:21, 10:35, 37,39,11:11; I Samuel 15:3.

In the Egyptian and Mesopotamian civilizations,[2] instead of being killed prisoners were enslaved. This was not based on any humane consideration for soldiers. It was based on economic considerations. The agricultural economy, which was just beginning to develop in these areas, required manpower and prisoners of war (POWs) constituted such manpower. This custom was, however, not widely followed by other civilizations until the advent of the Roman era.[3] In ancient Rome, a captive who surrendered voluntarily could become a freeman, enjoying a low form of civil freedom. When Greece became the centre of the Mediterranean civilization, it tried to regulate the treatment of prisoners, who had to be offered as ransom to the opponent after the battle. However, the fate of most prisoners of this period was mutilation and death. Only a few were enslaved or sold into slavery elsewhere. Sometimes, the inhabitants of whole towns and settlements were captured and enslaved, no distinction being made between combatants and civilians. At other times, there were massacres to suit the political purposes of the victorious party. By the beginning of the Christian era, exchanges of POWs between opposing generals and ransoming became quite common.

Two ancient civilizations that stand out as exceptions are those of China and India, which had legal codes with humanitarian provisions similar to those found in the modern laws of war. Sun Tzu, in *The Art of War*, the Chinese classic on military strategy written around BC 500, spoke of some important requirements relating to humanity during combat: a commander must show intelligence, sincerity, humanity, courage and dignity; he may utilize captured enemy equipment but must respect POWs. Sun Tzu was of the opinion that in the practical art of war…it was better to capture an army than to destroy it, to capture a regiment, a detachment or a company than to destroy them.[4] The captured soldiers should be treated and kept kindly, he advised.[5]

2 Egypt–Mesopotamia relations seem to have developed from the 4th millennium BCE, starting in the Uruk period for Mesopotamia and the Gerzean culture of Prehistoric Egypt (circa 3500–3200 BCE).

3 Levie Howard S, Preliminary Problems, Prisoners of War in International Armed Conflict, *International Law Studies*, Vol. 59, 1977, pp. 1-96.

4 Sun Tzu, The Art of War, Chapter III, Attack by Stratagem (Para 1), New York: Fall River Press, 2014.

5 Sun Tzu, The Art of War, Chapter II, Waging War (para 17), New York: Fall River Press, 2014.

In ancient India, the laws of war were based on the principle of humanity. Warfare was largely confined to combatants and only the armed forces were legitimate targets. Kautilya's *Arthashastra* (400 BC), one of the greatest political books of ancient India, advocates for the humane treatment of conquered soldiers and citizens. It states that prisoners who are captured in war must be set free by the king.[6] According to the code of Manu (*Manusmriti*),[7] persons not participating in a conflict or pursuing their special avocations or activities or diplomatic errands, unless they are engaged in war, must not be killed. It also says that a warrior must neither injure an enemy who folds his hands to ask for mercy nor the defenceless. The *Agni Purana* clearly mentions that POWs should not be enslaved. If soldiers were taken prisoner, they were to be released at the cessation of hostilities.[8]

A more humane approach developed with the growth of the Christian doctrines of equality and brotherhood. However, nonbelievers were killed with impunity. During the Crusades, both sides slaughtered enemies who fell into their hands.[9] Things improved further with the introduction of the principle of ransom, such as the ransoming of King Richard the Lion heart during the Crusades, and of prisoner exchanges. By the time the Treaty of Westphalia (1648) was signed to end the Thirty Years War, there was

6 Whenever a new country is conquered, when an heir apparent is installed on the throne, or when a prince is born to the king, prisoners are usually set free. Kautilya's *Arthashastra*, Translated into English by R. Shamasastry, Bangalore: Government Press, 1915, p. 212.

7 Smriti means "that which has to be remembered". Unlike the Vedas, which are considered of divine origin, the Smritis are human compositions meant to guide individuals in their daily conduct. They list the codes that should govern the actions of the individual, the community, the society and the nation. They are also called dharma sastras or laws of righteous conduct. *Manu Smriti* is one of the 18 smritis. It has been speculated that in its current form, *Manu Smriti* represents laws that have been added or modified throughout history.

8 Sinha,Manoj Kumar, Hinduism and International humanitarian law, *International Review of the Red Cross*, Vol. 87, No. 858, June 2005, pp. 285–294.

9 The term 'Crusade' designates a variety of military enterprises launched by Christendom from the late 11th to the 13th centuries. The Crusades are a very peculiar episode in the history of human violence that bears resemblance to some contemporary forms of conflict, but is also strikingly different in some respects. If combatants passed the dangerous aftermath of surrender or battle and were fortunate enough to be made POWs, they had to face extremely harsh conditions of detention. Torture and sexual abuse was quite common. Scheipers Sibylle, 2010, *Prisoners in War*, Oxford: Oxford University Press, p. 24–25.

general acceptance of the principle that a captive of war was to be regarded as being in the custody of the enemy state, rather than the individual captor, so that he could not be killed or enslaved. This principle became the basis for developing a code of humanitarian treatment of POWs.

Civilians in the defeated community were only infrequently taken prisoner, for as captives they were sometimes a burden upon the victor. Further, as they were not combatants it was considered neither just nor necessary to take them prisoner. The development of the use of the mercenary soldier also tended to create a slightly more tolerant climate for a prisoner, for the victor in one battle knew that he might be the vanquished in the next.[10]

There is very little literature on the treatment of POWs during the Mughal Empire in India. Akbar used POWs as labourers, who were called *shagirdpesha*. These prisoners were sometimes clad in costumes made from animal hides and paraded before spectators, underlining their status as human prey. By and large, however, the Mughals did not like to keep captives for extended periods. High profile political prisoners were an exception to this rule. Ordinary POWs were disposed of more quickly. Those not singled out for execution or other judicial punishments were released at the end of a war or campaign. The release and exchange of POWs were part of the formal proceedings when the Mughals and their opponents agreed to cease hostilities. Freed prisoners who were still fit and able rejoined the military labour market. Many former enemy soldiers joined the ranks of the Mughal army, especially if their commanders had already been pardoned and taken into service.[11]

In early modern European warfare (from the late fifteenth to the early nineteenth centuries), wounded enemy soldiers were either murdered by the victors or left to die.[12] In the 16th and early 17th centuries some European political and legal philosophers expressed their thoughts about

10 Monarchs who were at war with one another sometimes entered into agreements on the treatment of prisoners, as in the case of France, England and the Holy Roman Empire in 1528. However, the rules and practices of knighthood and chivalry did little in practice to mitigate the horrors of war. Neff Stephen C., 2005, *War and the Law of Nations: A General History*, Cambridge: Cambridge University Press, p. 73-74.

11 Garza Andrew de la, Mughals at War: Babur, Akbar and the Indian Military Revolution, 1500–1605, Unpublished Ph D Dissertation, The Ohio State University, 2010, p. 323.

12 Scheipers Sibylle, 2010, *Prisoners in War*, Oxford: Oxford University Press, p. 42.

the amelioration of the effects of capture upon prisoners.[13] In 1625 Hugo Grotius wrote *On the Law of War and Peace*, in which he explored the basic principles of the humanitarian treatment of the victims of war. He stated that victors had the right to enslave their enemies, but advocated exchange and ransom instead.

The 18th century witnessed new approaches to the question of treatment of POWs. Cornelius van Bynkershoek (1673-1743), who played a significant role in the development of international law, was of the view that "every force is lawful in war"; including the use of poison or incendiary bombs, as well as the hanging or enslaving of POWs.[14] The French philosopher Montesquieu, however, wrote in *The Spirit of Laws* (1748) that the only right that the captor had over a prisoner was to prevent him from doing harm. The captive was not to be treated as a piece of property to be disposed of at the whim of the victor, but was merely to be removed from the fight. Other writers, such as Jean-Jacques Rousseau and Emerich de Vattel expressed similar views, paving the way for the improvement of the treatment of POWs.

The 1785 Treaty of Commerce and Friendship between Prussia and the United States contained modernistic provisions concerning the treatment of POWs. This was perhaps the first international attempt to provide for the protection of POWs. The two contracting parties pledged that they would not send POWs to distant and inclement countries, the East Indies or any parts of Asia or Africa, but would place them in wholesome situations in some part of their dominions in Europe or America; and that they would not confine POWs in dungeons, prison ships, prisons, or put them in irons or otherwise restrain them in the use of their limbs.[15] However, there

13 In wars between sovereign European states, treatment depended on rank. Officers were normally permitted generous freedoms. Upon giving their word that they would not escape nor engage in combat until they were exchanged, officers lodged comfortably and unsupervised in private homes. Common soldiers' treatment depended on the availability of space and food. They were usually granted two-thirds of the daily rations of a soldier in the field and were confined in camps, stockades, or prison ships while they awaited exchange or the end of hostilities. Escape was considered a form of desertion for common soldiers and dishonorable oath-breaking for officers. Judith L. Van Buskirk, 2002, *Generous Enemies: Patriots and Loyalists in Revolutionary New York*, (check title) Philadelphia: University of Pennsylvania Press, pp. 73-75.

14 Neff Stephen C., 2005, *War and the Law of Nations: A General History*, Cambridge: Cambridge University Press, pp. 148.

15 The Treaty of Amity and Commerce between His Majesty the King of Prussia, and the

were grave violations of these humane provisions. In the Revolutionary War (1775–1783) the majority of American POWs, were confined under wretched conditions in floating British prison hulks around New York City. The provisions of this treaty were subsequently adopted by France, which in a decree made on 4 May 1792 declared that POWs were under the safeguard and protection of the nation.

The decree eliminated the three core practices that had been central to the prisoner regime in Europe: exchange cartels, release on parole and impressments into the captor's armed forces.[16] Policy-makers in

---

United States of America; 10 September 1785. Article XXIV of the Treaty provided: "And to prevent the destruction of prisoners of war, by sending them into distant & inclement countries, or by crowding them into close & noxious places, the two contracting parties solemnly pledge themselves to each other, & to the world, that they will not adopt any such practice; that neither will send the prisoners whom they may take from the other into the East-Indies, or any other parts of Asia or Africa, but that they shall be placed in some part of their dominions in Europe or America, in wholesome situations, that they shall not be confined in dungeons, prison-ships, nor prisons, nor be put into irons, nor bound, nor otherwise restrained in the use of their limbs; that the officers shall be enlarged on their paroles within convenient districts, & have comfortable quarters, & the common men be disposed in cantonments, open & extensive enough for air & exercise, and lodged in barracks as roomy & good as are provided by the party in whose power they are for their own troops; that the officers shall also be daily furnished by the party in whose power they are, with as many rations; & of the same articles & quality as are allowed by them, either in kind or by commutation, to officers of equal rank in their own army; & all others shall be daily furnished by them with such ration as they allow to a common soldier in their own service; the value whereof shall be paid by the other party on a mutual adjustment of accounts for the subsistence of prisoners at the close of the war; & the said accounts shall not be mingled with, or set off against any others, nor the balances due on them, be withheld as a satisfaction or reprisal for any other article, or for any other cause, real or pretended, whatever: that each party shall be allowed to keep a commissary of prisoners of their own appointment, with every separate cantonment of prisoners in possession of the other, which commissary shall see the prisoners as often as he pleases, shall be allowed to receive & distribute whatever comforts may be sent to them by their friends, & shall be free to make his reports in open letters to those who employ him; but if any officer shall break his parole, or any other prisoner shall escape from the limits of his cantonment, after they shall have been designated to him, such individual officer or other prisoner, shall forfeit so much of the benefit of this article as provides for his enlargement on parole or cantonment; & it is declared, that neither the pretence that war dissolves all treaties, nor any other whatever, shall be considered as annulling or suspending this & the next preceding article, but on the contrary, that the state of war is precisely that for which they are provided, & during which they are to be as sacredly observed as the most acknowledged articles in the law of nature or nations."

16 On 22 June 1793 the French National Convent passed a decree rejecting release on parole for officers. French officers were encouraged to break their word of honour and

Paris found exchange cartels (exchanging captured soldiers for money) unacceptable. On 19 September 1792 the French National Convent passed a decree stipulating that soldiers could only be exchanged man-for-man and officer-for-officer, but not for money. The French Revolutionary and Napoleonic Wars further transformed the POW protection regime by excluding irregular fighters from legal protection. Irregular fighters, denounced as "brigands", were enemies on a different moral footing. As such they were not deemed to benefit from the protections granted to captured or surrendered regular fighters, and were treated worse than their regular counterparts when they fell into the hands of the French armed forces.[17]

In 1805 the United States agreed that if a war should break out with Tripoli the POW captured by either party should not be made slaves, but should be exchanged, rank for rank, and if there were a deficiency on either side, it should be made up by the payment of 500 Spanish dollars for each captain and 300 Spanish dollars for each seaman. It was further agreed that POWs would be exchanged within 12 months after capture, and that the exchange might be made by any private individual, legally authorized by either of the parties.[18]

The cartel system for the exchange of POWS was well established by the early 19th century. It led to a cartel system for the exchange of POWs, even while the belligerents were at war. A cartel was usually arranged by the respective armed service for the exchange of like-ranked personnel. The aim was to achieve a reduction in the number of prisoners held, while at the same time alleviating shortages of skilled personnel in the home country. By the mid-19th century it was clear that a definite body of principles for the treatment of POWs was being generally recognized in the western world. During the Crimean War (1853-1856), the treatment of prisoners on both sides appears to have been in line with established usage. The sole major advance was the establishment at Constantinople of an organization

to return to the fighting upon their release. The common practice of inducing soldiers to swap sides and join the captor's armed forces was also prohibited by a National Convent decree of 25 May 1793.

17 ScheipersSibylle, Prisoners and Detainees in War, European History Online, 15 November 2011, available at: http://ieg-ego.eu/en/threads/alliances-and-wars/war-as-an-agent-of-transfer/sibylle-scheipers-prisoners-and-detainees-in-war.

18 Article XVI of the Treaty of Peace and Amity between the United States and Tripoli, concluded on 4 June 1805.

to facilitate the transmission of mail between Russian prisoners. In 1856 the United States entered into an agreement with Morocco that in case of war between the parties, the POWs might not be made slaves but should be exchanged, captain for captain, officer for officer, and private for private. The observances of the principles of war in the American Civil War (1861–65) and in the Franco-German War (1870–71) were responsible for introducing many humanitarian provisions for wounded soldiers and prisoners in war.

Lieber Code: In 1862, US President Abraham Lincoln asked Columbia University professor, Francis Lieber, to formulate rules of conduct in war for use by the Union army during the American Civil War. Lieber produced "Instructions for the Government of Armies of the United States in the Field" (also known as the Lieber Instructions or the Lieber Code). The Code was promulgated as General Order No. 100 by President Lincoln in 1863. Though the Lieber Code was not a treaty, it represented a codification of the current usages and customs of war in North America and Europe. The Code consisted of 157 articles and provided detailed rules on the entire range of land warfare, from the conduct of hostilities and the treatment of the civilians to the treatment of specific groups of persons such as prisoners of war, the wounded and so on.[19] According to the Lieber Code, "A prisoner of war is a public enemy armed or attached to the hostile army for active aid who has fallen into the hands of the captor, either fighting or wounded, on the field or in the hospital, by individual surrender or by capitulation, all soldiers of whatever species of arms; all men who belong to the rising en masse of the hostile country; all those who are attached to an army for its efficiency and promote the objects of the war directly, except such as are hereinafter provided for; all disabled men or officers

19 The Lieber Code was divided into ten sections relating to areas of conduct within conflict. **Section I**: Martial Law, Military jurisdiction, Military necessity, Retaliation; **Section II**: Public and private property of the enemy; Protection of persons, and especially of women, of religion, the arts and sciences; Punishment of crimes against the inhabitants of hostile countries; **Section III:** Deserters - Prisoners of war, Hostages, Booty on the battlefield; **Section IV**: Partisans, Armed enemies not belonging to the hostile army, Scouts-Armed prowlers, War-rebels; **Section V**: Safe-conduct, Spies, War-traitors, Captured messengers, Abuse of the flag of truce; **Section VI**: Exchange of prisoners, Flags of truce, Flags of protection; **Section VII**: The Parole; **Section VIII**: Armistice; Capitulation; **Section IX**: Assassination; and **Section X**: Insurrection, Civil War, Rebellion. The Lieber Code represented a codification of the international customary law of the time and would be heavily drawn upon as a basis for subsequent Hague and Geneva law.

on the field or elsewhere, if captured, all enemies who have thrown away arms and ask for quarter, are prisoners of war, and as such exposed to the inconveniences and entitled to the privileges of a prisoner of war."[20] The Code also provided that persons engaged in hostilities without satisfying the requirements for POW status could be captured and summarily shot.[21]

The rules formulated under General Order 100 were given effect in the trial of Capt Henry Wirz, the commandant of the Confederate Army. A special military commission comprising 10 military officers was appointed on 23 August 1865 to try Captain Wirz for the cruel treatment and murder of more than 1000 POWs in violation of the laws and customs of war. These prisoners were in his custody at the largest POW camp at Andersonville, Georgia. Captain Wirz was found guilty on all counts and was sentenced to death. He was hanged on 10 November 1865, at the Old Capitol Prison in Washington DC. This established the precedent of using the threat of punishment as a deterrent against the maltreatment of POWs.[22]

Geneva Convention: Until the middle of the 19th century, there was no multilateral agreement on the rights of POWs. The application of modern IHL to the treatment of POWs is often considered to be a consequence of Henry Dunant's account of the aftermath of the battle of Solferino between French, Italian, and Austrian forces in 1859.[23] In 1863, the Geneva Committee led by Henry Dunant persuaded the Swiss Government to

---

20 Article 49, The American Instructions, 1863 or Lieber Code.

21 The US Department of War, Instructions for the Government of the Armies of the United States in the Field by Order of the Secretary of War, General Orders No. 100, Article 57 (1863).

22 Trial of Henry Wirz, House of Representative, Ex Doc No. 23, 40th Congress, 2nd Session, pp. 850.

23 In 1859, Genevan businessman Henry Dunant travelled to Napoleon III's headquarters in northern Italy to seek land rights for a business venture. He got much more than he bargained for, however, when he found himself a witness to the aftermath of the Battle of Solferino, a gory battle in the Second War of Italian Independence. The horrific suffering Dunant saw impacted him so greatly he wrote a first-hand account in 1862 called *A Memory of Solferino*. But he didn't just write about what he'd observed, he also proposed a solution: All nations come together to create trained, volunteer relief groups to treat battlefield wounded and offer humanitarian assistance to those affected by war. A committee was formedin Geneva to explore ways to implement Dunant's ideas. In October 1863, delegates from 16 countries along with military medical personnel traveled to Geneva to discuss the terms of a wartime humanitarian agreement. This meeting and its resultant treaty signed by 12 nations became known as the First Geneva Convention of 1864.

convene a diplomatic conference in Geneva. The conference and adopted the "Convention for the Amelioration of the Condition of the Wounded in Armies in the Field" on 22 August 1864. This was the first international instrument to define the status of POWs based on the idea of humane treatment. Article 6 of the Convention dealing with wounded or sick combatants provided:

"Wounded or sick combatants, to whatever nation they may belong, shall be collected and cared for. Commanders-in-Chief may hand over immediately to the enemy outposts enemy combatants wounded during an engagement, when circumstances allow and subject to the agreement of both parties. Those who, after their recovery, are recognized as being unfit for further service, shall be repatriated. The others may likewise be sent back, on condition that they shall not again, for the duration of hostilities, take up arms. Evacuation parties, and the personnel conducting them, shall be considered as being absolutely neutral."

Article 8 stated that the details of the execution of the Convention shall be regulated by the Commanders-in-Chief of the belligerent armies, according to the instructions of their respective governments, and in accordance with the general principles laid down in the Convention.

The 1874 Congress of Brussels: On the initiative of Czar Alexander II of Russia the delegates of 15 European States met in Brussels on 27 July 1874 to examine the draft of an international agreement concerning the laws and customs of war submitted to them by the Russian Government.[24] Article 11 of the declaration stated that the armed forces of the belligerent parties may consist of combatants and non-combatants. In case of capture by the enemy, both would enjoy the rights of POWs. Article 21 further clarified that a spy who rejoined the army to which he belonged and who was subsequently captured by the enemy would be treated as a POW and incurs no responsibility for his previous acts. Articles 23 and 25 set out the laws of war which were benevolent and moderate, and they also set forth the modern conception of a POW.[25] Though the declaration was never ratified,

24 The 15 powers were Germany, Austro-Hungary, Belgium, Denmark, Spain, France, Great Britain, Greece, Italy, The Netherlands, Portugal, Russia, Sweden and Norway. The USA refused to participate, basing her objection upon the Monroe Doctrine.

25 Article 23 of the Brussels Declaration stated that POWs are in the power of the hostile government, but not in that of the individuals or corps who captured them. They must be humanely treated. Any act of insubordination justifies the adoption of such

it generated an opinion was for the humane treatment of POWs. As late as 1877 the ancient custom of making trophies of the heads of enemy soldiers was followed in Japan. This practice was also employed by the Chinese; however, in ancient China, prisoners were not always slaughtered.[26]

The Oxford Law: In 1880, the Institute of International Law at Oxford adopted a manual of the laws of war on land. Article 21 of the manual stated that individuals who formed a part of the belligerent armed force were to be treated as POW if they fell into the hands of the enemy. According to the manual, the confinement of POWs was not in the nature of a penalty for crime, nor an act of vengeance. It was only a temporary detention, entirely without penal character. Articles 61 to 78 of the manual provided that POWs were in the power of the hostile government, but not in that of the individuals or corps who captured them. They were subject to the laws and regulations in force in the army of the enemy and must be humanely treated. Their personal belongings, except arms, must remain their property. On capture, every POW was bound to give, if questioned on the subject, his true name and rank, and if he failed to do so, he could be deprived of all, or a part, of the advantages accorded to prisoners of his class. He could be interned in a town, a fortress, a camp, or other place, under obligation not to go beyond certain fixed limits; but was to be placed in confinement only as an indispensable measure of safety. Arms could be used, after summoning, against a POW attempting to escape.

The Oxford Manual specified that in case a POW was recaptured before being able to rejoin his own army or to quit the territory of his captor, he was only liable to disciplinary punishment, or subject to a stricter surveillance. But if, after succeeding in escaping, he was captured again, he was not liable to punishment for his previous flight. However, if the fugitive so recaptured or retaken had given his parole not to escape, he could be

measures of severity as may be necessary. All their personal belongings except arms shall remain their property. Article 25 stated that POWs may be employed on certain public works which have no direct connection with the operations in the theatre of war and which are not excessive or humiliating to their military rank, if they belong to the army, or to their official or social position, if they do not belong to it. They may also, subject to such regulations as may be drawn up by the military authorities, undertake private work. Their wages shall go towards improving their position or shall be paid to them on their release. In this case the cost of maintenance may be deducted from the said wages.

26 Flory William E.S., 1942, *Prisoners of War: A Study in the Development of International law*, Washington, DC: American Council on Public Affairs, pp. 179, at p. 11.

deprived of the rights of a POW. According to the Manual, the captivity of POWs ceased, as a matter of right, at the conclusion of peace; but their liberation was then to be regulated by agreement between the belligerents. Captivity also ceased as a matter of right for wounded or sick prisoners who, after being cured, were found to be unfit for further military service. They were then to be sent back to their country by their captor. POWs could be released in accordance with a cartel of exchange agreed upon by the belligerent parties. They could be set at liberty on parole, if the laws of their country did not forbid it. A prisoner could not be compelled to accept his liberty on parole. Similarly, the hostile government was not obliged to accede to the request of a POW to be set at liberty on parole. In 1906, the Swiss Government arranged a conference of 35 states to review and update the First Geneva Convention. The amendments extended protections for those wounded or captured in battle as well as volunteer agencies and medical personnel tasked with treating, transporting and removing the wounded and killed. It also made the repatriation of captured belligerents a recommendation instead of being mandatory. The 1906 Convention replaced the First Geneva Convention of 1864.

The Brussels Declaration and the Oxford Manual formed the basis of the two Hague Conventions on land warfare and the Regulations annexed to them, adopted in 1899 and 1907.

The Hague Conventions: The principles of humane treatment of POWs were formulated in the Hague Conventions of 1899, and revised in 1907 as the Hague Convention (IV) on the Laws and Customs of War on Land.[27] The 1907 Convention recognized that rights and responsibilities do not apply only to armies, but also to militia and volunteer corps, if they meet the following conditions: (i) have a commander who is responsible for his subordinates; (ii) have a fixed distinctive emblem recognizable at a distance;

27 Following the Crimean War, the American Civil War, and the Franco-Prussian War of 1870, mounting pressures for the codification of the laws of war and their embodiment in international agreements resulted eventually in a series of treaties known as The Hague and Geneva Conventions. Twenty-four nations, including the United States, adopted and ratified the Hague Convention of 1899 with Respect to the Laws and Customs of War on Land. It was supplemented by the second Hague Convention of 1907. These agreements contained identical provisions regulating the treatment and status of POWs and included articles providing for the possible internment of the sick and wounded in neutral countries and for parole. These provisions were applicable to warfare with the so-called civilized world, but not always considered applicable for colonial conflicts against non-white opponents.

(iii) carry arms openly; and (iv) follow the laws and customs of war in their operations. In countries where militia or volunteer corps constitute the army, or form part of it, they are included under the denomination "army".[28]

The inhabitants of a non-occupied territory, who, on the approach of the enemy, spontaneously take up arms to resist the invading troops without having had time to organize themselves in conditions specified above, shall be regarded as belligerents if they carry arms openly and if they respect the laws and customs of war.[29] Further, the armed forces of the belligerent parties may consist of combatants and non-combatants. In the case of capture by the enemy, both have a right to be treated as POWs.[30]

The Convention recognized that POWs were in the power of the hostile government, and not of the individuals or corps who capture them and advocated for the humane treatment of POWs. It said that all personal effects and articles of personal use (except for arms, horses, military equipment and military papers) were to remain in the possession of prisoners. Prisoners were to be detained in a camp or some other place only as a necessary measure to ensure safety and the State could utilize the labour of the prisoners, with the exception of officers, in accordance with their rank and ability. The work was not to have any relation to military operations and the prisoners had to be paid for their work.[31] On capture, every POW was required to declare his true name and rank. If he infringed this rule, he would expose himself to a restriction of the privileges accorded to prisoners of his category. Prisoners remained subject to the laws, regulations and orders in force in the armed forces of the detaining

28 Both the 1899 Convention II and the 1907 Convention IV included a preamble, a body of the Convention containing important administrative matters, and regulations annexed to the Convention containing the substantive rules of land warfare. Article 1 of the 1899 and the 1907 Annexed Regulations specified the criteria for irregulars to have privileged status in identical wording.

29 Article 2 of the 1899 Convention and 1907 Annexed Regulations dealt with the mass levy, i.e., the situation when inhabitants of an unoccupied territory take up arms spontaneously upon the approach of the invader. The 1899 Regulations required only that such inhabitants respect the laws and customs of war, whereas the 1907 Regulations required that they also carry arms openly. The requirements for mass levies to enjoy privileged combatant status omit the two additional requirements for other irregular combatants.

30 Article 3, the 1907 Annexed Regulations.

31 Article 4-6, the 1907 Annexed Regulations.

power, which was responsible for meeting their basic needs; upkeep, lodgings and victuals and, in the pay in case of officer prisoners. They were permitted complete freedom in the performance of their religious duties, including attending the services of their faith, on the sole condition that they complied with the routine and followed the regulations prescribed by the military authorities. After the conclusion of peace the prisoners were to be sent to their homeland as quickly as possible.[32] The Hague Convention of 1907 strengthened the legal status of POWs based on the premise that the capture of a hostile soldier was not an act of revenge or punishment, but a necessary measure to prevent him from participating in military actions.

The Martens Clause appeared in the Preamble to both the Conventions and was worded as follows in the 1907 Convention:

"Until a more complete code of the laws of war has been issued, the High Contracting Parties deem it expedient to declare that in cases not included in the Regulations adopted by them, the inhabitants and the belligerents remain under the protection and the rule of the principles of the law of nations, as they result from the usages established among civilized peoples, from the laws of humanity, and from the dictates of the public conscience."

The Second Hague Convention of 1899 and its Regulations were replaced by the Fourth Hague Convention of 1907 and the Regulations attached to that Convention. There were only very minor differences between the POW provisions of the Regulations attached to the two Conventions. There was only an indirect reference to direct repatriation during hostilities in the Annex to the Hague Convention of 1907. Article 21 thereof stipulated that the obligations of belligerents with regard to the handling of the sick and wounded were governed by the 1906 Geneva Convention for the Amelioration of the Condition of the Wounded in Armies in the Field.

It was specified in Article 2 that the exchange and internment of wounded POWs was optional, dependent upon bilateral exchange pacts:

> The belligerents remain free, however, to mutually agree upon such clauses, by way of exception or favor, in relation to the wounded or sick as they may deem proper. They shall especially have authority to agree: (1) To mutually return the sick and wounded left on the field of battle after an engagement; (2) To send back to their own country

32 Article 20, the 1907 Annexed Regulations.

> the sick and wounded who have recovered, or who are in a condition to be transported and whom they do not desire to retain as prisoners; and (3) To send the sick and wounded of the enemy to a neutral State, with the consent of the latter and on condition that it shall charge itself with their internment until the close of hostilities.

However, Article 2 of the Hague Convention of 1907 stipulated that the conventions would apply only between contracting parties and then only if all the belligerents were parties to the convention. As a result, the POW provisions of the Regulations were supplemented by a number of special multilateral and bilateral agreements[33] which were entered into during the course of a conflict. For instance, the agreement between the USA and Germany provided that the term "prisoners of war" would comprise those officers, officials, non-commissioned officers and enlisted or enrolled persons, male or female, of all branches and corps of the army, navy and marine corps, whether on the active, retired, or reserve lists, who were captured while in the active service of the armed forces of their State of origin. Sanitary personnel were excluded.[34]

The supplementary agreements between France, Britain, and Germany contained provisions regarding exchanges that can be summarized as follows: (1) All POWs (and internees) were to be exchangeable "head for head and rank for rank" after 18 months' confinement. (2) All enlisted POWs (and internees) over 48 years of age, or over 40 in the case of fathers with at least three children, were to be returned after 18 months of captivity. Officers in this category and those prisoners in "poor" health were to be interned in Switzerland or Holland. (3) Exchanged prisoners were prohibited from going within a specified distance of the front.

33 For example, the agreement between Great Britain and Germany concerning combatant and civilian POWs of 2 July 1917; the agreement between the British and German governments concerning combatant POWs and civilians of 14 July 1918; the Final Act of the Conference of Copenhagen, executed by Austria-Hungary, Germany, Rumania, Turkey and Russia on 2 November 1917; the agreement between the British and Turkish governments with respect to POWs and civilians, executed on 28 December 1917; the agreement between France and Germany concerning POWs, executed on 26 April 1918; and the agreement between the USA and Germany concerning POWs, sanitary personnel and civilians, executed on 11 November 1918.

34 Agreement between the USA and Germany concerning prisoners of war, sanitary personnel and civilian prisoners, Treaty No. 531–A, 11 November 1918, Annexure 7, para 1.

Most of the pre-war rules were inadequate in protecting POWs during World War I. Between 6.6 and 8.4 million men were taken prisoner in the war.[35] Germany's disregard of many of the provisions of the Hague Regulations was predicated upon grounds of military necessity and rationalized by the general participation clause. POWs suffered greatly from measures taken in reprisal for the unlawful acts allegedly committed by their respective states. Reprisals against POWs were not prohibited under international law. Germany and France opened 'reprisal camps' where prisoners were subjected to deliberately harsh or humiliating treatment for the alleged wrongdoing of their adversaries. Swiss physician Adolf Lukas Vischer described a psychiatric syndrome among POWs, the 'barbed-wire disease' (severe depression) that involved boredom, confusion, clouding of consciousness and amnesia. By 1917, the French, Germans and British held prisoners in front-line labour companies, in contravention of Article 6 of the 1907 Hague Regulations. The prisoners were subjected to physically exhausting and even life-threatening labour. Harsh measures of coercion, whether in the camps or on labour detachments, were widespread. The prisoners were employed in war-related tasks, often within range of their own guns, and denied access to relief parcels or inspection visits by neutral diplomats.[36] After the war, the German government admitted that it had broken international law, but claimed that both sides deployed prisoners at the front. During 1915–16, a typhus epidemic killed many prisoners on both the sides. On 2 July 1917, at The Hague, Germany and Britain reached an agreement regarding the exchange of seriously ill prisoners.

The War ended on 11 November 1918, but not the captivity of the POWs. The French and British governments continued to retain German POWs as forced labour to help restore the devastated regions. From January 1919 to January 1920, nearly 300,000 German prisoners worked under

35 In the First World War, there were various categories of internment and captivity. The distinction between combatant and non-combatant in relation to POWs was straight forward. With regular armies fighting other regular armies, it was usually clear that the men they captured were combatants who were accorded due rights as POWs under the Hague Law of Land Warfare. However, a large number of civilians were interned as enemy aliens. The forced labour, deportation, internment, and execution of civilians marked the erosion of the standards of legal protection previously afforded to noncombatants. Kramer Alan R., "Prisoners in the First World War", in Scheipers Sibylle (ed.), 2010, *Prisoners in War*, Oxford: Oxford University Press, p. 75-90.

36 Article 6 provided that the 'tasks shall not be excessive and shall have no connection with the operations of the war.'

French command, and some 200,000 under British command, in atrocious conditions, clearing ordnance and debris from fields, trenches and canals. While formally not breaching international law, this 'reparation labour' was a disproportionate punishment for men who had suffered double misfortune.

After the war, Germany faced Allied demands for the extradition for prosecution in war crimes of 52 suspects for the killing of captured soldiers, and 151 suspects for killings and other maltreatment in the camps. The Allies, due to political reasons, allowed Germany to conduct its own war crimes trials before the Reich Supreme Court at Leipzig, which turned out to be a farce.[37]

Several distinguishing features of modern POW law are rooted in the experience of captivity during World War I. In particular, the duration and intensity of wartime captivity gave rise to a conceptual shift in the way POWs were perceived – transforming their status from 'disarmed combatants', to 'humanitarian subjects'. It was also firmly established that there was no place for reprisals in POW law.[38]

The Geneva Convention of 1929

Soon after the War, the nations of the world met at Geneva to devise a new convention to afford civilized treatment to POWs. At the request of the Tenth International Conference of the Red Cross in 1921, the ICRC prepared a draft convention to correct the defects of the Hague Convention IV which emerged during World War I. This draft formed the basis for discussions at the Diplomatic Conference in Geneva in 1929. Unlike the

37 The Leipzig trials are principally remembered for the opportunity they gave the German military to expound its views upon such concepts as 'military necessity' and 'defence of superior orders' which was used to justify the violation of pre-war international norms. Two German soldiers were eventually found guilty of ill-treating British prisoners and were awarded the sentence of six and ten months of imprisonment. These wartime agreements, forty in all, encapsulated a wealth of state practice. Though they passed over some issues, and left others unresolved, they bequeathed to the post-war legislators a body of knowledge that fed directly into the post-war debates over POWs. Wylie Neville, "The 1929 Prisoner of War Convention and the Building of the Inter-war Prisoner of War Regime," in Scheipers Sibylle (ed.), 2010, *Prisoners in War*, Oxford: Oxford University Press, p. 93-94.

38 Wylie Neville and Lindsey Cameron, The Impact of World War I on the Law Governing the Treatment of Prisoners of War and the Making of a Humanitarian Subject, *The European Journal of International Law*, Vol. 29, No. 4, 2019, pp. 1327–1350.

Hague Conventions, the 1929 Convention specified that its provisions were to be effective between the contracting parties even though it had not been ratified by all of the belligerents. Article 89 of the 1929 Convention specified that it was to be complementary to Articles 4 to 20 of the Hague Regulations of 1907 and in fact covered the substance of these regulations except to the extent that they dealt with parole.[39] Forty-six states signed the 1929 Geneva Convention. Most of them, including Germany, Great Britain, France, and the US, had ratified it prior to the outbreak of World War II. The Soviet Union, however, had not. As a result, there were different legal requirements concerning the protection of POWs among the main parties in the War. The Convention of 1929 was the basis of the legal relationship between Germany and its western adversaries, whereas between Germany and the Soviet Union the applicable provisions were those of the Hague Conventions of 1907 and the rules of customary law.[40]

All of the basic principles of 1907 Hague Convention with respect to the Laws and Customs of War on Land remained intact in the 1929 Convention. The major difference was the clarification of those basic rights. Instead of the 16 articles of the Hague Convention, the 1929 Convention had 97 articles directly related to POWs. Article 1 made explicit reference to Articles 1, 2, and 3 of the Hague Convention to define lawful combatants who were to qualify as POW on capture. In addition to combatants covered by the Hague Convention, some civilians were also covered in the section called the "Application of the Convention to certain Classes of Civilians."[41] In Article 2 and 3, the Convention stated, "Prisoners of war are in the power of the hostile Government, but not of the individuals or formation which

39 Esgain Albert J. and Waldemar A. Solf, The Geneva Convention Relative to the Treatment of Prisoners of War 1949: Its Principles, Innovations, and Deficiencies, *North Carolina Law Review*, Vol. 41, 1963, pp. 537-596.

40 The Convention was signed in Geneva on 27 July 1929 and entered into force on 19 June 1931.

41 Article 1 of the 1929 Convention stated that it shall apply without prejudice to the stipulations of Part VII to the following categories of persons: (1) All persons referred to in Articles 1, 2 and 3 of the Regulations annexed to the Hague Convention (IV) of 18 October 1907, concerning the Laws and Customs of War on Land, who are captured by the enemy. (2) All persons belonging to the armed forces of belligerents who are captured by the enemy in the course of operations of maritime or aerial war, subject to such exceptions (derogations) as the conditions of such capture render inevitable. Nevertheless, these exceptions shall not infringe the fundamental principles of the present Convention; they shall cease from the moment when the captured persons shall have reached a POW camp.

captured them. They shall at all times be humanely treated and protected, particularly against acts of violence, from insults and from public curiosity. Measures of reprisal against them are forbidden. POWs are entitled to respect for their persons and honour. Women shall be treated with all consideration due to their sex. Prisoners retain their full civil capacity."

A good example of the changes made in the new 1929 Convention was Article 5. The Convention stated that on capture, a POW was required to state his name and rank, and his regimental number. If he infringed this rule, he would expose himself to a restriction of the privileges accorded to prisoners of his category. The interrogation of POWs to obtain information regarding the situation in their armed forces or their country was not permitted. Prisoners were not to be coerced to provide information related to the condition of their army or country. If, because of his physical or mental condition, a prisoner was unable to identify himself, he was to be turned over to the medical corps. All personal effects and articles of personal use; except arms, horses, military equipment and military papers, were to remain in the possession of a POW. Sums of money carried by prisoners could only be taken from them on the order of an officer and only after the amount had been recorded and a receipt given for the same. Identity tokens, badges of rank, decorations and articles of value were not to be taken from prisoners.

The Convention allowed prisoners to assign a representative, usually the highest ranking officer, to make complaints and recommendations to the detaining power and relief societies. The prisoner was subject to the laws, regulations, and orders of the detaining power. However, the Convention forbade the use of corporal punishment, isolation of a prisoner from his comrades or daylight, collective punishment for the actions of an individual prisoner, and in general any form of cruelty. The detaining power had the responsibility of informing the protecting power of the opening date of the trial of a prisoner. Also, it was to report the sentence immediately to the protecting power. In case of a death penalty, a detailed report concerning the nature and circumstances of the offence was to be forwarded to the protecting power and any interested power. Article 77 of the 1929 Convention dealt with the prisoner information bureau, the idea of which was originally put forth in the Hague Convention of 1899.

The Second World War: In the Second World War, approximately 35 million military personnel became POWs. Depending upon the nationalities of the captive and captor and the period of war, the treatment of prisoners varied from strict adherence to the 1929 Geneva Convention to privation and brutality at the hands of the captors.[42] There were violations of the existing rules, which included individual violations, as well as complete disregard for the humanitarian foundations of the provisions of the Geneva Convention and customary laws. Eastern Europe and the Far East were the two main theatres where customary laws and the Geneva Convention were, for all practical purposes, totally disregarded.[43] Some examples of the violations follow.

- The Geneva Convention stipulated that prisoners were not obliged to give their captors anything more than their 'name, rank, and serial number', but all belligerent powers saw the value of captured enemies as a source of battlefield and wider military intelligence. Thus, prisoners could find themselves subjected to interrogation, which included threats and the use of force if the information sought was required immediately.[44]
- About 9 million Germans, Finns, Italians, Slovaks, Croats, Spaniards, Poles, Hungarians, Romanians, Bulgarians and Soviets fell into captivity on the eastern theatre of operations during the Second World War. The Soviet Union and Germany had no

42 MacKenzie S.P., The Treatment of Prisoners of War in World War II, *The Journal of Modern History*, Vol. 66, No. 3, September 1994, pp. 487-520.

43 Generally, the 1929 Convention was disregarded by Japan in the Far East and the Soviet Union in Eastern Europe, since neither had ratified this Convention. This failure of the Soviet Union was used as an excuse for a German decree issued on 8 September 1941 by General Reinecke stating that the humanitarian rules relative to the treatment of POWs would not be applied to Soviet prisoners. Accordingly, Soviet prisoners were starved, tortured and shot during the winter of 1941-1942. German Admiral Canaris protested against this treatment in a memorandum to German General Keitel, who replied that the objections arose from the military concept of chivalrous warfare, and since there had beena destruction of the ideology, he approved and backed the measures. These gross departures from the minimum international standards of conduct constituted a major part of the indictmentof the Germans before the International Military Tribunal at Nuremberg in 1945–1946 and the Japanese before the International Military Tribunal for the Far East in Tokyo in 1946–1947.

44 Moore Bob, "The Treatment of Prisoners of War in the Western European Theatre of War, 1939–45," in Scheipers Sibylle (ed.), 2010, *Prisoners in War*, Oxford: Oxford University Press, pp. 111–125.

interest in submitting themselves to international law during war. In total nearly 4 million of the captured soldiers died in captivity.[45]

- Hundreds of British POWs were murdered 1940, tens of thousands of Soviet and German prisoners perished after battle on the Eastern Front. In Normandy, the largest war crime was committed in 1944, when 156 Canadian soldiers were murdered.[46] Nearly 1,500,000 Polish, German, Japanese and other prisoners taken by the Russian forces were never released and never accounted for. Countless thousands of others about whom there is information died in captivity, victims of starvation, brutalization, and overwork.[47]

- Soviet prisoners were the first victims of the Nazi policy of mass starvation. They received a ration of only 700 calories per day. Within a few weeks of this "subsistence" ration, as the German army termed it, they died of starvation. Many desperate POWs

---

45 Overman Rudiger, "The Treatment of Prisoners of War in the Eastern European Theatre of Operations, 1941–56," in Scheipers Sibylle (ed.), 2010, *Prisoners in War*, Oxford: Oxford University Press, pp. 127-140.

46 In the words of historian Howard Margolian, they were cold, calculated and systemic acts of mass murder ... a criminal slaughter of Canadian prisoners of war." Col. Kurt Meyer, commander of the 12th Panzer Division, was put on trial for war crimes. He was convicted and sentenced to death, but the punishment was commuted to life in prison. He served five years at the Dorchester Penitentiary in New Brunswick before being transferred to a prison in Germany. He was freed in 1954 with the blessing of the Canadian government, a way to curry favour in the blossoming post-war relationship between Canada and Germany. Margolian Howard, 1998, *Conduct Unbecoming: The Story of the Murder of Canadian Prisoners of War in Normandy*, Toronto: University of Toronto Press, pp. 279.

47 Joseph Stalin's Order 270 from Red Army High Command of 16 August 1941 demanded that: "Commanders and political officers who rip their insignias off during battle, retreat to the hinterlands or give themselves up to the enemy are to be seen as malicious deserters, whose families, as families of law breakers and treacherous deserters, are subject to arrest. All superior officers and commissars are ordered to shoot such men on the spot .... and when a commander or units of the Red Army prefer to surrender, then they are to be destroyed by any means necessary, such as ground or air attack. The families of captured Red Army personnel are to be denied any state assistance or support." It became clear to Soviet soldiers that they could expect no mercy should they return home from German prison camps. Stalin's son Jacob committed suicide in such a camp on 14 April 1943. In most cases, returning POWs were sent to labour battalions or Gulags after the war's end. Whoever collaborated with the Germans had to reckon with death. Overman Rudiger, "The Treatment of Prisoners of War in the Eastern European Theatre of Operations, 1941–56," in Scheipers Sibylle (ed.), 2010, *Prisoners in War*, Oxford: Oxford University Press, pp. 127–140.

tried to ease their hunger by eating grass and leaves. The Germans made little provision to shelter the prisoners, who often had to dig holes in the ground as improvised shelter. In September 1941, a draft order was circulated within the German High Command (OKW) stating that humanitarian rules relative to the treatment of POWs would not be applied to Soviet POWs because the USSR had not ratified the Convention. In many camps, POWs were shot dead when they could no longer keep up with the march because of hunger and exhaustion. In Sachsenhausen alone, 60,000 Soviet POWs died of hunger, neglect, torture, and shooting during the winter of 1941-42. By February 1942, 2,000,000 of the 3,300,000 Soviet soldiers in German custody up to that point had died from starvation, exposure, disease, or shooting.[48]

- On 18 October 1942, the OKW issued an order that Allied commando units were to be slaughtered to the last man, whether or not armed, even if they attempted to surrender. In March 1944, another order was issued for the execution upon their recapture of escaped officers and noncommissioned officers. In the same month, 50 British military officers who had escaped were killed. On numerous instances Allied air crews were handed over to civilians for mob action.[49]

- When 70,000 American and Filipino soldiers surrendered to the Japanese, on 9 April 1942, they were already close to starvation. They were marched 55 miles to San Fernando virtually without food or water. While on march, prisoners were hit with rifle butts, bayonets, lengths of bamboo, and looted golf clubs. They were

48 German political and military leaders regarded Soviet POWs not only as racially inferior, but as potential enemies, obstacles in the German conquest of "living space". The Nazi regime claimed that it was under no obligation for the humane care of POWs from the Red Army because the Soviet Union had not ratified the 1929 Geneva Convention, nor had it specifically declared its commitment to the 1907 Hague Convention. The Treatment of Soviet POWs: Starvation, Disease, and Shooting, June 1941-January 1942, United States Holocaust Memorial Museum, Washington, DC, available at: https://encyclopedia.ushmm.org/content/en/article/the-treatment-of-soviet-pows-starvation-disease-and-shootings-june-1941january-1942.

49 Esgain Albert J. and Waldemar A. Solf, The Geneva Convention Relative to the Treatment of Prisoners of War 1949: Its Principles, Innovations, and Deficiencies, *North Carolina Law Review*, Vol. 41, Number 3, 1963, pp. 541-542.

beheaded for having water stains on their trousers. Nearly 16,000 prisoners died of heat stroke and dehydration.

- After the surrender at Bataan, Japanese soldiers halted men from the 91st Filipino Division and tied their hands together with telephone wire. On the third day, they were all escorted to a ravine near the Pantingan River, where a Japanese officer said: "Dear friends, pardon us. If you had surrendered early, we would not kill you. But we suffered heavy casualties, so just pardon us. If you have any last wish before we kill you just tell us." The Japanese then proceeded to bayonet and behead the prisoners. The Japanese also conducted medical experiments on prisoners, whether they were American, British, Dutch, or Asian.[50]

- On the Allied side, from beginning to end, there was a reluctance to take prisoners. There were cases of American bomber pilots and submarine commanders using machine guns on the survivors of a sunken ship. American soldiers would boil the heads of Japanese captors and sometimes send the skulls back home. Australian soldiers were also known to gouge the gold teeth out of prisoners.

- The treatment of the non-white soldiers serving with the Allied armies on capture varied enormously. The Indians and Africans were singled out for especially bad treatment. Some were executed summarily, a small number taken to Germany either for medical

50 One of the most notorious examples of vivisection performed by Japanese medical practitioners occurred at Kyushu Imperial University. Eight captured American airmen had been placed in a detention barrack. On learning of the airmen's capture, one of the university's doctors cajoled the prison commander to turn the fliers over to the university's medical school for experimentation. Operations on the men were performed on four separate days in May and June 1945. In one operation, a lung was removed from each of two prisoners. On a second occasion, doctors removed the stomach, heart, and liver from two other prisoners. The third experiment led to the death of an airman whose brain was damaged in the course of surgery to examine the function of the trigeminal nerve. Three American fliers were used in the fourth and final test. The doctors operated on stomachs, gall bladders, livers and hearts. All eight men died on the operating table. Roland C.G., "Human vivisection: The intoxication of limitless power in wartime," in: Moore B. and Fedorowich K., (eds.) 1996, *Prisoners of War and Their Captors in World War II,* Oxford, p. 158. A US tribunal in Yokohama in 1948 indicted nine Japanese physician-professors and medical students for conducting vivisections upon captured American fliers. Two professors were sentenced to death and others to 15–20 years' imprisonment. Williams P, and Wallace D., 1989, *Unit 731: Japan's Secret Biological Warfare in World War II,* New York: Free Press, pp. 178–179.

research or as film stunt men, while most were made to work in construction or clearing bomb damage in France.[51]

- POWs were often executed for violations of the laws of the detaining power. A fair trial was rare, for example, prisoners were not permitted to defend themselves or to present evidence in their defence.[52]

- Although the 1929 Convention expressly prohibited reprisals against prisoners of war, even between parties to the Convention violations of protective rules were claimed to be justified as reprisals. For example, 80 German POWs were executed by the French authorities as a reprisal after the occupying German authority had executed 80 French hostages near Lyon in 1944.[53]

The serious violations of the provisions of the 1929 Geneva Conventions and customary laws of war revealed the necessity for the extension and clarification of the provisions to protect war victims. Immediately after the end of hostilities, the ICRC succeeded in securing the convening of another Diplomatic Conference in Geneva. This Conference drafted a new POW Convention with many novel provisions directed at filling the voids which were exposed during World War II.[54] This Convention has been ratified or adhered to by almost every country in the world and has been discussed in the next chapter.

51 Moore Bob, "The Treatment of Prisoners of War in the Western European Theatre of War, 1939–45," in ScheipersSibylle (ed.), 2010, *Prisoners in War*, Oxford: Oxford University Press, pp. 111–125.

52 Fischer Horst, "Protection of Prisoners of War," in Fleck Dieter (ed), 2009, *The Handbook of International Humanitarian Law*, Oxford: Oxford University Press, pp. 370.

53 Ibid.

54 The purpose of revising the Geneva Conventions of 1929 was to clarify ambiguities in order to ensure that belligerents adhere to the intent of international law during war. This required the expansion of existing articles, creation of new articles, and even the generalizing of articles into broader terminology. Three of the most significant revised matters are: the definition of combatant status, the clarification of the authority of protective powers and parties, and the standards for safety, health, and well-being of POWs. Huffman Stephen P., International Humanitarian Law in 21st Century Conflict: A Historical Examination of the Third Geneva Convention Relative to the Treatment of Prisoners of War (1949), and its Applicability in Future War, Master's Thesis, Vanderbilt University, Nashville, Tennessee, 2008, pp. 115.

Chapter II

Protection of Prisoners of War

The 1929 Geneva Convention was applied throughout the Second World War. However, it failed to provide effective protection to prisoners of war (POWs). This led to the perception that the Convention needed modification and expansion in the matters of: (i) widening the scope of the term "prisoners of war", (ii) bringing about changes in the conduct and the consequences of war, (ii) improving the living conditions of prisoners, (iv) providing for stricter regulations governing captivity, (v) assisting prisoners during judicial proceedings, (vi) Expatriating prisoners immediately at the end of hostilities, and (vi) defining the status and scope of agencies responsible for looking after the interests of POWs.

Even before the end of hostilities, the International Committee of the Red Cross (ICRC) embarked on a study of the possibility of revising the 1929 Convention. The available literature was compiled and the points of the law that needed to be expanded, confirmed or modified were highlighted. A draft convention was then drawn up with expert help from governments, national Red Cross Societies and other relief societies. This was used by the ICRC to draw up the complete text of the Geneva Convention Relative to the Treatment of Prisoners of War, which was presented to the XVII International Red Cross Conference at Stockholm in 1948. The Convention was adopted with certain amendments on 12 August 1949.[1] This chapter covers the protection of POWs under the 1949 Geneva Convention and the 1977 Additional Protocol I.

1 Pictet Jean S, 1960, Commentary, III Geneva Convention Relative to the Treatment of Prisoners of War of 12 August 1949, Geneva: ICRC, p.6–9.

Outline of the Geneva Convention III

The Geneva Convention (GC) III contains 143 articles and five annexures. The text of the Convention is divided into VI parts. Part I contains general provisions such as the obligation to respect the Convention, its applicability, categories of persons entitled to POW status, the role of the protecting powers and the activities of the ICRC. Part II (Articles 12–16) lists the provisions of general protection, including the responsibility of the detaining power regarding the treatment of POWs, respect for the person and honour of POWs and equality of treatment.

Part III of the Convention deals with the captivity of POWs and is divided into six sections: beginning of captivity (Articles 17–20), the interment of POWs (Articles 21–48), labour of POWs (Articles 49–57), financial resources of POWs (Articles 58–68), their relations with the exterior (Articles 69–77), and relations between POWs and the authorities (Articles 78–108). Section II, dealing with the interment of POWs, is further divided into eight chapters: general provisions relating to places and conditions of interment; quartering, food and clothing; hygiene and medical; rights of medical and religious personnel; religious, intellectual activities; discipline; ranks of POWs; and their transfer after arrival in POW camps.

Part IV of the Convention deals with the termination of captivity (Articles 109–121), Part V contains information about bureaux and relief societies for POWs (Articles 122–125) and Part VI has provisions relating to the execution of the Convention (Articles 126–143).

Respect for the Convention

Combatants have an obligation to respect international humanitarian law (IHL), which includes distinguishing themselves from the civilian population. Combatants are lawful military targets until they offer to surrender. Soldiers are allowed to kill enemy combatants, with a few limitations; and in exchange for the right to fight and kill others, they assume the risk of being killed themselves. Soldiers are legitimate targets even when they are asleep in their barracks, playing,[2] swimming in the

2 In 1993, Bosnian-Serb soldiers fired mortar rounds at Bosnian soldiers playing soccer in an improvised neighbuorhood field, killing and injuring civilian spectators nearby. The International Criminal Tribunal for the Former Yugoslavia in the case of *Prosecutor v. Galic*[Case No. IT-98–29-A, 30 November 2006], found the Bosnian-Serb commanders guilty of harming civilians, but found no legal violation in the targeting of the sporting soldiers.

lake,[3] retreating, and when they are on leave. Under international law, a child soldier is also a legitimate military target.[4] There is no duty to offer enemy combatants the chance to surrender or to warn them in advance of an attack, nor is there a duty to try to apprehend them alive.[5] Having said that, the state parties to a convention have certain obligations vis-a-vis themselves and vis-a-vis others.[6]

Article 1, common to all four of the Geneva Conventions of 1949, obligates the contracting parties "to respect and ensure respect for the present Conventions in all circumstances". This applies to the High Contracting Parties themselves, their armed forces, other persons and groups acting on their behalf, and their populations as a whole.[7] The obligation to

3 Naked soldiers taking a bath or swimming in a pool remain lawful military target. They may be ineffective or irrelevant in a given situation, but may directly contribute to the success or failure of the campaign. Walzer analysed the issue of targeting the 'naked soldier', first raised by Robert Graves (1929) in his memoir, *Good-bye to All That*. His answer to the question as to whether a soldier stripped naked and swimming in the lake is a legitimate target during an armed conflict is "Yes". Walzer Michael, 2006, *Just and Unjust Wars: A Moral Argument with Historical Illustrations*, USA: Basic Books, p. 139-140

4 If a child is enrolled in the armed forces of a party to an international armed conflict, there seems to be no apparent basis in current IHL to characterize that child as anything other than a combatant. International law prohibits the recruitment and use of children under the age of 15 to participate actively in hostilities. However, such child soldiers constitute military targets under IHL, and the prevailing view is that they may be targeted in the same way as their adult counterparts. There may be moral or pragmatic reasons for avoiding targeting child soldiers if possible, but there is no obligation under international law to treat them differently from an adult fighter. For more information, see: Dallaire Romeo, 2010, *They Fight Like Soldiers, They Die Like Children*, Canada: Arrow Books, pp. 307.

5 Blum Gabriella, The Dispensable Lives of Soldiers, *Journal of Legal Analysis*, Vol. 2, No. 1, 2010, pp. 69-124.

6 In order to fulfill the solemn undertaking it has given under a treaty, the Government must of necessity prepare in advance, that is to say in peace-time, the legal, material or other means of ensuring the faithful enforcement of the Convention when the occasion arises. The proper working of the system of protection provided by the Convention demands in fact that the States which are parties to it should not be content merely to apply its provisions themselves, but should do everything in their power to ensure that it is respected universally. Pictet Jean S., 1960, Commentary, III Geneva Convention Relative to the Treatment of Prisoners of War of 12 August 1949, Geneva: ICRC, p.18.

7 The obligation "to respect" and "to ensure respect" constitutes two different obligations. The duty to "ensure respect" expands the scope of state responsibility beyond liability for the conduct of non-state actors under control of the state. It creates obligations for states to not assist other states (or non-state actors) who violate their

ensure respect also has an external dimension related to ensuring respect for the Conventions by others that are party to a conflict. Accordingly, States, whether neutral, allied or enemy, must do everything reasonably in their power to ensure respect for the Conventions by others that are party to a conflict. The duty to ensure respect by others comprises both a negative and a positive obligation. Under the negative obligation, High Contracting Parties may neither encourage, nor aid or assist violations of the Conventions by parties to a conflict. Under the positive obligation, they must do everything reasonably in their power to prevent and bring such violations to an end.

The undertaking of each party to the Convention to respect it "under all circumstances", together with the concomitant obligation of all other Parties to the Convention to ensure respect for it, results in an obligation which is absolute in character and which is not based upon reciprocity. It is in the nature of a statutory obligation owed to all other Parties, rather than a contractual obligation owed only to a Party's adversary in an international armed conflict.[8] The Convention requires that in times of peace, all preparatory measures, including the enactment of legislation necessary to repress grave breaches, be taken and that the text of the Convention be disseminated, by means of educational programmes, among both the military and the civil community.

The fact that common Article 1 is part of an international treaty means that it is not a loose pledge but a commitment vested with legal force. This was affirmed by the International Court of Justice in the *Nicaragua* case in which the Court considered that the clause reflected a legal obligation.[9] The proper functioning of the system of protection provided by the Conventions demands that States Parties not only apply the provisions themselves, but also do everything reasonably in their power to ensure that the provisions are respected universally. The terms of Article 1 clearly indicate that the

---

obligations under the Geneva Conventions and to prevent and halt other states from violating the Conventions. Dormann Knut and Jose Serralvo, Common Article 1 to the Geneva Conventions and the Obligation to Prevent International Humanitarian Law Violations, *International Review of the Red Cross*, Vol. 96, No. 895/896, 2015, pp. 707–736.

8 Levie Howard S, Preliminary Problems, Prisoners of War in International Armed Conflict, *International Law Studies*, Vol. 59, 1977, p. 29–30.

9 ICJ, *Military and Paramilitary Activities in and against Nicaragua case*, Merits, Judgment, 1986, para. 220.

benefits and burdens of the Convention are to apply equally to both the aggressor and the victim of aggression. An illegal war therefore does not preclude the applicability of the Conventions to war victims.[10]

Applicability of the Convention

Article 2, common to the four Geneva Conventions is a key provision as it establishes the circumstances and conditions under which the Conventions apply. It was a major step forward as it addressed a lacuna in earlier IHL instruments.[11] The provisions of Article 2 were intended to make the GC III applicable in the following circumstances:[12] (i) All cases of war formally declared between two or more Parties; (ii) All other cases of armed conflict between two or more Parties; (iii) All cases of armed conflict between two or more Parties no matter what designation such conflict may be given; (iv) All cases of armed conflict between two or more Parties even if the existence of a legal state of war is not recognized, or is denied, by one or more of them;[13] (v) All cases of the occupation of a part or all of the territory of one Party by the armed forces of one or more other Parties, whether or not such occupation is preceded, accompanied, or followed by armed resistance; (vi) All cases of armed conflict between two or more Parties even if one Power, or more than one Power, to the armed conflict is not a Party; and (vii) All cases of armed conflict involving a Power, or Powers, not a Party, on a reciprocal basis, if the Power, or Powers, not a Party, accepts and applies the provisions thereof.[14]

10 Esgain Albert J and Waldemar A. Solf, The Geneva Convention Relative to the Treatment of Prisoners of War 1949: Its Principles, Innovations, and Deficiencies, *North Carolina Law Review*, Vol. 41, Number 3, 1963, pp. 544–45.

11 The 1899 and 1907 Hague Conventions as well as the 1864, 1906 and 1929 Geneva Conventions never specified under what conditions their application would be triggered. In the absence of any explicit indication, it was generally understood that these instruments applied only during a declared war, with recognition by the belligerents that a state of war existed between them.

12 Levie Howard S., Preliminary Problems, Prisoners of War in International Armed Conflict, *International Law Studies*, Vol. 59, 1977, p. 25-26.

13 Article II concludes with the phrase, "even if the state of war is not recognized by one of them." The literal wording of Article II of the GC III does not cover all of the possible contingencies. For example, during the armed conflict in Vietnam, neither the Democratic Republic of Vietnam nor the US, for different reasons, recognized the existence of a legal state of war.

14 The third paragraph of Article 2 deals with the problem created when one of the belligerents in an international armed conflict is not a party to the Convention. In

Under international law applicable at sea, States in certain circumstances may, lawfully use force against a vessel owned or operated by other States, or registered therein. For example, if the coast guards of a State, suspecting a violation of their State's fisheries legislation, or suspecting that a vessel is transporting illegal cargo, attempt to board such a vessel but meet with resistance.[15] The use of force in the course of such and other types of maritime law enforcement operations is regulated by legal notions akin to those regulating the use of force under human rights law.[16] Such measures, in principle, do not constitute an international armed conflict between the States with which the vessels are affiliated, in particular when force is exercised against a private vessel.[17]

Combatant Status and Prisoner of War

POWs are combatants who have fallen into the hands of the enemy, or specific non-combatants to whom the status of POW is granted by IHL. The fundamental importance of combatant status lies in the fact that combatants who fulfil the necessary requirements are legitimately permitted to participate in armed hostilities.[18] At the cessation of hostilities,

order to encourage belligerents to comply with the provisions of the GC III even if they are not Parties thereto, it provides that contracting parties shall "be bound by the Convention in relation to the said Power (non party), if the latter accepts and applies the provisions thereof."

15 For instance in December 2017, Dutch naval forces intercepted a Tanzania-flagged merchant vessel. The ship was escorted to Santo Domingo, Dominican Republic, where a thorough search was undertaken by the USCG law enforcement detachment (LEDET) who discovered 1,600 kilos of cocaine hidden in a space between the fuel tanks aboard the ship.

16 Maritime law enforcement agents bear responsibility not only for the safety and security of their own team and unit, but also for the safety and security of those under their control, such as the crew and passengers on board a detained vessel. Maritime Crime: A Manual for Criminal Justice Practitioners: United Nations Office on Drugs and Crime (UNODC), United Nations, 2017, pp. 127.

17 For more details on the issue see: Patricia Jimenez Kwast, Maritime Law Enforcement and the Use of Force: Reflections on the Categorization of Forcible Action at Sea in Light of the Guyana/Suriname Award, *Journal of Conflict and Security Law*, Vol. 13, No. 1, 2008, pp. 49-91.

18 The Inter-American Commission has stated that the combatant's privilege is in essence a licence to kill or wound enemy combatants and destroy other enemy military objectives. They cannot be prosecuted for lawful acts of war in the course of military operations even if their behaviour would constitute a serious crime in peacetime. Inter-American Commission on Human Rights, Report on Terrorism and Human Rights, OEA/Ser.L/-V/II.116 Doc. 5 rev. 1 corr., 22 October 2002, para. 68.

a legitimate combatant cannot be prosecuted for acts committed during the course of the armed conflict, unless such acts were in violation of the laws of armed conflict. The prisoners of war have been defined in Articles 4 of the GC III.[19] According to Article 4(A), [20] the following categories of persons, "who have fallen into the power of the enemy" in an international armed conflict are POWs:

A. Members of the Armed Forces: The first of the six categories is "members of the armed forces." This is the most significant category and refers to all military personnel under a command responsible to a party to the conflict. The requirement for membership in the armed forces is not prescribed in international law and is instead a matter of domestic regulation. This first category also includes members of militia or volunteer corps forming part of the armed forces. They are formally incorporated into the armed forces and under the responsible command of a party to the conflict. It may include paramilitary forces that are formally incorporated into the armed forces through the national law of a State. The members of the armed forces are required to distinguish themselves from the civilian population during military operations. Under customary IHL, failure to do so while engaged in an attack or in a military operation preparatory to an attack results in their forfeiting the right to POW status.[21]

B. Members of other militias and members of other volunteer corps, including those of organized resistance movements, belonging to a party to the conflict and fulfilling the four conditions: The second category of POWs consists of members of "other militias and members of other volunteer corps, including those of organized resistance movements, belonging to a Party to the conflict" and fulfilling four prescribed conditions.[22] This category concerns groups that are not incorporated into

19 The relevant treaty provisions regarding combatant status are contained in Geneva Convention I, Article 13(1)-(2), Geneva Convention II, Article 13(1)-(2), Geneva Convention III, Article 4A(1)-(2), and Articles 43-44 of Additional Protocol I.

20 Article 4(A) of GC III mirrors the list of protected persons in Article 13 of GC I and GC II, which provide protection for wounded, sick and shipwrecked military personnel. Wounded, sick and shipwrecked persons covered by GC I or GC II who fall into the power of the enemy are simultaneously protected by GC III as well as GC I or CG II.

21 Customary Rule 106, Jean-Marie Henckaerts and Louise Doswald-Beck (eds), 2005, *Customary International Humanitarian Law*, Vol. 1: Rules, Cambridge: Cambridge University Press, Cambridge, p. 384.

22 Article 4 A (2), GC III.

the armed forces but otherwise "belong" to a party to the conflict. The four criteria, derived from Hague Regulation IV of 1907, are: (a) being commanded by a person responsible for his subordinates; (b) having a fixed distinctive sign recognizable at a distance; (c) carrying arms openly; and (d) conducting operations in accordance with the laws and customs of war. For members of such militia or volunteer corps to be considered POWs upon falling into the power of the enemy, the militia and volunteer corps must collectively fulfil four conditions, each of which serves a protective purpose.[23]

C. Members of regular armed forces who profess allegiance to a government or authority not recognized by the detaining power: The third category consists of members of regular armed forces who profess allegiance to a government or an authority not recognized by the detaining power.[24]

D. Persons authorized to accompany or accompany the armed forces without being members thereof: The fourth category consists of persons authorized to accompany and in fact accompanying the armed forces without being members thereof. The list may include, civilian members of military aircraft crews, war correspondents or civilian contractors authorized to accompany the armed forces providing services such as laundry or transportation. The authorization of a person to accompany the armed forces is evidenced by the provision of an identity card of a similar model to that annexed to GC III.

23 A structured hierarchy can ensure internal discipline and that operations are planned, coordinated and carried out in a way that is consistent with the laws and customs of war. Having a fixed distinctive sign and carrying arms openly facilitates the distinguishing of combatants from the civilian population. The condition that the militia or volunteer corps conduct operations in accordance with the laws and customs of war serves as an additional encouragement for the groups to comply with IHL, in order for their members to receive protective POW status in the event that they fall into the power of the enemy. Arman Jemma, Jean-Marie Henckaerts, Heleen Hiemstra and Kvitoslava Krotiuk, The updated ICRC Commentary on the Third Geneva Convention: A new tool to protect prisoners of war in the twenty-first century, *International Review of the Red Cross*, Vol. 102, No. 913, 2020, pp. 389–416, at p. 397.

24 In the World War II, POW status was denied to certain groups on the basis that the authorities or governments to whom those armed forces pledged allegiance were not recognized by the enemy State. To avoid a repetition of this abusive interpretation, the definition of POWs in GC III expressly includes all members of regular armed forces, irrespective of whether the enemy recognizes the legitimacy of their government or authority. Ibid, p. 398.

E. Members of the crew of the merchant marine or civil aircraft of the parties to the conflict: The fifth category consists of members of the crew of the merchant marine or civil aircraft of the parties to the conflict who do not benefit from other more favourable treatment in international law.

F. Inhabitants of a Non-occupied territory (*Levee en masse*): The sixth category of POWs comprises any inhabitants of a non-occupied territory who, on the approach of the enemy, spontaneously take up arms to resist the invading forces, without having had time to form themselves into regular armed units, provided they carry arms openly and respect the laws and customs of war.[25] This category does not include persons or groups who organize or are organized in advance of the invasion.

In addition to these six categories, Article 4 also sets out two categories of persons who are not POWs per se, but are to be treated as POWs.[26] First, the former military personnel residing in occupied territory who are interned by the occupying power for security reasons because of their former membership in the opposing armed forces and their continued allegiance to an opposing belligerent in an ongoing armed conflict. Although such former military personnel must be regarded as civilians, once interned, they are treated as POWs. The second category of POWs under Article 4B are military internees in neutral countries. Neutral States receiving on their territory members of the armed forces of belligerent parties, including the wounded and sick, are obliged to intern such personnel and to provide them, as a minimum, with the humanitarian benefits and protection afforded to POWs.[27] An important consequence of their POW status is that, in principle, such prisoners may be interned by the detaining

25 The persons under this category do not belong to the State, nor do they require any level of organization, command structure or fixed distinctive sign. The circumstances in which the conditions for a *levee en masse* apply are limited. First, the term refers only to those that take up arms during an invasion period, where territory is not yet occupied, or in an area where the previous Occupying Power has lost control over the administration of the territory and is attempting to regain it. Second, the persons in question must have spontaneously taken up arms in response to the invading army. The persons in this category must carry their arms openly and must respect the laws and customs of war.

26 Article 4B(1) and (2), GC III.

27 Article 4(B)(1) and (2), GC III.

power until the end of active hostilities without any particular judicial or administrative procedure.[28]

The protection under the GC III is applicable to persons covered by Article 4 from the time they fall into the power of the enemy until they are released and repatriated. Should any doubt arise as to whether persons, having committed a belligerent act and having fallen into the hands of the enemy, belong to any of the categories enumerated in Article 4, such persons shall enjoy the protection of the Convention until such time as their status has been determined by a competent tribunal.[29]

Article 5 has two very important provisions. Its first paragraph provides that the Convention is applicable from the time the persons entitled to POW status fall into the power of the enemy until their final release and repatriation. The second paragraph of the article specifically provides that if there is any doubt as to the entitlement to POW status,[30] the individual is entitled to the protection of the provisions of the Convention until his status has been determined by a competent tribunal. The "competent tribunal" in Article 5 of the GC III is often called an "Article 5 Tribunal". In some cases, courts have undertaken to assess whether a detainee is entitled to POW status, but a "competent tribunal" generally means an administrative board consisting of military officers convened by the detaining power.[31]

28 Article 118(1), GC III.

29 Article 5 of GC III reads: "The present Convention shall apply to the persons referred to in Article 4 from the time they fall into the power of the enemy and until their final release and repatriation. Should any doubt arise as to whether persons, having committed a belligerent act and having fallen into the hands of the enemy, belong to any of the categories enumerated in Article 4, such persons shall enjoy the protection of the present Convention until such time as their status has been determined by a competent tribunal."

30 Article 5 only requires a tribunal if there is "any doubt" regarding a person's entitlement to POW status or treatment. For example, if there was no doubt that the armed group to which a person belongs fails to qualify for POW status, then the GC III would not require a tribunal to adjudicate the person's claim to POW status by virtue of membership in that group. Law of War Manual, Department of Defence, United States of America, June 2015 (updated December 2016), p. 182.

31 Regulations issued by the four branches of the US military in 1997 set out detailed procedures for tribunals consisting of three commissioned officers to make determinations of status where doubts arise in accordance with the GC III. Persons whose status is to be determined shall: be advised of their rights at the beginning of their hearings; be allowed to attend all open sessions and will be provided with an interpreter if necessary; be allowed to call witnesses if reasonably available, and to

There has been some misunderstanding about the role of and procedure to be applied by a competent tribunal under Article 5. The purpose of such tribunals, usually established close to the battle zone, is to determine the status of captured belligerents individually, and not to pronounce on their criminal guilt or innocence. The GC III is silent on the procedures to be followed by such a tribunal. Therefore, procedural issues fall within the purview of the detaining power. Article 5 does not specify what constitutes a competent tribunal, so it is left to the individual State's national (military) law to determine. Since the determination of POW status is a question of fact-finding rather than adjudication, it need not be carried out by a judicial body, and is often carried out by an administrative board or through a semi-judicial procedure conducted in the field in the proximity of the actual zone of operations where the individuals in question were captured and are being held. It is fairly clear that the tribunals were not envisaged as judicial bodies obliged to comply with fair trial guarantees. However, they are expected to determination the status of the captured persons on an individual basis, taking into account the available evidence and reasonable standards of objectivity and fair play.[32]

Medical personnel and chaplains retained by the detaining power to assist prisoners are not considered POWs. They are entitled, however, to receive as a minimum the benefits and protection of the GC III, and must also be granted all facilities necessary to provide for the medical care of, and religious ministration to POWs.[33] On a few occasions, governments have granted POW status to those who do not fulfil the conditions of a combatant as laid down in the GC III or AP I. In order to encourage the surrender of guerillas and spies, commanders have sometimes asked the political authorities of their state for special permission to treat unprivileged combatants as POWs. The United States granted limited POW status to

---

question those witnesses called by the tribunal; have a right to testify or otherwise address the tribunal; and not be compelled to testify before the tribunal. Following the hearing of testimony and the review of documents and other evidence, the tribunal shall determine the status of the subject of the proceeding in closed session by majority vote.

32 Gill Terry and Elies van Sliedregt, Guantanamo Bay: A Reflection on the Legal Status and Rights of 'Unlawful Enemy Combatants', *Utrecht Law Review*, Vol. 1, Issue 1, 2005, pp. 28–54.

33 The GC III, Articles 33–35.

enemy captives in the Civil War, the Philippines War, and the Vietnam War.[34]

Additional Protocol I and POW

The definition in Article 4 is supplemented by Additional Protocol I (AP I) of 1977 which excludes spies, saboteurs and mercenaries from POW status. Under the AP I, anyone whose status as a member of the organized armed forces of a party to a conflict is recognized is considered to be a combatant and is entitled to participate directly in hostilities.[35] AP I has simplified the legal position by defining armed forces as all organized armed forces, groups and units which are under a command responsible to a party to a conflict for the conduct of its subordinates. Such armed forces shall be subject to an internal disciplinary system which shall enforce compliance with the rules of international law applicable in armed conflicts.[36] Further, whenever a party to a conflict incorporates a paramilitary or armed law enforcement agency into its armed forces it shall so notify the other parties to the conflict.[37] Any combatant, as defined by AP I, who falls into the power of an adverse party must be treated as a POW.[38] The basic rule is that combatants must distinguish themselves from the civilian population while they are engaged in an attack or in a military operation preparatory to an attack. However, a uniform is not a compulsory attribute of combatants. In case of any doubt, POW status has to be determined by a competent tribunal.[39] A person who fails the tests laid down in Articles 43 and 44 of AP I, after due determination of status, and who would not be entitled to the status of POW under the IHL, would thus be a civilian, protected by the basic humanitarian guarantees laid down in Articles 45(3) and 75 of AP I.

Protecting Power

Article 8 of the GC III is concerned with the operations of the Protecting Power, the neutral power which represents a belligerent in the territory

34 Solis Gary D., 2016, *The Law of Armed Conflict: International Humanitarian Law in War*, Cambridge: Cambridge University Press, p. 225.

35 Article 43(2), Additional Protocol I of 1977.

36 Article 43(1), Additional Protocol I of 1977.

37 Article 43(3), Additional Protocol I of 1977.

38 Article 44 (1), Additional Protocol I of 1977.

39 Article 45(1), Additional Protocol I of 1977.

of its enemy and which has the very important responsibility of ensuring that POWs receive humane treatment and other protections to which they are entitled under the provisions of the GC III. A Protecting Power is selected by the belligerent which it is to represent and must be acceptable to the belligerent in whose territory it is to operate. The mere existence of a Protecting Power is sufficient to ensure more humane treatment of POWs.

Article 9 of the GC III provides that nothing in the Convention is to be considered as adversely affecting the humanitarian activities of the ICRC, or of any other impartial humanitarian organization, the activities of which are, however, subject to the consent of the belligerent concerned. During the Iran-Iraq War there were not only no Protecting Powers, but both countries frequently denied the ICRC access to its POW camps. The Government of Iran held 46, 262 Iraqi POWs, while Iraq had 9,206 Iranian POWs. Finally, the UN Secretary-General sent a special mission to inspect the POW camps in both countries. The special mission reported numerous violations of the provisions of the GC III committed by both sides.[40]

General Protection

Prisoners of war are in the hands of the enemy power, but not of the individuals or military units that capture them. Irrespective of the individual responsibilities that may exist, the detaining power is responsible for the treatment given to such prisoners. Prisoners of war may only be transferred by the detaining power to a power which is a party to the Convention and after satisfying itself of the willingness and ability of such transferee power to apply the GC III. When POWs are transferred under such circumstances, the responsibility for the application of the Convention rests on the power accepting them while they are in its custody.[41]

Prisoners of war must at all times be treated humanely. Any unlawful act or omission by the detaining power causing the death of or seriously endangering the health of a POW in its custody is prohibited and regarded

40 Prisoners of War in Iran and Iraq: The Report of a Mission Dispatched by the Secretary-General, January 1985, S/16962, 22 February 1985. The report stated, "In the interest of the two Governments concerned, conditions should be created to enable the ICRC effectively to carry out all its functions under the Geneva Conventions for the protection and relief of POWs and other victims of war in both countries. The Committee should be enabled, as a matter of priority, to look into the matter of missing persons.

41 Article 12, GC III.

as a serious breach of the Convention. In particular, no POW may be subjected to physical mutilation or to medical or scientific experiments of any kind which are not justified by the medical, dental or hospital treatment of the prisoner concerned and carried out in his interest. They must at all times be protected, particularly against acts of violence or intimidation and against insults and public curiosity. Measures of reprisal against POWs are prohibited.[42]

POWs are entitled to respect for their persons and their honour. Other than the provisions of the GC III relating to rank and sex and any privileged treatment which may be accorded to them by reason of their state of health, age or professional qualifications, all prisoners of war are to be treated alike, without any adverse distinction based on race, nationality, religious belief or political opinion. Women POWs are to be treated with the regard due to their sex.[43] The power detaining POWs is bound to provide, free of charge, for their maintenance and for the medical attention required by their state of health. Under no circumstances can POWs renounce in part or in entirety the rights secured to them by the third Geneva Convention.[44]

Captivity of Prisoners of War

Questioning of prisoners: A POW is expected to be thoroughly searched immediately upon his capture, both to ensure that he has no hidden weapons/ articles which might facilitate escape, and to ascertain whether he has in his possession any documents or other items of intelligence value. The GC III preserves to him his own personal property as well as certain types of equipment of military issue. Article 17 of the GC III is the key provision relating to the questioning of POWs. It stipulates that captured combatants are only required to give a minimal amount of identifying information. APOW, when questioned, is bound to give his surname, first

42 Article 13, GC III.

43 Nine different provisions of the GC III have provisions related specifically. They have two basic aims: (i) to guarantee to women POWs treatment as favourable as that accorded to male POWs; and (ii) to afford them protection from sexual molestation to the maximum extent possible. Article 25 provides that if women are interned in a POW camp with men, they are to be billeted in separate dormitories. Article 29 states that toilet facilities (conveniences) are to be available for the use of POWs day and night, and such facilities shall be separately provided for women POWs.

44 Articles 14-16, GC III.

name and rank, date of birth, and army, regimental, personal or serial number, or equivalent information.[45]

Article 17 of the GC III replaced the provision in the 1929 Geneva Convention that no pressure shall be exerted on prisoners to obtain information regarding the situation in their armed forces or their country. According to the ICRC commentary, the many violations that occurred during World War II led drafters of the 1949 Convention to expand the provision to cover "information of any kind whatever," and prohibit not only "coercion" but also "physical or mental torture". Thus, no physical or mental torture, nor any other form of coercion, is to be inflicted on POWs to secure from them information of any kind whatever. Coercion is also prohibited to elicit confessions to be used against POWs during their trial. Prisoners of war who refuse to answer may not be threatened, insulted, or exposed to unpleasant or disadvantageous treatment of any kind. It must be noted that the provision does not prohibit the detaining power from seeking any particular kind of information. It prohibits only the methods mentioned. A POW could therefore be questioned on his involvement in alleged war crimes. POW status does not prevent a prisoner from being tried for crimes committed before capture.

The questioning must be done in a language which the POW understands. If he willfully refuses to answer these questions, he may render himself liable to a restriction of the privileges accorded to him by virtue of his rank or status.

POWs are free to provide more information than is required by Article 17 and this can be done at any time, whether at the point of capture or afterwards. Such information could include the names and addresses of

45 In practice, immediately upon capture POWs are disarmed and searched for concealed weapons by the capturing troops and all articles which could be turned into dangerous weapons or tools for escape are removed. Sometimes, due to hostile action or a large number of prisoners, an immediate search is impracticable, but the process is not be delayed too long; otherwise prisoners might have the chance to dispose of some valuable documents they may be carrying. Capturing forces especially guard against the destruction of documents, many of which are highly useful as information sources or aids in the questioning/ interrogation process. As soon after capture as possible, enemy officers, non-commissioned officers, lower ranks, deserters, and civilians are segregated to the extent possible. These segregated groups are maintained throughout the journey to the rear. This step is taken in order to prevent the surreptitious whispering of orders or threats by POWs of higher rank to their subordinates and to maintain the breakdown of morale.

their next of kin, so that these can be notified of their capture; their blood group; or their religion. Information on religion is to be taken into account in matters of food and daily routine and to enable prisoners to enjoy "complete latitude in the exercise of their religious duties", have access to ministers of their religion and have the appropriate rites performed in case of death.

Prisoners who, owing to their physical or mental condition, are unable to state their identity, are to be handed over to the medical service. Each party to a conflict is required to furnish POWs with an identity card containing at least the bearer's surname, first name, date of birth, rank, and army/regimental/personal/serial number or equivalent information. Additional information may be added to the card at each party's discretion.

The identity of a POW must be communicated without delay to their country of origin and their families through national information bureaux and the ICRC's Central Tracing Agency. The same channels of communication are to be used throughout captivity for notification of transfers, releases, repatriations, escapes, hospitalizations and deaths, and to respond to any enquiries concerning the fate of individual POWs.[46]

Property of POWs: All effects and articles of personal use, except arms, military equipment and documents, must remain in the possession of a POW. A POW must be in possession of identity documents issued by the detaining power. Badges of rank and nationality, decorations and articles having personal or sentimental value must not be taken from a POW. A receipt for the sum of money held by a POW must be issued to the POW by an officer of the detaining power and a record of it must be made in a register. The detaining power may withdraw articles of value from POWs only for reasons of security. The procedure laid down for sums of money impounded applies to such articles. Such articles and money must be returned to POWs at the end of their captivity.[47] One of the issues which have not been dealt with in the GC III is whether a POW has the right to sell his personal belongings and the right of the military personnel of the detaining power to buy such articles from POWs.

46 Articles 70, 122 and 123 of GC III.

47 Article 18, GC III.

Evacuation

The detaining power is responsible for the well-being of its POWs from the moment they fall into its power. This includes not only refraining from prohibited acts, but also protecting the prisoners' lives and well-being. POWs must be evacuated, as soon as possible after their capture, to camps situated far enough from the combat zone for them to be out of danger. Only those who, owing to wounds or sickness, would run greater risks in being evacuated than in remaining where they are, may be temporarily kept back in a danger zone. They should not be unnecessarily exposed to danger while awaiting evacuation from a fighting zone.

The evacuation of POWs must be effected humanely and in conditions similar to those for the change of station of the forces of the detaining power. Article 22 of the GC III sets forth the general requirements and prohibitions governing the selection of POW camp sites. They must be located on land and must afford every guarantee of hygiene and health fulness. They must not, except in unusual circumstances, be located in a penitentiary and must not be in unhealthful areas, or where the climate is injurious for the POWs. The third paragraph of Article 23 requires the detaining power to provide "the powers concerned", i.e., the power of origin of the POWs and its allies, information on the geographical location of POW camps. The camps must be marked with the letters "PW" so as to be visible from the air.[48] The detaining power must supply POWs with sufficient food, drinking water, necessary clothing and medical attention and must ensure their safety during evacuation. If POWs must pass through transit camps during evacuation, their stay in such camps must be brief.[49]

Internment

During their internment, POWs benefit from a detailed regime of rights and protections contained in the Third Geneva Convention. The detaining power may intern POWs and impose on them the obligation of not leaving, beyond certain limits, the camp where they are interned, or if the said camp

48 No such provisions were contained in the 1929 Geneva Convention, and POW camps were sometimes attacked by aircraft of their own forces, or of its allies, unaware of the actual nature of the installation being attacked. However, the height at which modern bombers fly and the speed at which low-flying aircraft travel may make it difficult to identify POW camps.

49 Articles 19-20, GC III.

is fenced in, of not going outside its perimeter. POWs may not be held in close confinement except where necessary to safeguard their health. The may be partially or wholly released on parole or promise, however, they cannot be compelled to accept liberty on parole or promise. Upon the outbreak of hostilities, each party to the conflict is to notify the adverse party of the laws and regulations allowing or forbidding its own nationals to accept liberty on parole or promise.[50]

Quarters, food and clothing: POWs must be quartered under conditions as favourable as those for the forces of the detaining power who are billeted in the same area, making allowances for the habits and customs of the prisoners, and in no case prejudicial to their health. The premises provided for the use of POWs must be protected from dampness and adequately heated and lighted, in particular, between dusk and lights out. All precautions must be taken against the danger of fire. Separate dormitories must be provided for women POWs in mixed camps.

The daily food rations must be sufficient in quantity, quality and variety to keep POWs in good health and to prevent loss of weight or the development of nutritional deficiencies. POWs who work must be supplied with such additional rations as are necessary for the labour on which they are employed. Sufficient drinking water must be supplied to POWs. They should be associated with the preparation of their meals and may be employed in the kitchens. The habitual diet of the various national groups must be taken into consideration. The use of tobacco is permitted. Adequate premises should be provided for messing. Collective disciplinary measures affecting food are prohibited.[51]

50 Article 21, GC III.

51 Article 26, GC III provides: "The basic daily food rations shall be sufficient in quantity, quality and variety to keep POWs in good health and to prevent loss of weight or the development of nutritional deficiencies." Collective disciplinary measures affecting food are prohibited. However, the use of food as an inducement to recalcitrant POWs to restore order in a POW camp is permissible. During the rioting at Koje-do in Korea in 1952, in order to move recalcitrant Communist POWs to smaller, more manageable, POW compounds, the military authorities of the United Nations Command made food available in the small compounds and refused to make it available in the old, large compounds. If the POW wanted to eat, he had to move to the new compound. The ICRC delegate took the position that this was collective punishment involving food. The UN Command took the position that as food was available in the new compounds, to which the POWs were free to move, there was no denial of food to them.

Clothing, underwear and footwear must be supplied to POWs in sufficient quantities by the detaining power, making allowance for the climate of the region where they are detained. The regular replacement and repair of the clothing articles must be ensured. In addition, POWs who work must be provided clothing that is appropriate for the nature of the work.

All camps must have canteens where POWs may procure foodstuff, soap, tobacco and articles of daily use. The tariff must never exceed local market prices. The profits made by canteens must be used for the benefit of the prisoners, and a representative[52] of the prisoners must be associated with the management of the canteen and its funds.[53]

Hygiene and medical attention: The detaining power is bound to take all sanitary measures necessary to ensure the cleanliness and hygiene of camps and to prevent epidemics. Prisoners must have for their use, day and night, conveniences which conform to the rules of hygiene and are maintained in a constant state of cleanliness. In camps in which women POWs are accommodated, separate conveniences are to be provided for them. Prisoners must be provided with sufficient water and soap for their personal toilet and for washing their personal laundry.

Every camp must have an adequate infirmary where prisoners may receive the required medical attention and appropriate diet. Prisoners suffering from a serious disease or condition necessitating special treatment, surgical operation or hospital care, must be admitted to a military or civilian medical unit where such treatment can be administered. Special facilities should be afforded for the disabled, in particular the blind. Prisoners must not be prevented from presenting themselves to the medical authorities for examination. The detaining authorities must, upon request, issue to every prisoner who has undergone treatment, an official certificate indicating the nature of his illness or injury, and the duration and kind of treatment

52 At every POW camp where there are no officers, prisoners freely elect spokesmen by secret ballot to represent them before the military authorities, the Protecting Powers, the ICRC and other organizations which may assist them. In camps for officers and persons of equivalent status, or in mixed camps, the senior officer is recognized as the representative. In officer camps, he is assisted by one or more advisers chosen by the officer prisoners. In mixed camps the assistants are elected by the prisoners who are not officers. Every representative elected must be approved by the camp commander before he has the right to commence his duties.

53 Articles 25-28 GC III.

received. A duplicate of this certificate should be forwarded to the Central Prisoners of War Agency.

Prisoners must have opportunities for taking physical exercise, including sports and games, and for being out of doors. Sufficient open spaces must be provided for this purpose in all camps. Regular medical inspections of prisoners must be held at least once a month, during which the weight of each prisoner must be checked and recorded. Also, the general state of health, nutrition and cleanliness of prisoners must be examined to detect contagious diseases, especially tuberculosis, malaria and venereal disease. The most efficient methods available shall be employed for this purpose, e.g. periodic mass miniature radiography for the early detection of tuberculosis.

If any prisoner considers himself incapable of working, he must be permitted to appear before the medical authorities. The medial authorities may recommend that prisoners who are unfit for work, be exempted. Prisoners have the right to make requests regarding their conditions of captivity to the military authorities in whose power they are. Their representatives may send periodic reports on the situation in the camps and the needs of the prisoners to the representatives of the protecting powers.[54]

Religious duties: The detaining power may retain religious personnel of the opposing armed forces and require them to exercise their spiritual functions for the benefit of their captured comrades. POWs must be allowed to freely exercise their religion and to attend the services of their faith in premises adequate for that purpose. Retained religious personnel are ministers of their religion and must be allowed to freely exercise their ministry.[55]

Recreation, sports and games: The detaining power must encourage POWs to engage in intellectual, educational, and recreational activities, including sports and games, and provide them with the time, premises and equipment necessary for that purpose.[56]

Discipline, administration and saluting: Every POW camp must be put under the immediate authority of a commissioned officer belonging to

54 Articles 29-32, GC III.

55 Articles 34-37, GC III.

56 Article 38, GC III.

the regular armed forces of the detaining power and responsible for the application of the GC III. POWs, except officers, must salute and show respect to all officers of the detaining power. POWs who are officers must salute the camp commander regardless of his rank. The wearing of badges of rank and nationality, as well as of decorations, must be permitted. Every order and command addressed to POWs must be given in a language they understand. The text of the GC III and of any special agreement concluded between the belligerent parties must be posted inside the POW camp in a language the prisoners understand. Throughout their captivity, POWs remain subject to camp discipline. The detaining authority may, within the terms of the GC III, take all reasonable measures to prevent or suppress riots, escapes or similar acts of disobedience. However, the use of weapons against POWs, especially against those who are escaping or attempting to escape, constitutes an extreme measure and must always be preceded by warnings appropriate to the circumstances.[57]

Transfer of POWs: When deciding to transfer POWs, the detaining power must take into account the interests of the prisoners. The transfer must be effected humanely, and POWs must be issued with sufficient food, drinking water and necessary clothing during the transfer. Sick or wounded prisoners must not be transferred as long as their recovery may be endangered by the journey, unless their safety imperatively demands it. In the event of transfer, POWs must be officially informed of their departure and their new postal address to facilitate packing and to inform their next of kin. The costs of the transfer must be borne by the detaining power.[58]

Labour: The detaining power may utilize the labour of POWs who are physically fit, taking into account their age, sex, rank and physical aptitude. Non-commissioned officers who are POWs shall only be required to do supervisory work. Officers must not be compelled to work under any circumstances. Besides work connected with camp administration, installation or maintenance, POWs may be compelled to do work of the following classes: agriculture; industries connected with the production or extraction of raw materials and other building operations; transport and handling of stores; commercial business and public utility service; provided they have no military character or purpose. POWs must be provided with suitable working conditions. Unless a POW volunteers, he

57 Articles 39-42, GC III.

58 Articles 46-48, GC III.

may not be employed on labour which is of an unhealthy or dangerous nature, for example, the removal of mines or similar devices. POWs must not be assigned to labour which would be looked upon as humiliating for a member of the detaining power's own forces. The duration of daily labour must not be excessive and must not exceed that of nationals of the detaining power employed on the same work.[59]

POWs must be paid a fair rate of pay by the detaining authorities. All POWs are entitled to receive from the detaining power a monthly advance of pay commensurate with their rank in their country of origin. Prisoners must also be allowed to receive supplementary payments from their country of origin, and to receive or send funds through money transfers. In all cases, however, the detaining power may limit the maximum amount of money in cash that prisoners may have in their possession.[60]

Relations of POWs with the exterior: As soon as POWs have fallen into its power, the detaining power must inform of their capture to the powers to which they belong through the protecting power. Immediately upon capture, or not more than one week after arrival at a camp, every POW must be enabled to write to his family and to the Central Prisoners of War Agency, about his capture, address and state of health.[61] Prisoners undergoing confinement must be granted the right to read and write and to send and receive correspondence. They must also be allowed to receive, by post or by any other means, individual parcels or collective shipments containing foodstuff, clothing, medical supplies and articles of a religious, educational or recreational character, including books, devotional articles, scientific equipment, examination papers, musical instruments, sports outfits and materials allowing them to pursue their studies or their cultural activities. All POW correspondence is censored, and all mail addressed to POWs is examined in accordance with the Geneva Convention and military regulations.

All correspondence to and from POWs is exempt from postal dues, both in the countries of origin and destination and in any intermediate countries. No paper, document, note, or written message may be delivered by a POW, directly to any person visiting a camp. Mail must be conveyed by

59 Articles 49-54, GC III.

60 For more details of financial resources of POWs see Article 58-68, GC III.

61 Article 123, GC III.

the most rapid method at the disposal of the detaining power and may not be delayed or retained for disciplinary reasons. The censoring of correspondence addressed to POWs or dispatched by them must be done as quickly as possible. Mail may be censored only by the dispatching State and the receiving State, and once only by each.[62]

Relations of POWs with the authorities: POWs must have an unrestricted right to make requests and complaints regarding their conditions of internment to the detaining power, the representatives of the protecting power or ICRC delegates. They should be represented by the most senior officer among them or, in the absence of officers, by a prisoner elected by his comrades and approved by the detaining power. The detaining power must afford such "prisoners' representatives" the time, facilities and freedom of movement necessary to accomplish their duties in terms of inspection, representation and communication.[63]

Penal and disciplinary sanctions

There is a possibility that POWs may commit or violate provisions of the laws, rules, and regulations of the detaining power specifically governing their conduct. The detaining power shall be justified in taking judicial or disciplinary measures in respect of any offence committed by a POW against such laws or regulations.[64] The GC III is based on the principle that POWs subjected to disciplinary or judicial proceedings and sanctions should be given the same rights, protection and treatment as members of the armed forces of the detaining power in the same situation. This applies not only to the question of whether the case should be adjudicated by a military or civilian court, but also to the nature of the penalties and to the treatment and living conditions of prisoners during the execution of such penalties.

The GC III provides necessary safeguards to protect POWs against arbitrary and inhumane action on the part of the detaining power. No

62 Articles 69–77, GC III.

63 For more details, see Articles 78–81, GC III.

64 The 1907 Hague Regulations deal with the subject of the punishment of POWs in Article 8 in a general manner. The Geneva Convention of 1929 includes 23 articles (Articles 45–67) on the subject. The GC III of 1949 includes 27 such articles (Articles 82–108). Most of these provisions are procedural in nature, imposing additional restrictions on the imposition of punishment on POWs by the detaining power.

proceedings or punishments contrary to Chapter III of the GC III are permitted. In deciding whether proceedings concerning an alleged offence shall be judicial or disciplinary, the detaining power must ensure that the competent authorities exercise the greatest leniency and adopt, wherever possible, disciplinary rather than judicial measures. Article 82, paragraph 2, places a specific limitation upon the detaining power with respect to any laws, regulations, or orders promulgated by it to govern the conduct of POWs. If such a law, regulation, or order makes punishable acts that are not punishable when committed by a member of the armed forces of the detaining power, the maximum punishment imposable may be of a disciplinary nature only.

A POW must be tried only by a military court,[65] unless the existing laws of the detaining power expressly permit civil courts to try a member of the armed forces of the detaining power in respect of the alleged offence committed by the POW. A prisoner must never be tried by a court which does not follow the essential guarantees of independence and impartiality and does not afford the accused the rights of defence provided in Article 105. Article 96 of the GC III prohibits the delegation of disciplinary powers over POW to another senior POW. A prisoner must not be punished more than once for the same act or on the same charge. Article 88 provides that once a POW has completed his punishment he "may not be treated differently from other POWs". Collective punishment for individual acts, corporal punishment, imprisonment in premises without daylight and, in general, any form of torture or cruelty, are forbidden. A prisoner must not be deprived of his rank by the detaining power, or prevented from wearing his badges.

POWs undergoing a disciplinary or judicial punishment must not be subjected to more severe treatment than that applied in respect of the same punishment to members of the armed forces of the detaining power of equivalent rank. A woman POW must not be sentenced to a punishment

---

65 In practice, every POW camp is placed under the command of a commissioned officer of the armed forces. Copies of the Geneva Convention and its annexes and special agreements are posted in every camp in the language of the POWs. Copies must be supplied, upon request, to those prisoners who cannot have access to the posted copy. All regulations, orders, and notices must be issued or addressed in a language which is understood by the prisoners. Disciplinary measures are normally imposed by the military commander designated as the POW camp commander, who may delegate his disciplinary powers to one of his officers.

more severe or treated more severely than a woman member of the armed forces of the detaining power dealt with for a similar offence.[65]

Article 75(4) is particularly significant. It provides: "No sentence may be passed and no penalty may be executed on a person found guilty of a penal offence relating to the armed conflict except pursuant to a conviction pronounced by an impartial and regularly constituted court respecting the generally recognized principles of regular judicial procedure."

Disciplinary punishments: Disciplinary punishments must not be inhuman, brutal or dangerous to the health of prisoners. Article 89 specifies the four types of punishment that may be imposed upon a POW: (i) Fine, which shall not exceed 50% of the advances of pay and working pay which the POW would otherwise receive under the provisions of Articles 60 and 62 during a period of not more than 30 days; (ii) Discontinuance of privileges granted over and above the treatment provided for by the GC III; (iii) Fatigue duties, but not applicable to officers;[67] and (iv) Confinement. These four types of punishment are exclusive; no other punishment may be imposed as a result of disciplinary proceedings, even if the laws of the detaining power permit the imposition of additional types (or more severe punishment) upon members of its armed forces.

Articles 97 and 98 of the GC III contain detailed and specific rules concerning the conditions under which confinement imposed upon a POW as disciplinary punishment is to be served. POWs undergoing disciplinary punishment may not be confined in a penitentiary type of establishment; the establishment in which they are confined must meet the sanitary requirements of Article 25 of the GC III and the confined POWs must be able to maintain their personal cleanliness as required by Article 29. They must be permitted to attend the daily medical inspection, to receive any appropriate medical treatment and, if necessary, to be removed to a medical facility. POWs must be allowed at least two hours of exercise daily in the open air; they must continue to be accorded the benefits of the Convention including the rights granted by Article 78 to make complaints

66 Article 88, GC III.

67 This punishment consists of extra duty, which may be beyond regular working hours and beyond normal duty-roster assignments, such as policing of the POW camp grounds, cleaning activities and kitchen duties. Extra fatigue duty as disciplinary punishment is limited to 2 hours per day; and Article 90 limits the overall duration to 90 days.

with respect to the conditions of their confinement and to confer privately with representatives of the protecting power.

Officer POWs may not be confined in the same quarters as non-commissioned officers or enlisted men; and no POW may be deprived of the prerogatives attached to his rank. Article 90 specifies that this rule is applicable even if the disciplinary proceedings are connected with several different acts of misconduct, related or unrelated, of the POWs. It is necessary that the disciplinary punishment be put into effect within one month of being imposed. When a second disciplinary punishment is imposed upon a POW (for example, for some act committed while he is serving the punishment imposed earlier), and either of the two punishments exceeds 10 days in duration, a period of at least 3 days must elapse between the conclusion of the first punishment and the commencement of the second.

Article 97 of the GC III provides that women POWs undergoing disciplinary punishment shall be confined in separate quarters from male POWs. Article 108 contains the same provision with respect to women POWs undergoing punishment after conviction of a penal offence. Both of these articles provide further that women POWs so confined shall be under the supervision of women.

Judicial proceedings: Articles 99–108 of the GC III deal with judicial proceedings against a POW. A POW must not be tried or sentenced for an act which is not forbidden by the law of the detaining power or by international law in force at the time the said act was committed.[68] No moral or physical coercion may be exerted on a prisoner to induce him to plead guilty of the act of which he is accused. He may not be convicted without having had an opportunity to present his defence and the assistance of a qualified counsel.

Article 103 of the GC III directs that the judicial investigation of an alleged offence committed by a POW be conducted as rapidly as circumstances permit so that the trial, if any, may take place as soon as possible. Article 103 prohibits placing a POW in pretrial confinement unless a member of the armed forces of the detaining power charged with a similar offence

68 Article 99 of the GC III places a ban on *ex post facto* criminal laws. It prohibits the punishment of a POW for the commission of an act that was not an offence against the law of the detaining power or against international law at the time it was allegedly committed.

would be so confined. The prisoner is entitled to a bundle of rights for his defence.[69] He must be advised of these rights by the detaining power before the trial. Failing a choice by the prisoner, the protecting power must provide a counsel for his defence at the trial. The prisoner must have the right to appeal against a sentence, in the same manner as do the members of the armed forces of the detaining power. He must be informed of his right to appeal and of the time limit within which he may do so. The GC III contains very little with respect to the actual conduct of the trial of a POW.

Death sentence: Article 100 of the GC III requires that POWs and the protecting power be informed "as soon as possible" of the offences punishable by death under the laws of the detaining power. This accomplishes the double purpose of making such offences known to the protecting power and freezing the list as on the date of the notification. Other offences shall not thereafter be made punishable by the death penalty without the concurrence of the power on which the POWs depend.

Before pronouncing the death sentence the court must consider that: (i) the POW is not a national of the detaining power; (ii) he owes it no duty of allegiance; and (iii) he is in its power through circumstances beyond his control. Article 107 requires that as soon as possible after a death sentence has been passed, the detaining power must communicate it to the protecting power and also inform the latter as to whether the accused POW has the right of appeal with a view to the quashing of the sentence

69 Article 105 of the GC III provides certain rights to a POW facing judicial proceedings. A copy of the charges on which he is to be tried, together with any other documentation that, under the law of the detaining power, would be furnished to a member of its armed forces being tried under the same circumstances, must be served upon him "in good time before the opening of the trial" and in a language that he understands, while an identical copy thereof must be provided to his counsel. An accused POW is entitled to the assistance of a fellow POW, of a qualified counsel of his own choice, and of a competent interpreter if he considers this latter necessary; and he must be advised of these rights by the detaining power far enough prior to the trial to make them meaningful and to ensure compliance with other provisions containing time limitations. In case the POW cannot, or does not, himself obtain the assistance of a counsel, the protecting power must do so for him, being allowed one week to accomplish this, and being authorized to call upon the detaining power for a list of qualified counsels if it so desires; and if the protecting power does not select a counsel within the time allotted, the detaining power is obligated to appoint a competent counsel for the POW. Once appointed, the counsel must be allowed a minimum of two weeks prior to the beginning of the trial in which to prepare the defence and he must be afforded adequate facilities for this purpose, being permitted to consult his client freely and in private, and also to interview witnesses for the defence.

or the reopening of the trial. This information must also be given to the accused POW and his representative. Article 101 prohibits the execution of the death sentence prior to the expiration of at least six months from the date upon which the protecting power actually receives the notification.

Escape

According to Article 91 of the GC III, the escape of a POW shall be deemed to have succeeded when: (i) he has joined the armed forces of the power on which he depends, or those of an allied power; (ii) he has left the territory under the control of the detaining power, or of an ally of the said power; (iii) he has joined a ship flying the flag of the power on which he depends, or of an allied power, in the territorial waters of the detaining power, the said ship not being under the control of the last named power.

Prisoners of war who have made good their escape and who are recaptured, are not be liable to any punishment in respect of their previous escape. A prisoner who has made an unsuccessful attempt to escape is liable only to a disciplinary punishment, even if it is a repeated offence. The record of disciplinary punishments must be maintained by the camp commander, which must be open to inspection by representatives of the protecting power.

Release and Repatriation

Direct repatriation: The GC III provides for the direct repatriation or accommodation in neutral countries of certain wounded and sick POWs during hostilities. Parties to a conflict have an obligation to send back to their own country, regardless of number or rank, certain seriously wounded and seriously sick POWs, after having cared for them until they are fit enough to travel.[70] No sick or injured POW who is eligible for repatriation under this provision may be repatriated against his or her will during hostilities. Throughout the duration of hostilities, parties to the conflict shall endeavour, with the cooperation of the neutral powers concerned, to

70 According to Articles 109 and 110, the following categories of POWs shall be repatriated directly:(a) incurably wounded and sick whose mental or physical fitness seems to have been gravely diminished; (b) wounded and sick who, according to medical opinion, are not likely to recover within one year, whose condition requires treatment, and whose mental or physical fitness seems to have been gravely diminished; and (c) wounded and sick who have recovered, but whose mental or physical fitness seems to have been gravely and permanently diminished.

make arrangements for the accommodation in neutral countries of certain sick and wounded POWs.[71]

Interning POWs in neutral territory: The detaining power, the power on which the POWs depend, and a neutral power agreed upon by these two powers, shall endeavour to conclude agreements that will enable POWs to be interned in the territory of that neutral power until the close of hostilities.[72]

Repatriation from a neutral state: POWs who have been accommodated in a neutral country, should be repatriated if they belong to the following categories,: (a) those whose health has deteriorated so far as to fulfil the conditions for direct repatriation; and (b) those whose mental or physical powers remain, even after treatment, considerably impaired.[73]

No prisoner on whom a disciplinary punishment has been imposed and who is eligible for repatriation or for accommodation in a neutral country may be kept back on the plea that he has not undergone his punishment. Prisoners must be released and repatriated without delay after the cessation of active hostilities.[74] There is one exception to immediate repatriation. In case a POW is convicted or prosecuted for criminal offence, he may be detained until the end of the legal proceedings and if necessary, until he has completed his sentence.[75]

---

71 Under Article 110, the following categories of POWs may be accommodated in a neutral country: (a) wounded, injured, or sick whose recovery may be expected within one year of the date of the wound or the beginning of the illness, if treatment in a neutral country might increase the prospects of a more certain and speedy recovery; and (b) those whose mental or physical health, according to medical opinion, is seriously threatened by continued captivity, but whose accommodation in a neutral country might remove such a threat.

72 Article 111, the GC III.

73 Article 110, the GC III.

74 After the 1971 Indo-Pak war, the Indian government initially refused to repatriate more than 85,000 Pakistanis held as POWs, on the grounds that a renewal of hostilities could not be excluded. Repatriation started in late 1973, almost two years after the cessation of hostilities.

75 Article 119 of the GC III: Prisoners of war against whom criminal proceedings for an indictable offence are pending may be detained until the end of such proceedings, and, if necessary, until the completion of the punishment. The same shall apply to prisoners of war already convicted for an indictable offence. Parties to the conflict shall communicate to each other the names of any prisoners of war who are detained until the end of the proceedings or until punishment has been completed.

The rule against employment on active military service applies to POWs repatriated by the detaining Power pursuant to Articles 109 and 110 of the GC III. For example, able-bodied POWs who are voluntarily repatriated by the unilateral decision of the detaining power during hostilities may be employed on active military service.[76] The repatriation of POWs against their will has been a contentious issue. The UK follows a policy that POWs should not be repatriated against their will. However, an attempt to insert such a provision into the GC III failed as it was felt that the proposal might give rise to the exercise of undue influence on the part of the detaining power.

Death

Article 121 of the GC III takes into account the possibility of a sentry or other member of the armed forces killing or seriously wounding a POW. Article 121 explicitly provides that every death of or serious injury to a POW that is caused or suspected to have been caused by a sentry, another POW, or any other person, as well as any death the cause of which is unknown, "shall be immediately followed by an official enquiry by the detaining power".[77] This article, however, does not provide specific punishments in such a scenario. Instead, it leaves the responsibility of punishing those individuals to the detaining power. Violence against persons who are *hors de combat*, which expressly includes detainees, is prohibited by treaty and customary humanitarian law in international and non-international armed conflicts alike and can amount to a war crime. The obligation under IHL to prosecute war crimes logically presupposes an obligation to investigate. The GC III specifies the conditions of burial or cremation, as appropriate, to ensure

76 The British Military Manual (2004) states, "Despite its apparent general application, Art 117 is taken to apply only to POW repatriated under the special rules laid down in Arts 109–110. It does not apply to able-bodied POW who are voluntarily repatriated by the unilateral decision of the detaining power during hostilities." The UK sent members of the Royal Marine garrison of the Falkland Islands, who had been captured and then repatriated by Argentina, back into combat with the Task Force that re-took the Islands in 1982, Para 8.155.1, footnote 417.

77 Article 121 of GC III further provides, "A communication on this subject shall be sent immediately to the Protecting Power. Statements shall be taken from witnesses, especially from those who are POW, and a report including such statements shall be forwarded to the Protecting Power. If the enquiry indicates the guilt of one or more persons, the Detaining Power shall take all measures for the prosecution of the person or persons responsible." For more details refer to *Guidelines for Investigating Deaths in Custody*, October 2013, Geneva: ICRC.

respect for the dead and to safeguard the interests of their families and stipulates that a death certificate must be forwarded as rapidly as possible to the POW Information Bureaux. A POW is entitled to make a will.

The burial or cremation of a POW must be preceded by a medical examination of the body with a view to confirming death and enabling a report to be made and, where necessary, establishing identity. The detaining authorities shall ensure that POWs who have died in captivity are honourably buried, if possible according to the rites of the religion to which they belonged, and that their graves are respected, suitably maintained and marked so as to be found at any time. Deceased POWs must be buried in individual graves unless unavoidable circumstances require the use of collective graves.[78] Bodies may be cremated only for imperative reasons of hygiene, on account of the religion of the deceased or in accordance with his express wish to this effect. In case of cremation, the fact shall be stated and the reasons mentioned in the death certificate of the deceased.[79]

Information Bureaux and Central Tracing Agency

The Central Tracing Agency (CTA) is an institution that was originally established for situations of international armed conflict in accordance with the provisions of the four Geneva Conventions and Additional Protocol I of 1977, and with the Statutes of the Movement. Later resolutions of the International Conference have widened the range of its activities to non-international armed conflicts and other situations of violence. More recently, the CTA has begun to assist in restoring family links (RFL) during natural disasters and in other situations in which the national Red Cross and Red Crescent Societies (National Societies) are involved. The CTA carries out four types of activities:

(i) Activities to benefit persons affected and services that are provided directly to them: RFL, efforts to clarify the fate of the

78 Article 120 of GC III provides, "In order that graves may always be found, all particulars of burials and graves shall be recorded with a Graves Registration Service established by the Detaining Power. Lists of graves and particulars of the POWs interred in cemeteries and elsewhere shall be transmitted to the Power on which such POWs depended. Responsibility for the care of these graves and for records of any subsequent moves of the bodies shall rest on the Power controlling the territory. These provisions shall also apply to the ashes, which shall be kept by the Graves Registration Service until proper disposal thereof in accordance with the wishes of the home country."

79 Article 120, GC III.

missing, the transfer of people, and the provision of travel and other documents.

(ii) Activities and services for the benefit of National Societies, particularly coordination and technical assistance for their tracing services.

(iii) Activities for States (e.g. assisting in the establishment of national information bureaus as provided for by IHL).

(iv) Management of data on persons who require individual follow-up.

On the basis of the 1997 Seville Agreement and its 2005 Supplementary Measures adopted by the Council of Delegates of the Movement, the ICRC has been entrusted with the lead role for activities related to the work of the CTA. Broadly speaking, this covers all activities associated with RFL. A CTA must be created in a neutral country. The ICRC may propose the organization and location of such an Agency to the powers concerned. To facilitate the work of the CTA, States must grant them free postage and exemptions/reduced rates for communication charges.

Customary International Humanitarian Law

The long-standing rule of customary IHL is that upon capture, combatants are entitled to POW status. They may neither be tried for their participation in the hostilities nor for acts that do not violate IHL. Customary rules provide that combatants must distinguish themselves from the civilian population while they are engaged in an attack or in a military operation preparatory to an attack. If they fail to do so, they do not have the right to POW status. Combatants who are captured while engaged in espionage do not have the right to POW status. However, they may not be convicted or sentenced without previous trial. Mercenaries, as defined in the Additional Protocol I, do not have the right to combatant or POW status. They too may not be convicted or sentenced without previous trial.[80]

ICRC and Prisoners of War

The First World War led to a considerable expansion of the ICRC's activities. During the war, the ICRC monitored compliance with the 1906 Geneva Convention and the 1907 Hague Convention for the Adaptation to

80 Customary Rules 106–108, IHL.

Maritime Warfare of the Principles of the Geneva Convention (a revised version of the Geneva Convention of 22 August 1864). In October 1914, the ICRC opened its International Agency in Geneva. During the conflict, it listed almost five million POWs, visited many of them and enabled families to send relief parcels. The Agency made out more than 4.8 million index cards and dispatched over 1.8 million parcels and consignments of collective relief. Throughout the conflict, the ICRC protested against the inhumane treatment to which both combatants and civilians were subjected. In particular, it led a vigorous campaign against the use of chemical weapons. On 31 December 1919, after the peace treaties had been signed, the ICRC closed down the Agency. In the period between the two World Wars it was replaced by a special department at the ICRC which was responsible for handling individual inquiries, making representations concerning missing persons and providing former prisoners with certificates enabling them to claim benefits.

The specific rules protecting POWs were provided for the first time in the 1929 Geneva Convention. However, during World War II, a large number of POWs suffered inhumane and degrading treatment and death at the hands of Nazi and Soviet forces. Casualty figures of captured POWs varied considerably and sometimes went as high as 95%. The provisions relating to the protection of POWs were thereafter refined in the third Geneva Convention of 1949, as well as the Additional Protocol I of 1977.

The Geneva Convention of 1949 and AP I also provide extensive protection to civilian internees during international armed conflicts. If justified by imperative reasons of security, a party to the conflict may confine civilians in an assigned residence or subject them to internment. Internment of civilians as a security measure is justified, but cannot be used as a form of punishment. This means that each interned person must be released as soon as the reasons which necessitated his internment no longer exist. Rules governing the treatment and conditions of detention of civilian internees under IHL are similar to those applicable to POWs. In non-international armed conflicts, Article 3 common to the 1949 Geneva Conventions and AP II provide that persons deprived of liberty for reasons related to the conflict must be treated humanely in all circumstances. In particular, they are protected against murder, torture and cruel, humiliating or degrading treatment. Those detained for participation in hostilities are not immune from criminal prosecution under the applicable domestic law.

Mandate to ICRC

The ICRC is mandated by the international community, under the Geneva Conventions, to visit POWs and civilian internees to verify whether they are being treated according to the relevant international standards. In addition, it seeks to visit those held in situations of internal violence.

The objective of the ICRC's activities for people deprived of their freedom is purely humanitarian, to ensure that their physical and mental integrity is fully respected and that their conditions of detention are in line with internationally recognized standards or IHL. The ICRC strives to prevent forced disappearances or extrajudicial executions, ill-treatment and failure to respect fundamental judicial guarantees, and, whenever necessary, takes action to improve conditions of detention. This involves in particular:

- Negotiating with the authorities to obtain access to people deprived of their freedom wherever they may be held;
- Visiting all detainees, assessing their conditions of detention and identifying any shortcomings and humanitarian needs;
- Monitoring individual detainees for specific protection, medical or other purposes;
- Maintaining family links such as facilitating family visits;
- Providing material and medical relief supplies to detainees or engaging in cooperation on specific projects with the detaining authorities.

Trained ICRC staff visit places of detention, talk with the authorities concerned, hold private interviews with detainees/internees and prepare an overall analysis of their findings. ICRC findings, assessments and related recommendations are discussed confidentially with the authorities at the appropriate levels.

Visits to places of detention are carried out by the ICRC under the following conditions: (i) delegates must be provided with full and unimpeded access to all detainees falling within the ICRC's mandate and to all places where they are held; (ii) delegates must be able to hold private interviews with the detainees of their choice; (iii) delegates must be able to repeat their visits; (iv) detainees falling within the ICRC's mandate must be notified individually to the ICRC, and the ICRC must be able to draw up lists of their names; and (v) at the end of each visit, the delegates hold a final talk with the detaining authorities to inform them about their findings and recommendations. .

Health during detention: The ICRC is concerned with the welfare of persons detained in connection with armed conflicts or internal disturbances that require intervention by a neutral organization. Its objective is to ensure acceptable conditions of detention and to safeguard the physical and mental welfare of prisoners. It monitors their situation in detention and, where appropriate, prior to detention through direct visits to the victims and dialogue with their captors.

The ICRC emphasizes the responsibility of the detaining authority to respect and protect detainees. It draws attention to any breaches of international law and standards and recommends remedial action. In emergency situations where the basic needs of detainees cannot be met by the authorities, it can provide temporary assistance in the form of water and food supplies or basic medical items.

ICRC doctors, nurses and delegates who visit places of detention to evaluate factors bearing on the health of the detainees need to have experience in prison and public health issues, knowledge of environmental hygiene, epidemiology, nutritional needs, and of the inter-relationship between nutrition, sanitation, health care, violence and overcrowding. Their aim is to advise on improvements to the overall functioning of the health system in detention centres, rather than individual diagnosis and treatment. When torture and other forms of ill-treatment are evident, ICRC physicians document individual situations to strengthen the case for formal intervention by the organization. This documentation is not in itself part of any judicial investigation, but aims to trigger such action by the relevant authority.

Protecting Powers

To ensure that the Geneva Conventions are respected, the parties to a conflict should secure the cooperation and admit the supervision of protecting powers, in other words neutral States. For this purpose, the protecting powers may appoint, apart from their diplomatic or consular staff, delegates from amongst their own nationals or the nationals of other neutral powers.[81]The representatives or delegates of the protecting powers must have permission to go to all places where POWs are detained, particularly to places of internment, imprisonment and labour. They must have access to all premises occupied by POWs and be allowed to go to the places of departure, passage and arrival of prisoners who are being transferred. They must be authorized to interview the prisoners/ their representatives, without witnesses, either personally or through an interpreter. Representatives and delegates of the protecting powers must have the liberty to select the places they wish to visit. The duration and frequency of these visits must not be restricted. The delegates of the ICRC enjoy the same prerogatives.[82]

Dissemination

The State Parties have an obligation to disseminate the text of the GC III in times of peace as well as war as widely as possible in their respective countries. They must also include the study of the GC III in the training programmes of military and civil instruction, so that the principles of the Convention are known to all the members of the armed forces and to the entire population. The military or other authorities who assume responsibilities in respect of POWs must possess the text of the Convention and be specially instructed to apply its provisions. [83]

Grave Breaches and Penal Sanctions

Breaches of the GC III are classified into: breaches of the laws of war and grave breaches.[84] The State Parties are under obligation to enact legislation necessary to provide effective penal sanctions for persons committing, or ordering to be committed, any of the following grave breaches of the GC III: (i) wilful killing; (ii) torture or inhumane treatment, including biological experiments; (iii) wilfully causing great suffering or serious injury to body or health; (iv) compelling a POW or a protected civilian to serve in the armed forces of the hostile power; and (v) wilfully depriving a POW or a protected person of their rights or fair and regular trial prescribed by the

81 Article 8, GC III.

82 Article 126, GC III.

83 Article 127, GC III.

84 Grave Breaches are addressed in all four Geneva Conventions of 1949 and are Common Articles 50/51/130/147 respectively.

Convention. If an offence is not explicitly defined as a grave breach by the GC III, then no act, no matter what it may be, can be considered as such.

The State Parties are under obligation to search for persons who are alleged to have committed or ordered for the committing of grave breaches, and should put them through trial in courts; regardless of the nationality of the accused. Grave breaches of the Geneva Conventions constitute war crimes under the Rome Statute of the International Criminal Court.[85] During the trial the accused is to be provided with judicial safeguards and should have the right to defend himself as contained in Article 105 of the GC III. The State Party must also take necessary measures for the suppression of all acts contrary to the provisions of the third Geneva Convention.[86]

It must be noted that there are no specific prohibitions or definitions of maltreatment provided in the GC III. For instance, Article 17, which prohibits exposure to disadvantageous or similar forms of treatment, does not specify what constitutes such acts.[87] Maltreatment may be in the form of causing mental or physical suffering, brutality or threat of imminent death.[88]

Denunciation

The State Parties to the GC III have the liberty to denounce the Convention. The denunciation should be notified in writing to the Swiss Federal Council, which shall transmit it to the Governments of all the States Parties. The denunciation shall take effect one year after the notification. However, a notification of denunciation which has been made at a time when the denouncing power is involved in an armed conflict shall not take effect until peace has been concluded, and until after operations connected with the release and repatriation of the persons protected by the GC III have

85 Article 8, para 2 (a) (i), (ii), (iii), (v) and (vi) of the Rome Statute; killing or wounding a combatant who, having laid down his arms or having no means of defence, has surrendered at discretion would amount to a war crime under Article 8, para 2 (b) (vi).

86 Articles 129 and 130, GC III.

87 Hardwick Patrick A, The Geneva Conventions in Modern Warfare, Master's Thesis, Texas State University-San Marcos, 2012, p. 88–89.

88 In accordance with the Geneva Conventions of 1949, the US has criminalized the grave breaches of torture and cruel treatment on detained individuals under the War Crimes Act of 1996 (18 U.S.C. section 2441). "Persons convicted for an offense under the Act may be sentenced to life imprisonment or, if death results from the breach, be executed."

been terminated. Even after the denunciation, the Parties to the conflict shall remain bound by the principles of the law of nations, as they result from the usages established among civilized peoples, from the laws of humanity and the dictates of public conscience (i.e. Martens Clause).

Conclusion

In the context of an international armed conflict involving the armed forces of two or more parties, persons who have fallen into the power of an adverse party to a conflict are entitled to POW status if they qualify as: (a) combatants (members of the armed forces or participants of a *levee en masse* effort); (b) civilians formally authorized to accompany the armed forces; (c) demobilized military personnel in occupied territory; (d) military personnel interned in neutral territory.[89] In addition, members of organized militias, volunteer corps and, resistance movements who meet the criteria stipulated above also qualify for POW status if they fall into the hands of the enemy party.[90] The concept of POW does not exist in a non-international armed conflict.

The GC III is significant in that it provides a code of legal rules both fundamental and detailed for the protection of POWs. It vests in POWs the right to humane treatment. It attempts to restrict abuses and embrace the principle of universal jurisdiction for the trial of grave breaches. It also provides a comprehensive role for the protecting power, the ICRC and other relief organizations. It prohibits reprisals against POWs and precludes the use of POWs as slave labour. The GC III has removed the doubts which existed during World War II as to what acts or omissions were punishable as war crimes and the manner in which such crimes were to be adjudicated. It is a significant step forward in the development of rules of humanitarian practice in the treatment of POWs.

Nearly all the States have ratified the Geneva Convention of 1949 and many military manuals direct their armed forces to observe unconditionally the obligations embodied in the Convention. A party may denounce the GC III, but if such denunciation is made during a conflict in which the party is

---

89 Articles 4(A)(1), (2), (3), (4), (5) and (6); 4(B)(1) and (2) of GC III; Article 44 (1) AP I and Hague Convention No. V, Article 11.

90 Gill Terry and Elies van Sliedregt, Guantanamo Bay: A Reflection On The Legal Status and Rights Of 'Unlawful Enemy Combatants', *Utrecht Law Review*, Vol. 1, Issue 1, 2005, pp. 28-54.

involved, it cannot take effect until peace has been restored and operations connected with the release and repatriation of the persons protected by the Convention have been concluded. The denunciation has effect only in respect of the party that denounces.

In 2019, the ICRC released its updated Commentary on the Third Geneva Convention of 1949. The Commentary analyses how the application and interpretation of the four Geneva Conventions of 1949 have evolved in the past decades. It also provides a fresh interpretation of the Convention, taking into consideration the legal and technological developments that have occurred since the publication of the first Commentary 60 years ago. The highlights of the updated Commentary are covered in the last chapter.

Chapter III

Prisoner of War Status: Certain Specific Groups

The question of "unlawful" combatants gained prominence after the decision of the United States in 2002 to deny prisoner of war (POW) status to Taliban and Al Qaeda fighters. Former US President George W. Bush authorized the arrest of members of the Taliban movement in Afghanistan and their detention at the US military base of Guantanamo Bay as "unlawful" combatants. In the following months, the scope of this term was broadened to include, at first, detained members of Al Qaeda and later, all other international terrorists around the world and supporters of such terrorists. The US declared that such individuals did not enjoy combatant privileges, which grants combatants the right to participate in hostilities without undergoing the risk of prosecution for such participation. In the view of the US, once detained, these individuals were not entitled to either the status of POW, or of civilians (protected by the Geneva Conventions of 1949). They constituted an autonomous category of persons named "unlawful, combatants," who were excluded from international protection and not covered by minimal humanitarian standards. This chapter looks into the POW status of certain specific groups, namely, spies, saboteurs, deserters, mercenaries, unlawful combatants, private military and security company (PMSC) personnel, and foreign fighters.

Spies

No international convention addresses the legality of espionage in peacetime, though it has been practiced by all nations for centuries. Espionage is, however, not prohibited by the international community as a fundamentally wrong activity. International humanitarian law recognizes the practice of employing spies. However, they may be severely punished under domestic law when they are captured by the enemy. There is only one explicit reference to spies in Article 5 paragraph 2 of the 1949 Geneva Convention IV. It states that civilian spies do not lose their civilian status if they are detained during espionage. However, if military security requires so, they shall be regarded as having forfeited their rights of communication. At the very least, they should be treated with humanity and should be provided with the right of fair trial. Also, a death sentence may be carried out only after a six-month waiting period.

The Additional Protocol (AP) I states that any member of the armed forces of a party to the conflict who falls into the power of an adverse party while engaging in espionage may be treated as a spy. Further, spies are not entitled to POW status (AP I/46, paragraph 1). Article 46 of AP I, states that a member of the armed forces of a party to the conflict who, on behalf of that party and in territory controlled by an adverse party, gathers or attempts to gather information shall not be considered as engaging in espionage if, while so acting, he is in the uniform of his armed forces. A member of the armed forces wearing another uniform (through an act of false pretence or in a clandestine manner) under the same circumstances may be treated as a spy. A distinction has to be made between military and civilian spies. Civilian spies are granted the protection of the GC IV, if they meet the nationality criteria. If not, they can rely on Article 75 of AP I. Military spies, however, do not fall under the scope of the GC IV since the Convention is only applicable to civilians. Nonetheless, military spies are also entitled to protection under Article 75 of AP I.

Saboteurs

Saboteurs are generally understood to be persons who act clandestinely or under false pretences behind enemy lines to commit acts of destruction or damage against objects and material belonging to the enemy. An act of sabotage may also include killing and kidnapping of the enemy. Whether the use of sabotage against the enemy is legitimate or otherwise depends on three factors: the category of persons committing it; the target; and the means and methods used. As regards the category of persons, in an international armed conflict only combatants (i.e. specially trained and equipped units of the regular forces (commandos), members of resistance movements and participants in a *levee en masse*) may commit acts of sabotage; no person who does not have combatant status may lawfully commit sabotage. Sabotage is a clandestine activity, generally carried out by individuals or small formations operating in enemy-controlled territory and using surprise and ruses of war. It is generally carried out with great precision and therefore, does not usually harm the civilian population. The targets of sabotage must form part of the enemy's material infrastructure, that is, they must be military objectives.

Although not expressly mentioned in Article 4 of the Third Geneva Convention, there is a well-established practice that saboteurs are treated in the same way as spies and are not entitled to POW status. Members of armed forces who are not in uniform while engaged in sabotage are unlikely to be given POW status if captured. An individual who is not entitled to protection as a POW under the Third Convention is entitled to protection under the Fourth Convention, if he meets the conditions laid down in Article 4 of that Convention. In any case, the protections in Article 75 of AP I apply as a minimum. These protections are today considered part of customary international law. The following case is relevant as regards the POW status of saboteurs.[1]

> On 10 March 1965, two women employed in a bank in Singapore were killed by the explosion of a bag containing 25lb of nitroglycerine placed on the stairs of the building by two saboteurs. The saboteurs were rescued from the sea some distance from Singapore by a bumboat. They were not in uniform when arrested and had no identification papers. They were charged with the murder of the two girls and of another person who succumbed to injuries due to the explosion and tried by the High Court of Singapore. The accused claimed to be members of the Indonesian armed forces and entitled to protection under the Third Geneva Convention. The trial judge ruled that they were not entitled to the status of POW, convicted them for the murder of three civilians and sentenced them to death.
>
> Their appeals to the Federal Court of Malaysia were dismissed on 5 October 1966, and they further preferred an appeal by special leave. The Federal Court held that there could not, "be the least doubt that the explosion at MacDonald House was not only an act of sabotage but one totally unconnected with the necessities of war".

1 *Osman Bin Haji Mohd Ali and another v. The Public Prosecutor*, House of Lords (P.C.) Law Reports, Vol. 1, 1969, Appeal Cases, pp. 430–455 (PC).

The Federal Court further held, "It seems to us clear beyond doubt that under international law a member of the armed forces of a party to the conflict who, out of uniform and in civilian clothing, sets off explosives in the territory of the other party to the conflict in a non-military building in which civilians are doing work unconnected with any war effort forfeits his right on capture to be treated as a prisoner of war." The Court consequently held that the appellants were not POWs within the meaning of the Convention.

Deserters and Defectors

Members of armed forces who desert but subsequently fall into the hands of the enemy are entitled to POW status. This issue is not expressly addressed in the Third Geneva Convention, however, under domestic law, generally an act of desertion does not amount to a unilateral termination of one's membership of a State's armed forces. It is common practice for persons to be punished for acts of desertion by the State on which they formerly depended. The deserter's relationship with his armed forces is a question of that State's domestic law and not international law.[2] The POW status of deserters must be maintained until their final release and repatriation, and POWs may not renounce their rights.[3] Deserters who are subsequently captured by their own armed forces are not POWs because they are not in the power of the enemy. A deserter who is interned by a neutral State would also be treated as a POW.[4]

2 "States generally forbid members of their armed forces from desertion and generally regard deserters as continuing to be members of their armed forces." The United States Law of War Manual, 2016, p. 114-115, para. 4.5.2.5. The Regulations for the Indian Army, 1987, para 376 provides, "A person subject to the Army Act, who is declared absent under section 106 of the Act, does not thereby cease to belong to the corps in which he is enrolled though no longer shown on its returns, and can, if subsequently arrested, be tried by court-martial for desertion. When arrested he will be shown on returns as rejoined from desertion."

3 In circumstances where deserters find themselves in the power of the enemy, certain protective measures must be taken. For example, it may be safer not to assemble them in the same camp as other members of the same armed forces.

4 It has been suggested that the deserter is not entitled to POW status on the basis of either of two reasons: (i) that the failure to mention deserters specifically in the enumeration contained in Article 4 was a deliberate omission; and (ii) that deserters do not "fall" into the power of the enemy. The first argument is unconvincing because a member of the armed forces who deserts and surrenders to the enemy is, nevertheless, a member of the armed forces within Article 4A (1) of the Third Geneva Convention, hence, it was no more necessary to include deserters as specifically being within that

Defectors are persons who desert their own armed forces and voluntarily join the armed forces of the opposing side.[5] Because they have not "fallen into the power of the enemy", they are not POWs while serving in their new armed forces. Those who defect after capture, however, retain their POW status because they may in no circumstances renounce the protection of the Third Geneva Convention. A question that comes up is what will be the status of persons who have defected and have been subsequently captured by other armed forces. The fact that they have become members of the armed forces by defecting from another State's armed forces does not alter the application of Article 4A(1). Therefore, if they fall into the power of the enemy, be it the State from which they defected or another State, they become POWs. A few States exclude defectors from their own armed forces from POW status.[6] Whether an individual is a deserter or a defector may be uncertain and a determination will need to be based on the available facts. If there is doubt about a person being a POW, his status would be determined by a competent tribunal.[7]States may not compel POWs, retained personnel, or protected persons in their power to defect and serve in their armed forces.

Mercenaries

Concerns have been raised over the question of considering mercenaries[8] as combatants under the Third Geneva Convention. A mercenary is a person

category than it was to include cooks, artillerymen, or non-commissioned officers, all of whom are equally members of the armed forces. And the second argument is also unconvincing becausethe words "fallen into the power of the enemy" were substituted for the word "captured," previously used, precisely in order to ensure POW status to those who surrender voluntarily. Levie Howard S., Prisoners of War in International Armed Conflict: Preliminary Problems, *International Law Studies*, Vol. 59, 1977, p. 78.

5 A defector has been defined as one who seeks refuge with the enemy because, in effect, ideologically he supports its objectives and opposes those of his own country.

6 The United States Department of Defence, Law of War Manual, 2016, p. 114, para. 4.5.2.6 states, "Defectors serving in the forces of the enemy who are captured by the State to which they originally owed an allegiance generally would not be entitled to POW status because the privileges of combatant status are generally understood not to apply, as a matter of international law, between nationals and their State of nationality." Also see New Zealand, Military Manual, 2019, Vol. 4, p. 6-10, para. 6.3.26.

7 Article 5(2), the Third Geneva Convention, 1949.

8 There is no expert consensus on who exactly is a 'mercenary'. In the simplest terms, a mercenary is an armed civilian paid to do military operations in a foreign conflict zone. Switzerland has been famous for providing mercenaries. The Swiss Guard is known as striped-uniformed protectors of the Pope in the Vatican, but their history

who takes a direct part in hostilities motivated essentially by the desire for private gain. Mercenaries have existed since the earliest recorded armed conflict and were treated as respected professionals. The Roman Empire made extensive use of mercenaries. In the Christian society, mercenaries served as knights and retainers and became an integral part of the social system. The mercenary was treated no differently than other men-at-arms even when captured. With the advent of large conscript armies, mercenaries became very important as elite fighting units, cadre for training large units, and strategic advisors to commanders. They were treated with respect as experts in warfare and were generally treated with cordiality when captured because often hirelings from the same native land were employed by both sides to a conflict. However, in the modern era, mercenaries are looked upon with disdain, for instance, in June 1976, 13 mercenaries who were captured while participating in the civil war in Angola were placed on trial. The tribunal trying the mercenaries treated them as war criminals and sentenced them to death. They were subsequently executed.[9]

The Hague Conventions of 1907 as well as the four Geneva Conventions of 1949 do not refer to mercenaries. The Diplomatic Conference on the Reaffirmation and Development of IHL Applicable in Armed Conflicts (1974-1977) accepted the demands of the Organization of African Unity (OAU) and socialist nations to insert a provision dealing specifically with mercenary activity. Accordingly, the first core IHL instrument to deal specifically with mercenaries was the 1977 AP I. Article 47.2 of AP I spells out six cumulative conditions for a person to be a mercenary. The person must:

(a) be specially recruited locally or abroad in order to fight in an armed conflict;

---

stretches back to bands of mercenaries that flourished during the Renaissance. More than one million Swiss adventurers fought in Europe's armies between the 15th and 19th centuries, and they fought and died in large numbers during the French Revolution. Recently, the Nigerian government secretly turned to mercenaries to fight Boko Haram. These mercenaries arrived with Special Forces teams and Mi-24 Hind helicopter gunships—flying tanks. Conducting search and destroy missions, they drove out Boko Haram in a few weeks. The Nigerian military could not achieve this task in 6 years. McFate Sean, Mercenaries and War: Understanding Private Armies Today, National Defence University Press, December 2019, pp. 51.

9 Cotton John Robert, Comments: The Rights of Mercenaries as Prisoners of War, *Military Law Review*, Vol. 77, Summer 1977, p. 143-166.

(b) take a direct part in the hostilities;

(c) be motivated to take part in the hostilities essentially by the desire for private gain and to be promised, by or on behalf of a Party to the conflict, material compensation substantially in excess of that promised or paid to combatants of similar ranks and functions in the armed forces of that Party;

(d) not be a national of a Party to the conflict or a resident of territory controlled by a Party to the conflict;

(e) not be a member of the armed forces of a Party to the conflict; and

(f) not have been sent by a State which is not a Party to the conflict on official duty as a member of its armed forces.

The definition of mercenary in AP I is so narrow that it is virtually impossible to find an individual who falls within the Article 47.2 definition of a mercenary.[10] However, the ICRC considers Article 47 of AP I as reflecting customary IHL. The ICRC's Customary Rule 108 provides that mercenaries, as defined in AP I, do not have the right to combatant or POW status; however, they may not be convicted or sentenced without previous trial.[11]

The 1989 International Convention against the Recruitment, Use, Financing and Training of Mercenaries extends the above definition to persons recruited for the purpose of participating in a concerted act of violence aimed at overthrowing a government or otherwise undermining the constitutional order of a State, or at undermining the territorial integrity of a State.[12] Under Article 10 of the treaty, mercenaries are treated as criminals and to be taken in custody for extradition. The African Union's Convention for the Elimination of Mercenarism in Africa, 1985, attempts to eliminate mercenaries by criminalizing them. The main rationale for criminalizing mercenarism in these two Conventions is that financial

10 Fallah Katherine, Corporate actors: the legal status of mercenaries in armed conflict, *International Review of the Red Cross*, Volume 88, No. 863, September 2006, pp. 599-611.

11 Jean-Marie Henckaerts and Louise Doswald-Beck, Customary IHL: Vol. 1: Rules, ICRC and Cambridge University Press, Geneva, 2005, pp. 391-195.

12 The International Convention against the Recruitment, Use, Financing, and Training of Mercenaries was adopted by the United Nations on 4 December 1989, pursuant to UNGA Resolution A/RES/44/34, and entered into force on 20 October 2001.

greed drives mercenaries, while patriotism and honour motivate a regular combatant. A national of a neutral state who enlists in the armed forces of a party to the conflict is not a mercenary.

Though Article 47.1 of AP I does not give mercenaries the rights of a combatant or POW status, it does not criminalize mercenary activity. The 1989 Mercenary Convention, on the other hand, says that mercenaries may be criminally punished for their status as mercenaries, as well as for any other criminal conduct in the course of being mercenaries. They can be prosecuted for being mercenaries only under the national law of the detaining power if it contains such provisions designating mercenarism as a distinct crime. However, mercenaries are still entitled to AP I's fundamental guarantees contained in Article 75. These guarantees are broad in scope and include the right to be treated humanely in all circumstances and the right to be protected against murder, torture, corporal punishment and outrages upon person dignity. Article 75.4 guarantees the right to a fair trial and due process in respect of penal offences.[13]

The attitude of the US towards American mercenaries has varied. In the past, the Department of State has sought the release of captured American mercenaries. Later, the attitude has been to take a neutral stance and let the mercenary take care of his own problem. More recently, American mercenaries have been regularized as members of private security companies now governed by the Montreaux Document of 2008.[14]

Unlawful Combatants

The term 'unlawful combatant'[15] became better known after the US attack on Afghanistan in 2001. The Bush administration announced its decision to classify the captured Taliban soldiers and al-Qaeda fighters as unlawful combatants and, as a consequence, to deny them POW status.[16] The US

13 Fallah Katherine, Corporate actors: the legal status of mercenaries in armed conflict, *International Review of the Red Cross*, Volume 88, Number 863, September 2006, pp. 599-611.

14 The Montreux Document is the first international document to reaffirm the international legal obligations of States regarding the activities of the private military and security companies present in armed conflicts.

15 Various other terms like "unprivileged belligerents", "illegitimate warriors" and "illegal combatants" have also been used in literature.

16 The term "unlawful combatant" was first used by the US Supreme Court in 1942 *[Ex parte Quirin*, 317 US 1 (1942)]. The case related to a group of eight German agents who,

transferred a large number of suspected terrorists to its naval base in Guantanamo Bay, Cuba. The US authorities claimed that the laws relating to armed conflict were not applicable to these detainees because they were not POWs and were not entitled to protection under the Geneva Convention III, but were 'unlawful enemy combatants', a term not used in the Geneva Conventions.[17] Unlawful combatants are persons who, by engaging in hostilities, have incurred one or more of the corresponding liabilities of combatant status (*e.g.*, being made the object of attack and subject to detention), but who are not entitled to any of the distinct privileges of combatant status such as combatant immunity and POW status.[18] Unlawful combatants generally receive less favourable treatment than lawful combatants under the Geneva Convention.

The term 'unlawful combatants' does not fit into the traditional categorization of persons in an armed conflict. Under IHL, persons in an armed conflict can be divided into two categories: combatants and civilians.[19] In defining these categories, the AP I has adopted a 'negative

disguised in civilian clothes, penetrated the territory of the US in a submarine, with the purpose of committing acts of espionage and sabotage there. They were arrested before committing any hostile act and were brought to trial before a military commission, which sentenced them to death. In appeal, the US Supreme Court held, "by universal agreement and practice, the law of war draws a distinction between the armed forces and the peaceful populations of belligerent nations and also between those who are lawful and unlawful combatants." The Court added that while the former 'are subject to capture and detention as POW by opposing military forces, the latter, including spies and saboteurs are likewise subject to capture and detention, but in addition they are subject to trial and punishment by military tribunals for acts which render their belligerency unlawful.

17 A White House legal counsel recommendation, endorsed by President George W. Bush, denied POW status to Taliban captives on the grounds that the Taliban was a "failed state." Further, because Taliban units reportedly did not follow the Geneva Convention, they could expect no quarter from capturing forces. A clarification, issued on 7 February 2002, announced that the United States would substantially adhere to the Convention regarding the maintenance of Taliban captives, but would not accord them POW status. Steven Strasser (ed.), 2004, *The Abu Ghraib Investigations: The Official Reports of the Independent Panel and the Pentagon on the Shocking Prisoner Abuse in Iraq*, New York: Public Affairs, pp. 4-5.

18 The United States Department of Defence, Law of War Manual, 2016, page 102, para 4.3.1.

19 The principle of distinction between "combatants" and "civilians" formed the basis of early codification efforts resulting in the Hague Regulations of 1907. Though the distinction was whittled down by the demands of military necessity (during the World Wars), the principle continued to be seen as the primary vehicle for the humanizing of

approach', to ensure that each person in an armed conflict belongs to one category or another, i.e., there are no uncertainties, and no one is left out. After first defining who combatants are,[20] Article 50 (1) of the AP I explains that all persons who are not combatants are then inevitably civilians. If there are doubts as to whether a person is a combatant or a civilian, that person must be considered to be a civilian. Such an approach is not only justified but also demanded by the fact that the concepts of the civilian population and of the armed forces are only conceived in opposition to each other, and the latter constitutes a category of persons clearly defined in international law.[21]

According to Prof Dinstein (2003), a person is not allowed to wear simultaneously two caps: the hat of a civilian and the helmet of a soldier. A person who engages in military activities by night, while purporting to be an innocent civilian by day, is neither a civilian nor a combatant. He is an unlawful combatant. Upon being captured by the enemy, an unlawful combatant is subject to automatic detention and will not be entitled the benefits of the status of a POW.[22]

In the last two decades, the term 'unlawful combatant' has been used frequently in different contexts without there being a clear understanding of the issue. The typical view is that unlawful combatants are terrorists who are not entitled to POW status or any other protection under IHL. For example, ISIS, al-Qaeda or Taliban terrorists have organized themselves as unlawful self-styled fighters and have disregarded the fundamental requirement of distinguishing themselves from civilians. They are, therefore, not entitled to POW status when captured. However, this does not mean that they are completely outside the protection of IHL. Unlawful combatants who meet the nationality criteria qualify as civilians and are entitled to protection under the Fourth Geneva Convention. This depends

war. Contemporary reinforcement of the principle of distinction is reflected in Article 48 of Additional Protocol I. Watkin Kenneth, Warriors without Rights? Combatants, Unprivileged Belligerents, and the Struggle Over Legitimacy, HPCR Occasional Paper Series, Winter 2005, pp. 77.

20 Article 43, AP I.

21 Sandoz Y., Swinarski C., and Zimmermann B., 1987, *Commentary on the Additional Protocols of 8 June 1977 to the Geneva Conventions of 12 August 1949*, Geneva: International Committee of the Red Cross, p. 610.

22 DinsteinYoram, Unlawful Combatancy, *International Law Studies*, Vol. 79, 2003, pp. 151-174.

not on the place where the unlawful combatants were captured but on the situation in which such persons find themselves in enemy hands. The ICRC Commentary on Article 45 of AP I states: “In armed conflict with an international character, a person of enemy nationality who is not entitled to POW status is, in principle, a civilian protected by the GC IV, so that there are no gaps in protection.”[23]Article 75 of AP I further guarantees fundamental rights where no exceptions are allowed.

In addition, Common Article 3 to the four Geneva Conventions applies to all persons in a non-international armed conflict (NIAC).[24] While the term ‘combatant’ is sometimes used when referring to NIAC, such usage is colloquial; as a matter of law, ‘combatant’ or ‘prisoner of war’ status does not exist in NIAC. Those fighting against the state in NIAC remain criminals subject to detention, arrest and prosecution.

Private Military and Security Companies

The extensive use of contractors by the United States on the battlefields of Iraq and Afghanistan initiated debate on the employment of private companies and their employees in an armed conflict. This gave rise to a new term, ‘private military and security companies (PMSCs)’, so far not mentioned in any IHL instrument.[25] PMSCs supply manpower to a growing transnational market created by the needs of governmental and intergovernmental actors. They have participated in most UN operations since the 1990s and provided security guards in peace operations where IHL applies.[26]

23 Ibid, p. 558.

24 The Common Article 3 requires high contracting parties to follow certain rules even if other parties to the conflict, such as insurgent groups, are not signatories to the Geneva Convention.

25 There is a close similarity between mercenaries and PMSCs. The PMSCs have, however, tried to portray themselves as different from mercenaries by choosing their own label, Private Security Company, in the Montreux Document. The media continued to utilize terms like mercenary, cowboys, and hired guns when referring to PMSC personnel in the industry. Mitchell Sommer, Becoming Legitimate: How PMSCs are Seeking Legitimacy in the International System, Graduate Thesis and Dissertations, University of South Florida, 2018, pp. 142.

26 The PMSC industry increasingly offers services that penetrate some of the core activities and tasks of the UN and supplements the tasks often performed by UN in humanitarian and peacekeeping operations, political missions or as part of regular country office work. The practice of the UN buying PMSC services is, however, rarely a topic open to discussion, and there has been little public acknowledgement

The tasks assigned to PMSCs have included reconstruction, logistics and base support services, escorting convoys, intelligence gathering, providing interpreters and bodyguards and security guards outside military bases, and even interrogation of prisoners. The executive staff and employees of a PMSC may be of different nationalities. Most of the employees of PMSCs holding private weapons are former military or police personnel from the US, European countries including the UK, Australia, and South Africa.[27] Some PMSCs have also employed Iraqis, mainly in reconstruction activities.

Concerns about the risk of human rights violations by PMSCs came to the fore after the massacre of civilians by Blackwater private military contractors in Nissour Square, Baghdad in 2007.[28] Though there is specific reference to mercenaries in IHL, there is no reference to PMSCs in IHL treaties and they are not specifically regulated by customary international law. The fact that PMSCs were outside the chain of military command and their activities were not strictly regulated, was becoming a matter of great concern until the Swiss Government and the ICRC formulated the Montreux Document in 2008. The document, which was non-binding,

---

of it whatsoever. The controversial nature of the issue appears to have prevented the formulation of a coherent political and practical approach to PMSCs among UN bodies. It also seems to have contributed to an *ad hoc* contracting culture in contrast with other goals set by the UN. Ostensen Ase Gilje, UN Use of Private Military and Security Companies: Practices and Policies, The Geneva Centre for the Democratic Control of Armed Forces, SSR Paper, 2011, p. 5-6.

27 A large number of former soldiers and police officers from Britain, the US, Australia and South Africa were earning wages as high as £600 a day to protect government officials, oil company executives and construction firm bosses in Iraq. The British Special Forces, SAS, was suffering an unprecedented loss of personnel as its soldiers were lured by lucrative work. According to experts, between 1,200 and 1,500 former British soldiers and police officers were working in Iraq. With business of around £1bn, British companies were estimated to have the biggest share of private security contracts in Iraq. Robert Fisk and Severin Carrell, Britain's secret army in Iraq: thousands of armed security men who answer to nobody, *The Independent*, 28 March 2004, available at: http://www.sandline.com/hotlinks/Independent-Secret_army.html.

28 On 16 September 2007, a convoy of Blackwater personnel guarding US State Department employees entered a crowded square in Baghdad, Iraq and opened fire, killing innocent civilians. The Blackwater employees claimed that they were attacked by gunmen and responded by firing. However, a jury in the US Federal District Court found that the deaths of the 17 Iraqis in the shooting, which began when a convoy of the guards suddenly began firing in a crowded intersection, was not a battlefield tragedy, but the result of a criminal act. Matt Apuzzo, Blackwater Guards Found Guilty in 2007 Iraq Killings, *The New York Times*, 22 October 2014.

contained IHL rules and proposed 'best practices' applicable to PMSCs operating in armed conflict and post-conflict situations.[29]

PMSCs and POW status: The main issue is whether members of PMCs should be considered as combatants or civilians.

Under Article 4 of the Third Geneva Convention, persons belonging to three categories are entitled to POW status as a result of recognition of their right to use force. The first category is "members of the armed forces of a Party to the conflict as well as members of militias or volunteer corps forming part of such armed forces". If PMSCs are formally incorporated into the army, then there is no doubt they would be covered by this provision. The second category includes "inhabitants of a non-occupied territory, who on the approach of the enemy spontaneously take up arms to resist the invading forces". This provision is not relevant to PMSCs. The third category is, "members of other militias and members of other volunteer corps, including those of organized resistance movements, belonging to a Party to the conflict and operating in or outside their own territory even if this territory is occupied, provided that such militias or volunteer corps, including such organized resistance movements, fulfil the following conditions: (a) being commanded by a person responsible for his subordinates; (b) having a fixed distinctive sign recognizable at a distance; (c) carrying arms openly; (d) conducting their operations in accordance with the laws and customs of war".

It is most unlikely that PMSCs would meet the definition of militias or volunteer corps. Although some PMSCs carry arms openly, their status is questionable due to their command structure and failure to wear distinctive symbols or emblems that would help differentiate them from the civilian population. While failing to wear a distinctive symbol is easily corrected, scholars are divided regarding whether the corporate structure of modern

29 Seventeen States jointly finalized the "Swiss Initiative" at a concluding meeting in Montreux, Switzerland. The Montreux Document was adopted in September 2008 by consensus by: Afghanistan, Angola, Australia, Austria, Canada, China, France, Germany, Iraq, Poland, Sierra Leone, South Africa, Sweden, Switzerland, United Kingdom of Great Britain and Northern Ireland, Ukraine, USA. The Document is directed at States and international organizations, rather than the industry itself, and applies only to armed conflict. A closer look at the document leads to the understanding that it does little actually to regulate the industry. Mitchell Sommer, Becoming Legitimate: How PMSCs are Seeking Legitimacy in the International System, Graduate Thesis and Dissertations, University of South Florida, 2018, pp. 142.

PMSCs is sufficient to meet the requirements of Article 4(A)(2).[30] Thus, Article 4(A)(2) does not appear to provide POW status for most modern PMSCs who provide military services.[31]

Article 44 of AP I specifies that any combatant, as defined in Article 43,[32] who falls into the power of an adverse party shall be a POW. For this, the combatants are required to distinguish themselves from the civilian population with some external sign; where this is not possible; combatants must carry their arms openly during the preparation and commission of each military engagement. If they do not do so, they forfeit their right to POW status. The members of the PMSCs are not within the military's chain of command. In case, the members of PMSCs are expected to perform role of a combatant, the general view is that they would not be entitled to POW status. This means that in the event they are captured, the enemy does not have to return them to their state at the end of hostilities.

Members of PMSCs who do not perform any task related to a combatant are entitled to POW status under Article 4 A(4) of the Third Geneva Convention. Article 4 A(4) provides, "Persons who accompany the armed forces without actually being members thereof, such as civilian members of military aircraft crews, war correspondents, supply contractors, members of labour units or of services responsible for the welfare of the armed forces, provided that they have received authorization from the armed forces which they accompany, who shall provide them for that purpose with an identity card." Typically, such persons do not have any combatant

30 The criteria set forth in Article 4 A(2): (i) members must belong to an organized group; (ii) the group must belong to a party to the conflict; (iii) it must be commanded by a person responsible to the conflict; (iv) its members must have a fixed, distinctive sign recognizable from a distance; (v) the members must carry arms openly; and (vi) the group must ensure that its members conduct their operations in accordance with the laws and customs of war.

31 Kochheiser Steven R., Silent Partners: Private Forces, Mercenaries, and International Humanitarian Law in the 21st Century, *U. Miami Nat'l Security & Armed Conflict L. Rev.*, Vol. 2, Issue 1, 2012, pp. 88-109.

32 Article 43, AP I provides: 1. The armed forces of a Party to a conflict consist of all organized armed forces, groups and units which are under a command responsible to that Party for the conduct of its subordinates, even if that Party is represented by a government or an authority not recognized by an adverse Party. Such armed forces shall be subject to an internal disciplinary system which, inter alia, shall enforce compliance with the rules of international law applicable in armed conflict. 2. Members of the armed forces of a Party to a conflict (other than medical personnel and chaplains) are combatants, that is to say, they have the right to participate directly in hostilities.

function and if they fall into the power of the enemy would be entitled to POW status.[33]However, they would not be entitled to receive combatant privilege.[34]

In 2007, the US amended its Uniform Code of Military Justice, formally incorporating PMSC personnel into the armed forces chain of command.[35] The Congress eliminated the "in time of war" restriction on jurisdiction over civilians and replaced it with a broader grant of military jurisdiction "in time of declared war or a contingency operation [over] persons serving with or accompanying an armed force in the field". The new law reflects a more realistic understanding of PMSCs and the nature and scope of their activities in modern battlefields, as it provides military officers with a direct recourse for any crimes they witness and avoids some of the logistical problems associated with international prosecution under civilian law.[36] The employees of PMSCs serving with the US military are also subject to the federal court jurisdiction.[37]

Private military companies assert that they are not mercenaries and that they play a number of beneficial roles in armed conflicts. They do not operate in a legal vacuum.[38] The States which hire PMSCs must be aware

33 Doswald-Beck Louise, "Private Military Companies under International Humanitarian Law," in Chesterman Simon and Lehnardt Chia (ed.), 2007, *From Mercenaries to Market: The rise and regulation of private military companies*, Oxford: Oxford University Press, pp. 115–138.

34 Combatant privilege generally relieves combatants from criminal responsibility for lawful acts of war such as killing enemy soldiers in battle. Without this privilege, the members of the PMSC may be held criminally liable for directly participating in hostilities. Ridlon Daniel P., Contractors or Illegal Combatants? The Status of Armed Contractors in Iraq, *Air Force Law Review*, Vol. 62, 2008, pp. 199–205.

35 Uniform Code of Military Justice (UCMJ), 10 U.S.C. §§ 801–946.

36 Ebrahim Adam, Going to War with the Army You Can Afford: The United States, International Law, and the Private Military Industry, Boston University International Law Journal, Vol. 28, 2010, p. 181–218.

37 Jennifer Elsea, Moshe Schwartz and Kennon H. Nakamura, Private Security Contractors in Iraq: Background, Legal Status and Other Issues, *Congressional Research Services,* 25 August 2008, available at: http://www.fas.org/sgp/crs/natsec/RL32419.pdf.

38 If a member of a PMSC is captured and does not qualify for POW status, he would qualify for protection under the Fourth Geneva Convention as civilian; which provides "protected persons" status to those who do not qualify for POW status and are from neutral or co-belligerent states with normal diplomatic representation. Those who fall outside the Fourth Geneva Convention and without POW status would "still have the benefit of fundamental customary rules relating to the prohibition of

that they will be responsible, under the doctrine of state responsibility, for violations of IHL committed by the personnel of such companies.

Foreign Terrorist Fighters

Individuals involved in armed violence outside their habitual country of residence are called foreign terrorist fighters (FTFs).[39]Thomas Hegghammer has defined a foreign fighter as an unpaid combatant, physically involved in a conflict with no prior links other than religious kinship.[40] The distinguishing features of FTFs are: (i) they are not overtly State-sponsored; (ii) they operate in countries which are not their own; (iii) they use insurgent tactics to achieve their ends; (iv) their principal objective is to overthrow a single government/occupier within a given territory; and (v) their principal motivation is ideological rather than material reward.[41]The term has not been used in the laws relating to armed conflict. Foreign terrorist fighters increase the intensity, duration and intractability of conflicts and may pose a serious threat to their States of origin, the States they transit and the States to which they travel, as well as States neighbouring zones of armed conflict in which they are active. There is no specific regime under IHL dealing explicitly with FTFs and their families. IHL deals with these individuals as it does with any other

torture, inhumane treatment, and hostage-taking, as well as the right to a fair trial." Kochheiser Steven R., Silent Partners: Private Forces, Mercenaries, and International Humanitarian Law in the 21st Century, *U. Miami Nat'l Security & Armed Conflict L. Rev.*, Vol. 2, Issue 1, 2012, pp. 88-109.

39 Security Council Resolution 2178, S/RES/2178 (2014) has defined "foreign terrorist fighters" as individuals who travel to a State other than their States of residence or nationality for the purpose of the perpetration, planning, or preparation of, or participation in, terrorist acts or the providing or receiving of terrorist training, including in connection with armed conflict, and resolving to address this threat.

40 Thomas Hegghammer, The Rise of Muslim Foreign Fighters: Islam and Globalisation of Jihad, *Quarterly Journal: International Security*, Vol. 35, No. 3, Winter 2010/11, pp. 53-94.

41 It has been reported that most FTFs in Syria lack a basic understanding of Islam. Also, most individuals who attempted to join terrorist organizations but were stopped by their government came from large, dysfunctional families in the deprived parts of cities, where they were isolated from mainstream social, economic and political activity. Economic incentives rather than religious belief seem to have played a greater role in their motivation. ISIS propaganda videos showing smiling militants engaging in activities like bee-keeping and farming attracted young men who felt they had few prospects at home, especially when combined with perceived grievances and a wish to protect Sunni Muslims in areas of Syria targeted by the government.

person involved in or affected by armed conflict. It governs the actions of FTFs and their families, as well as any measures taken by States in relation to them, when these actions and measures are taken in the context of an ongoing armed conflict.[42]

Status of POW to FTFs: International humanitarian law distinguishes between two types of armed conflict—international armed conflict (IAC) and non-international armed conflict (NIAC). Most FTFs are active in NIACs and only in rare cases are they involved in IACs.[43] The nationality of FTFs is irrelevant for determining whether they can qualify as combatants and hence are entitled to POW status in an IAC. If they do not qualify as combatants then they must be considered civilians as under IHL, any person who does not fall under the definition of combatant/POW is considered a civilian.[44]

In the case of a NIAC, Common Article 3 governs the conduct of the parties to the conflict. These are fundamental rules from which no derogation is permitted. They include the requirement that persons not actively participating in the conflict (including armed forces which have surrendered or are *hors de combat*) must be treated humanely. The article specifically prohibits violence to life and person, including murder, mutilation, cruel treatment, and torture. It also prohibits the taking of hostages, outrages upon human dignity, and the imposition of sentences and executions without the judgment of a regularly constituted court with appropriate judicial guarantees. In addition, it provides that the wounded

42 The phenomenon of 'foreign terrorist fighters and their families' has grown in recent years. An unprecedented influx of foreign fighters to the ISIS has been worrisome for several countries as it is feared that these fighters would be a major threat after returning to their state of nationality or habitual residence. With their experience in handling weapons and explosives they may carry out terrorist acts on their return, or may set up terrorist cells, recruit members or provide funds for terrorist acts or movements. This threat is commonly known as 'blowback'.

43 Combatants captured in IACs are entitled to POW status under the third Geneva Convention and Article 43(2) of AP I. IHL does not directly define the term 'combatant', beyond recognizing that under AP I, combatant status confers the right to participate directly in hostilities. The Third Geneva Convention includes extra categories of combatants entitled to POW status. Combatant status carries two important consequences. First, combatants are immune from criminal prosecution for belligerent acts they commit that comply with IHL. Second, they are entitled to POW status if they fall into the hands of the enemy. Article 4, 1949 Geneva Convention III; and Article 44(1), 1977 AP I.

44 Article 50, 1977 Additional Protocol I.

and sick must be collected and cared for, and an impartial humanitarian body such as the ICRC, may offer its services to the parties to the conflict. There are no combatants in NIACs, which implies that FTFs would get protection under Common Article 3, but may be punished for taking up arms under the national laws.[45]

IHL does not prevent States from prosecuting FTFs for violations of law. Only States that are parties to the armed conflict in which FTFs and their families are involved are bound by IHL rules. These rules apply first of all in the territory in which the armed conflict is taking place. In addition, they also apply throughout the territories of all the States involved in the NIAC extraterritorially, even if hostilities related to the conflict are not taking place in their territory. In the ICRC's view, FTFs and their families who are in the territory of these intervening States (through transfer or repatriation) benefit from the protection afforded by the applicable IHL rules. In any other situation, measures against FTFs and their families taken by States that are not party to an armed conflict are governed by human rights law. The ICRC is of the firm view that authorities who hold FTFs and/or their family members must treat them humanely and in accordance with international law.

Dilemma of FTFs in Syria: A non-state alliance of Kurdish, Arab, Syriac Christian, and Turkmen fighters in Syria called the Syrian Democratic Forces (SDF) was assembled with the assistance and support of the United States in late 2015 to counter the Islamic State of Iraq and Syria

45 On 24 September 2014, at a high-level summit chaired by US President Barack Obama, the Security Council adopted Resolution 2178. The operative paragraphs of the Resolution confirm that the Council was treating FTFs as actors in an armed conflict. The Resolution stipulates that States shall suppress and prevent the recruitment, organization, transport and equipment of 'FTFs in accordance with their obligations under international law'. To do so, States are requested to adopt legislation to prosecute their nationals who travel abroad to participate in terrorist acts or terrorist training. According to Gikel (2014) the scope of Resolution 2178 is not clear and precise. Instead of clearly defining the category of activities or persons that would fall under its scope and within the broad definition the Council provides of 'foreign terrorist fighters', the resolution states that it concerns all forms and manifestations of terrorism. The Council does not limit the scope to international terrorism, and it certainly does not define what terrorism means. It once again leaves it to states to decide and identify who falls under this category. Ginkel Bibi van, The New Security Council Resolution 2178 on Foreign Terrorist Fighters: A Missed Opportunity for a Holistic Approach, *ICCT Journal*, 4 November 2014, available at: https://icct.nl/publication/the-new-security-council-resolution-2178-on-foreign-terrorist-fighters-a-missed-opportunity-for-a-holistic-approach/.

(ISIS) in Syria. It has around 60,000 fighters from diverse origins and has the support of an international coalition of 74 nation states (the Global Coalition to Defeat ISIS). By 2019, the SDF controlled almost one-third of the territory of Syria. The SDF has captured nearly 10,000 FTFs who have committed a wide range of crimes, including slavery, genocide and war crimes. However, it is in dilemma about the treatment and disposal of the detained FTFs. IHL is not clear on whether these FTFs are to be prosecuted in their country of origin, or in another country; or kept under long-term detention under the law of armed conflict; or could be simply released. The other problem is that the States of origin have refused to accept the repatriation of the detainees. A number of European countries have stated that they do not have adequate laws to try their nationals who have committed terrorist offences on foreign soil, and that they do not have supportive evidence for their prosecution in court. Some countries have stripped the FTFs of their citizenship or have expressed the view that they should be tried in the country where they have committed the crimes. The inability of non-State partners to detain FTFs indefinitely and the refusal of States to repatriate their nationals has increased the risk posed by FTFs. Interestingly, the SDF is itself a non-State armed group and is not a party to the core international instruments that comprise IHL.[46]

Mercenaries and FTFs: There are some similarities between the definitions of mercenaries and FTFs. Both are external actors who intervene in an armed conflict. Mercenaries are neither nationals of a party to the conflict nor residents of a territory controlled by a party to the conflict. Similarly, FTFs, while they may or may not be nationals of a party to the conflict, do not reside in the State affected by the conflict and have travelled from abroad to join the insurgency. Both mercenaries and FTFs may be recruited abroad or locally. FTFs and mercenaries have many things in common, ranging from links to acts of terrorism and participation in armed conflicts that may negatively impact human rights, as well as to other criminal activities, including organized crime and smuggling networks.

There is no internationally agreed legal definition of FTFs, nor a specific regime governing them. During an armed conflict, FTFs are obliged, as are all other members of State armed forces or non-State armed groups

46 For more details see: Stigall Dan E., The Syrian Detention Conundrum: International and Comparative Legal Complexities, *Harvard National Security Journal*, Vol. 11, 2020, pp. 54-105.

party to the conflict, to respect the applicable rules of IHL, in particular the minimum standards, enshrined in Article 3 common to the four Geneva Conventions of 1949, concerning the treatment and protection of civilians and others who are not or are no longer actively participating in hostilities. This includes the prohibition of murder, torture and the taking of hostages. Customary IHL requires all parties to a conflict to respect the principle of distinction and proportionality in their military operations and prohibits attacks whose primary purpose is to spread terror. Serious violations of humanitarian law, including acts of terrorism, may amount to war crimes, triggering individual criminal responsibility. In NIACs, non-State armed groups, including FTFs, do not enjoy combatant immunity and may be prosecuted under domestic law for mere participation in hostilities. Regardless of their status under IHL, foreign fighters are protected under human rights law, including its prohibition of refoulement.

The participation of mercenaries, non-State actors, private military actors, terrorist groups and organized FTFs in armed conflict is growing and challenging the fundamental rules of warfare. The US has employed mercenaries to fight its wars in Iraq and Afghanistan because renting an army is cheaper than owning one. Keeping a contractual military is about 10–50% cheaper than keeping a traditional army.[47] Mercenaries and PMSCs are currently employed in wars around the globe, for example, in Syria, Yemen, Nigeria, Libya and Ukraine.

47 Qureshi Wasim Ahmad, Fourth- and Fifth-Generation Warfare: Technology and Perceptions, *San Diego International Law Journal*, Vol. 21, 2019, pp. 187-216.

Chapter IV

Children as Prisoners of War

Introduction

Throughout the history of war children have been recruited as combatants. In 1792, Carl Clausewitz began his career in the Habsburg army as a lance corporal at the age of twelve.[1] Nearly two hundred years later, on 27 November 1985, a 17-year-old girl exploded a car bomb at a joint post of Israeli troops and pro-Israeli militiamen in southern Lebanon, killing herself and at least 20 Israelis and members of the Israeli-backed South Lebanon Army. A statement by the pro-Syrian Arab Baath Party named the suicide bomber as Hamida Mustafa al-Taher. Clausewitz carried out a philosophical examination of war in all its aspects. Hamida became a national hero, and schools, parks, youth Baathcentres, and numerous events were named after her.[2] The first US soldier killed in Afghanistan was reportedly a 14-year-old boy. Palestinian Islamic Jihad and Hamas have recruited children as young as 13 to be suicide bombers and children as young as 11 to smuggle explosives and weapons.[3] The United States-backed Syrian Democratic Forces (SDF) has been accused of recruiting and using children in the ongoing armed conflict. Tens of thousands of children

1 Clausewitz was a professional combat soldier who was involved in numerous military campaigns, but he is famous primarily as a military theorist interested in the examination of war, utilizing the campaigns of Frederick Great and Napoleon as frames of reference for his work. The result was his principal book, *On War*, a major work on the philosophy of war. Clausewitz's work is still studied today, demonstrating its continued relevance.

2 Suicide Bomber Strikes Israeli Post in Lebanon, *The New York Times*, 27 November 1985.

3 Singer Peter W., The New Children of War, *ASPJ Africa & Francophonie*, 2nd Quarter 2010, pp. 77-90.

are thought to be involved in conflicts in Syria, Iraq, Mali, Myanmar, Nigeria, Yemen, Central African Republic, Libya, and elsewhere. Children are recruited as soldiers because they are easier to manipulate and more obedient than adults. They require minimal maintenance and do not have a developed sense of danger. They serve as combatants in a variety of roles: infantrymen, raiders, sentries, spies, trench diggers, and porters. They may also be used as sexual slaves by their superiors.[4]

Contemporary Reality

In 2008, it was estimated that military recruitment of children and their use in hostilities takes place in one form or another in at least 86 countries and territories worldwide.[5] The number of child soldiers, especially girls, recruited around the world has risen dramatically in recent years.[6]An estimated 300,000 children are reported to be serving as soldiers in various situations of armed conflict worldwide.[7] However, the cumulative total could be much higher – as children are killed or wounded, or manage to grow older, their places are taken by new children. A number of States recruit children into their armed forces after they finish schooling and are below 18 years of age;[8] however, the most recent instances of children taking part in hostilities have been for non-State actors. The UN has identified 14 countries where children have been widely used as soldiers. These are Afghanistan, Colombia, the Central African Republic, the Democratic

4 In the case of child soldiers, rape and other forms of sexual violence remained significantly under reported, particularly when perpetrated against boys. Children express reluctance to report such violations owing to the fear of reprisal or rejection by their families and communities, stigmatization, the weak rule of law and the lack of holistic services for survivors. Report of the Special Representative of the Secretary-General for Children and Armed Conflict, UNGA, A/75/203 of 20 July 2020, para 14.

5 Coalition to Stop the Use of Child Soldiers, Child Soldiers Global Report: 2008, p. 12.

6 Wulfhorst Ellen, Global Count finds cases of child soldiers more than doubling, *Reuters*, 13 February 2019.

7 UNICEF and international NGOs are working hard to free child soldiers but do not give any estimates of child soldiers around the world. The first global study on the prevalence of child soldiering was the 1996 UN study, Impact of Armed Conflict on Children (Machel 1996).IT estimated that there were 250,000 child soldiers. Subsequent reports, such as Child Soldiers Global Report 2001 of the International Coalition to Stop the Use of Child Soldiers, estimated that there were about 300,000 child soldiers at any point in time.

8 For instance in the case of the US and India, the minimum age for recruitment in the armed forces is sixteen-and-a-half years, but these recruits can be deployed only after completing a training of about 18 to 24 months.

Republic of the Congo, Iraq, Mali, Myanmar, Nigeria, the Philippines, Somalia, South Sudan, Sudan, Syria, and Yemen. The 2016 Annual Report of the United Nations Special Representative for the Secretary-General on Children and Armed Conflict listed nine State armed forces and nearly fifty non-State armed groups (NSAGs) that currently recruit and use children.[9] Child soldiers have also been used in conflict areas where the US has deployed its armed forces or provides aid to governments.[10]

Age Criteria

Children are generally understood as persons below the age of 18.[11] According to the Convention on the Rights of the Child (CRC), a child is "every human being below the age of 18 years unless under the law applicable to the child, majority is attained earlier".[12] The definition of child soldier used by the UNICEF is based on the Cape Town Principles (1997), which state: A child soldier "is any person under 18 years of age who is part of any kind of regular or irregular armed forces in any capacity, including but not limited to cooks, porters, messengers, and those accompanying such groups, other than purely as family members. Girls recruited for sexual purposes and forced marriage are included in this definition." International organizations which aim to eliminate the use of children as soldiers have widely adopted the definition proposed in the Cape Town

9 Children and armed conflict: Report of the Secretary-General, UN Doc A/70/836-S/2016/360 dated 20 April 2016.

10 The Child Soldiers Prevention Act of the US aims to hold governments accountable for the recruitment or use of children by their forces or their support to militias or paramilitaries that recruit or use children. Those on the list are ineligible for key US military assistance programs, unless they receive a waiver from the White House. US Presidents have routinely used their waiver authority to continue military aid to countries still using child soldiers,for example, in 2019, waivers allowed Afghanistan, Democratic Republic of Congo, Iraq, Mali, and Somalia to receive $17 million in military training and assistance.

11 109 countries have a 'Straight-18' policy for military recruitment in practice, meaning a minimum age of 18 for enlistment as well as deployment. 46 States (23%) still recruit under-18s into their armed forces in practice. Child Soldiers International Annual Report 2017-2018, p. 21.

12 Article 1 of the Convention on the Rights of the Child (CRC), 1989. Until adoption of the CRC, although the term "child" had appeared in some international documents, there was no legal definition of a child. The CRC Article 1(1) filled that gap. Article 38 (2) of the CRC, provides: "State parties shall take all feasible measures to ensure that persons who have not attained the age of 15 years do not take a direct part in hostilities."

Principles. The Paris Principles (2007) state, "A child associated with an armed force or armed group" refers to "any person below 18 years of age who is or who has been recruited or used by an armed force or armed group in any capacity, including but not limited to children, boys and girls, used as fighters, cooks, porters, messengers, spies or for sexual purposes. It does not only refer to a child who is taking or has taken a direct part in hostilities."[13]In this case, the term "child soldier" has been replaced by "a child associated with an armed force or armed group", but the essence of the definition is the same.[14]

The 1977 AP I urges the parties to a conflict to prohibit the recruitment and participation of children below 15 years of age in the hostilities.[15] In case children under the age of 15 are recruited by the armed forces and take part in armed conflict, they shall, if captured, be detained under conditions which take their age into consideration. Such special conditions shall be afforded whether or not they are recognized as POWs. In particular, such 'child soldiers' shall be detained separately from adults, except where families are accommodated as family units.[16]

The 2000 *Optional Protocol on the Involvement of Children in Armed Conflict* raised the 1977 standard by barring the use of anyone under the age of 18 in conflict.[17] The Optional Protocol states that individuals under the age of 16 cannot be enlisted to fight and individuals between the ages of 16 and 18

13 UNICEF, The Paris Principles: the Principles and guidelines on children associated with armed forces and armed groups, February 2007, p. 7.

14 The Cape Town and Paris conferences led to the adoption of non-binding instruments that have since obtained widespread professional, operational, and political currency. The initial development and subsequent circulation of these influential instruments owes much to the involvement of NGOs, United Nations agencies, donors, and activists. Drumbl Mark, A., 2012, *Reimagining Child Soldiers in International Law and Policy*, Oxford University Press, p. 3.

15 Article 77(2), AP I. AP I does not define the notion 'child' and, in particular, does not fix an age limit, a deliberate omission. In this way, varying views of different cultures may be taken into consideration. It should be accepted, however, that from the point of view of IHL anyone who has not attained the age of 18 should not take part in hostilities. Hans-Peter Gasser, 'Protection of the Civilian Population', in Fleck Dieter (ed), 2009, *The Handbook of International Humanitarian Law*, Oxford: Oxford University Press, p. 245.

16 Article 77 (3) and (4), AP I.

17 Article 2, The Optional Protocol to the Convention on the Rights of the Child on the Involvement of Children in Armed Conflict, 2000.

cannot be compelled to join an armed force. Under the Protocol, children must be fully informed of their duties and they cannot be combat-related until they attain the age of 18. The Optional Protocol requires States parties to make a binding declaration upon ratification, setting the minimum age for voluntary recruitment in the armed forces at 16 years or above.[18] The armed groups that are distinct from the armed forces of a state should not under any circumstances, recruit or use in hostilities persons under the age of 18. The state parties have an obligation to take measures to prevent such recruitment and use, including the adoption of legal measures necessary to prohibit and criminalize such practices by the armed groups. [19] The Statute of the ICC, adopted in Rome on 17 July 1998, includes in its list of war crimes within the Court's jurisdiction the active involvement in hostilities of children under 15 or their recruitment into national armed forces during an international armed conflict[20] or into the national armed forces or other armed groups during a non-international armed conflict.[21]The obligations of a State in relation to its use of child soldiers therefore vary according to the treaties it has ratified.

Children in International Armed Conflict

A significant number children were engaged in hostilities during World War II. However, the Geneva Conventions of 1949 did not prohibit the recruitment and participation of children in armed conflict.[22] Children carrying guns are legitimate targets in international armed conflict, but that may not be easy for a soldier who has to fight with them. Soldiers

18 Article 3(2), The Optional Protocol to the Convention on the Rights of the Child on the Involvement of Children in Armed Conflict, 2000. In addition, Article 3(1) of the same Protocol reads: "States Parties shall raise in years the minimum age for the voluntary recruitment of persons into their national armed forces from that set out in article 38 paragraph 3, of the CRC, taking account of the principles contained in that article and recognizing that under the Convention persons under the age of 18 years are entitled to special protection." Article 3(3) provides that state parties that permit voluntary recruitment into their national armed forces under the age of 18 years shall maintain certain safeguards contained therein.

19 Article 4 (1) and (2), The Optional Protocol to the Convention on the Rights of the Child on the Involvement of Children in Armed Conflict, 2000.

20 Article 8, para 2b [xxvi], the Rome Statute of the International Criminal Court.

21 Article 8, para 2e [vii], the Rome Statute of the International Criminal Court.

22 The third Geneva Convention of 1949 in Article 16 provides that the age of the person could give reason for privileged treatment as POW.

are most likely to experience post-traumatic stress disorder after such incidents.[23] Very little has been written about the controversial issue of the targeting of child soldiers in an armed conflict. International lawyers have conveniently avoided commenting on the rules of engagement (ROE) with child soldiers. For any professional force, child soldiers present a complicated question, which is more difficult than the issue of civilian casualties. Members of State armed forces and UN peacekeeping forces are often faced with a moral dilemma while contemplating the use of force against child soldiers. According to Lt General Dallaire, former force commander of the United Nations Assistance Mission for Rwanda (UNAMIR), "For soldiers with any sense of honour at all, fighting children offers a no-win situation. To be defeated by children would almost certainly bring death, derision and disgrace, while to win would carry the taint of having killed mere children."[24]

Targeting child soldiers raises two distinct legal questions: first, whether child soldiers are combatants like any other combatants, and second, if so whether the means used to target them should follow the same rules as for adult combatants. Since children have special rights under IHL and human rights treaties, every action of troops against them remains open to external monitoring and scrutiny. Children who take direct part in international armed conflict are recognized as combatants and in the event of their capture are entitled to POW status under GC III.[25] In addition, they are entitled to certain rights under the human rights treaties, ratified by the detaining power.

The 1977 AP I was the first international treaty to offer protection to children in armed conflicts. Without defining the term 'children', it stipulated that children under the age of 15 may not be enrolled in the armed forces or take part directly in hostilities. As for persons between 15 and 18 years of

23 The NATO forces which operated in Bosnia and in West Africa faced serious problems of clinical depression and post-traumatic stress disorder among soldiers who had faced child soldiers. Child Soldiers as the Opposing Force, Final Report of the HFM-159/RTO Task Group, The Research and Technology Organization of NATO, AC/323(HFM-159)TP/222, January 2011, p. 2.6.

24 Reeves Darin (ed.), 2017, *Child Soldiers: A Handbook for Security Sector Actors,* Canada: The Romeo Dallaire Child Soldiers Initiative, p. vii.

25 Female child soldiers are entitled to specific treatment in quartering, sanitation, health and medical care, execution of penalty, etc., under the GC III. This has been discussed in the next chapter.

age, it provided that recruitment priority should be given to those who are oldest. Article 77 of AP I dealing with the protection of child soldiers is as follows:

1. Children shall be the object of special respect and shall be protected against any form of indecent assault. The Parties to the conflict shall provide them with the care and aid they require, whether because of their age or for any other reason.
2. The Parties to the conflict shall take all feasible measures in order that children who have not attained the age of 15 years do not take a direct part in hostilities[26] and, in particular, they shall refrain from recruiting them into their armed forces. In recruiting among those persons who have attained the age of 15 years but who have not attained the age of 18 years, the Parties to the conflict shall endeavour to give priority to those who are oldest.
3. If, in exceptional cases, despite the provisions of paragraph 2, children who have not attained the age of 15 years take a direct part in hostilities and fall into the power of an adverse Party, they shall continue to benefit from the special protection accorded by this Article, whether or not they are prisoners of war.
4. If arrested, detained or interned for reasons related to the armed conflict, children shall be held in quarters separate from the quarters of adults, except where families are accommodated as family units as provided in Article 75, paragraph 5.
5. The death penalty for an offence related to armed conflict shall not be executed on persons who had not attained the age of 18 years at the time the offence was committed.

Article 77 is not subject to any restrictions as regards its scope of application. It applies to all children who are in the territory of the States at war, whether or not they are affected by the conflict.[27] The ICRC, during discussions on

26 To take "direct part in hostilities" means activities which adversely affect military operations of an adversary or directly inflict death, injury or destruction on persons or objects. Not only direct and personal involvement in such activities but also preparation of military operations may suspect immunity of a civilian. Gasser Hans-Peter, "Protection of the Civilian Population," in Dieter Fleck, (ed.), 2009, *The Handbook of International Humanitarian Law*, New York: Oxford University Press, pp. 261-262.

27 Sandoz Yves, Christophe Swinarski and Bruno Zimmermann. 1987. *Commentary on the Additional Protocols of 8 June 1977 to the Geneva Conventions of 12 August 1949*, Geneva: ICRC (henceforth: ICRC Commentary) p. 899.

the drafting of AP I, decided not to place specific age limits in paragraphs 1 and 4 as there was no precise definition of the term 'children' at that time.[28] The aim of the first paragraph is to assert that children are entitled to special respect and must be protected against any form of indecent assault. The second sentence places an obligation on the Parties to a conflict to provide children with the care and aid they require.

The second paragraph has direct implications for the armed forces and is related to other provisions of the AP I, including those dealing with combatants and POWs, and protection of persons who have taken part in hostilities. It is primarily concerned with the nationals of the recruiting State, though it does not exclude nationals of other States. In other words, this article applies to a State's nationals, and to some extent protects them from their own authorities. According to the ICRC, it is conceivable on the basis of Article 77(2) of AP I for a person to oppose the recruitment of his child under the age of 15 or to request that in the event of his child's voluntary enrolment, it should not be accepted. According to the ICRC, the participation of children and adolescents in combat is an inhumane practice that should be ended. However, it has been observed that in occupied territories and in wars of national liberation, it would not be realistic to totally prohibit the voluntary participation of children under 15 years of age.[29]Accordingly, paragraph 77(2) provides guidelines for exceptional cases where children under 15 years of age are likely to participate in hostilities. In such situations, the authorities employing them should be conscious of the heavy responsibility they are assuming and should give such children appropriate instructions on handling weapons, the conduct of combatants and respect for the laws and customs of war.[30]

28 According to the ICRC Commentary on the Additional Protocols of 1977, the word 'children' is not clarified in any way, and this omission is intentional as the Committee decided not to place specific age limits in paragraphs 1 and 4 of Article 77. Yves Sandoz, Swinarski Christophe and Zimmermann Bruno, 1987, Commentary on the Additional Protocols of 8 June 1977 to the Geneva Conventions of 12 August 1949, Geneva: ICRC, p. 899.

29 As regards the interpretation of "taking a direct part in hostilities", the ICRC Commentary indicates that "the intention of the drafters of the article was clearly to keep children under 15 outside armed conflict, and consequently they should not be required to perform such services....as gathering and transmission of military information, transportation of arms and munitions, provision of supplies, etc." Ibid, p. 901.

30 Ibid, p. 900-901.

Article 77 paragraph 3 does not do away with the obligation to refrain from recruiting children younger than 15 years of age; voluntary enrolment is not explicitly mentioned in AP I. Today, the minimum age for recruitment in the armed forces in a majority of the States is 18 years. Only a few States recruit at the age of 16. In paragraph 4, relating to the arrest or detention of children, however, no age limit has been specified. According to the ICRC, it is reasonable to assume that children under 15 years of age must be detained in quarters separate from those of adults, except where families are accommodated as family units.[31]

A child soldier displaying distinguishing signs and combatant status must be treated as a POW, if he is captured. In fact, there is no age limit for the right to such treatment. However, according to Article 16 of the GC III, age is a factor which justifies privileged treatment. Children under 15 years of age, even when they are POWs, will continue to have the benefit of the provisions of Article 77, particularly paragraphs 1, 4 and 5. The death penalty cannot be pronounced on them, and they must be interned in quarters separate from those of adults. If a child under 15 years of age participates in hostilities under such conditions that he does not have the right to POW status, he may fall under the GC IV if he is a protected person within the meaning of that Convention. Finally, if he does not have the right to POW treatment, and he is not a protected person either, he is entitled, according to Article 45 (Protection of persons who have taken part in hostilities), paragraph 3, to the protection of Article 75 (Fundamental guarantees), which is referred to in paragraph 4 of Article 77.

The provision contained in Article 77 paragraph 5 is similar to Article 68 (4) of the GC IV, which provides that, in any case, the death penalty may not be pronounced by the courts of the Occupying Power on a protected person who is under 18 years of age.[32]Paragraph 5 does not use the word 'children', but the more general term 'persons'. This is probably the most important paragraph as the provision is not subject to any restriction. In territories at war, no person under the age of 18 years may be executed for an offence related to the armed conflict. The inclusion of the term

31 Yves Sandoz, Swinarski Christophe and Zimmermann Bruno, 1987, Commentary on the Additional Protocols of 8 June 1977 to the Geneva Conventions of 12 August 1949, Geneva: ICRC, p. 903. This provision is similar to Article 82 of the GC IV.

32 Article 6 of the International Covenant on Civil and Political Rights (1966) also provides that the death sentence cannot be imposed for crimes committed by persons below 18 years of age.

'executed' caters to the penal provisions of States where legislation permits the death penalty being pronounced on persons below the age of 18 years, though a prohibition of its execution could be possible.[33] Article 26 of the Rome Statutes also provides that: "The Court shall have no jurisdiction over any person who was under the age of 18 at the time of the alleged commission of a crime."

According to Waschefort (2015), the aim of Article 77 is twofold. It prohibits the 'use' and 'recruitment' of children as soldiers. However, Article 77 does not absolutely ban the recruitment and use of children in armed conflict. For instance under paragraph 2, it is not unlawful for a State to recruit and use children between 15 and 18 years of age; it is merely the State's recruitment practice that violates AP I.[34] The International Criminal Court (ICC) Trial Chamber in the *Lubanga case* concluded that 'conscription', 'enlistment' and 'use' are three separate offences. Thus, the Chamber held that a child might be enlisted or conscripted, irrespective of whether she or he is later used to participate in hostilities. It rejected the defence's submission that enlistment and conscription were necessary for the purpose of using a child to participate actively in hostilities.[35] The highest level of protection for children is the interpretation that children under the age of 15 years cannot legally give consent to join an armed group. In the case of children, voluntary enlistment may not be an expression of free choice, but may be driven by social, political or economic pressure. They may have very little choice but to volunteer in order to provide for their family. According to Singer, the notion of voluntary recruitment for a child is misleading, because children of a tender age are incapable of making mature decisions.[36]

33 Yves Sandoz, Swinarski Christophe and Zimmermann Bruno, 1987, Commentary on the Additional Protocols of 8 June 1977 to the Geneva Conventions of 12 August 1949, Geneva: ICRC, p. 903-905.

34 Waschefort Gus, 2015, *International Law and Child Soldiers*, Oregon: Oxford and Portland, pp. 60-71.

35 *The Prosecutor v. Thomas Lubanga Dyilo*, Judgment, ICC-01/04-01/06 (Trial Chamber I), 14 March 2012; Decision on Sentence, ICC-01/04-01/06 (Trial Chamber I), 10 July 2012, paragraphs 38-39.

36 Singer Peter, 2006, *Children at War*, University of California Press, p, 62.

Child Soldiers in Non-international Armed Conflicts

The Common Article 3 to the 1949 Geneva Conventions and the 1977 Additional Protocol II (AP II) deal with non-international armed conflict. The Common Article 3 states that every person not taking an active part in hostilities is to be treated humanely without any discrimination on the basis of race, colour, religion or faith, sex, birth or wealth, etc., by all parties of the conflict. Any violence to life, health or the physical and mental well-being of persons is prohibited. Further, all parties to the conflict are prohibited to commit: murder, mutilation, torture and cruel, inhuman and degrading treatment or punishment at any time. AP II prohibits the recruitment of children under the age of 15 years into armed groups or forces and the participation of children in hostilities, regardless of direct or indirect participation. It also states that even if children take direct part in hostilities, they still have to be provided with the care and aid they require.[37] One of the main weaknesses of the Common Article 3 and AP II is that POW status is not recognized in these treaties, although they afford suitable protection to children participating in conflicts.

Customary law

Customary IHL prohibits the recruitment of children and their participation in hostilities in both international and internal armed conflicts. Though there is no universal accepted age limit for recruitment, it is clear that children should not be below 15 years of age.[38] Children affected by armed conflict are entitled to special respect and protection and States have the major responsibility for the realization of this right. This protection includes among other things protection from any form of sexual violence and from separation from the family, access to education, food and health care, evacuation to safety zones established by States, and reunification with the family.[39]

Pursuant to the Security Council Resolution 1315 of 2000, the Special Court for Sierra Leone (SCSL) was established by an agreement between

37 Article 4 (3), the 1977 Additional Protocol II.

38 Rules 136-137, Recruitment and participation of Child Soldiers; ICRC: Customary IHL.

39 Rules 135, Children affected by armed conflict are entitled to special respect and protection; ICRC: Customary IHL.

the UN and the Government of Sierra Leone.[40] The Court had the power to prosecute persons responsible for serious violations of IHL in the territory of Sierra Leone since 1996. The jurisdiction of the SCSL comprised crimes against humanity, violations of Article 3 common to the Geneva Convention and of Additional Protocol II and other serious violations of IHL as well as some crimes under Sierra Leonean law. The last category of crime included 'conscripting or enlisting children under the age of 15 years into armed forces or groups or using them to participate actively in hostilities' (Article 4 of the SCSL Statute).The Appeal Chamber of the Special Court held in the Hinga Norman decision of May 2004 that the recruitment of child soldiers, namely the conscription, enlistment and use to participate actively in hostilities creates a crime under customary international law attracting individual criminal responsibility. It was the first time that such a criminal act was charged before an international court or tribunal.

A central concern of IHL is to prevent children from serving as combatants, lawful or otherwise. In addition, IHL seeks to extend special POW privileges to captured children who are lawful combatants. It also seeks to protect captured children who have served as unlawful combatants or committed war crimes from the severest punishments of the law. The four Geneva Conventions of 1949 did not address the issue of child soldiers. Prohibitions against the use of child soldiers began with the 1977 Additional Protocols. Now, provisions criminalizing the recruitment of child soldiers are part of the 1998 Rome Statute of the ICC. Other international treaties also contain provisions that call for partial or total bans on the use of child soldiers, although none of these provide for criminal sanctions against violators. These include the 1990 African Charter on the Rights and Welfare of the Child, and the 1999 International Labour Organization Worst Forms of Child Labour Convention 182.

---

40 The special characteristic of the civil conflict in Sierra Leone between 1996 and 2002 was the presence of children, especially young boys under the age of 15,in the ranks of the armed factions, such as the Civil Defense Forces (CDF), the Revolutionary United Front (RUF), the Armed Forces Revolutionary Council (AFRC), the AFRC Junta and the Liberian fighters. It is estimated that more than 7000 young boys and girls took part in the fighting. In most cases, they had been seized from their families and were unable to escape from their captors. These children were often given military training and were taught to handle and fire weapons, to lay ambushes and evade detection. Topa Ilona, Prohibition of child soldiering – international legislation and prosecution of perpetrators, *Hanse Law Review*, Vol. 3, No. 1, 2007, pp. 105–117.

The Common Article 3 of the four GCs permits rebels, including armed children, to be treated as criminals. The sharp differences between the treatment of combatants in inter-State conflicts and domestic conflicts are reflected in the treatment of child soldiers. States promote a stringent legal rule for child protection when it comes to suppressing rebel movements but adopt a far more relaxed standard in regulating the recruitment and use of children in their armed forces. The phrases "all feasible measures", "direct part in hostilities" and "endeavour to give priority to those who are the oldest" in the AP I are vague enough to allow each State to read meanings that suit them. Another drawback is that Article 77(5) of the AP I provides that the death penalty must not be imposed on any person who was under the age of18years when the offence was committed. This blanket immunity might lead child soldiers to commit the most heinous war crimes. The ICC does not have any jurisdiction over a person who was under 18 years of age at the time of the alleged commission of a war crime.[41]

The AP II which applies to civil wars between the armed forces of a state and dissident armed forces or other organized armed groups, makes it clear that "children who have not attained the age of 15 years shall neither be recruited in the armed forces or groups nor allowed to take part in hostilities". It places a comprehensive ban on the use of any person under 15 years of age as a soldier in all civil wars and insurgencies. It also prohibits the death penalty for offences committed by persons under the age of 18years and gives protected status to children under the age of 15 years.

The 2000 Optional Protocol adopts double standards. It permits sovereign States to recruit child soldiers but bars rebel groups from doing the same. It requires States to "take all feasible measures to ensure that members of their armed forces who have not attained the age of 18 years do not take a direct part in hostilities". However, in the case of armed groups it states, "armed groups, distinct from the armed forces of a State, should not, under

41 There is no customary norm prohibiting the prosecution of children who have committed war crimes. However, the prosecution should be limited to extreme cases only: (i) those who refuse to take part in a post-conflict restorative accountability mechanism and thus refuse to acknowledge their crimes and (ii) those who are 'most responsible' or have committed the 'most serious crimes'. The aim should be educational, making them understand that what they have done is wrong and that such behavior cannot be tolerated, thereby ensuring that in the future they will not follow a criminal path on the basis that such behaviour is tolerated. Quenivet Noelle, Does and Should International Law Prohibit the Prosecution of Children for War Crimes? *The European Journal of International Law*, Vol. 28, No. 2, 2017, pp. 433–455.

any circumstances, recruit or use in hostilities persons under the age of 18 years." In other words, the recruitment of child soldiers by non-State armed groups is presumed to be involuntary and thus, illegal.

Child soldiers who are members of the armed forces of a party to an international armed conflict are combatants entitled to participate directly in hostilities. They benefit from 'combatant privilege' and cannot be punished for bearing arms and taking part in hostilities, provided that their actions are in accordance with international humanitarian law. If captured, they are entitled to POW status and all the protections set out in the GC III. The GC III says nothing about the age of a combatant.[42]

The Case of Omar Khadr

Omar Khadr, a Canadian citizen, was born in 1986. It is alleged that his father was a high-ranking member of the Egyptian Islamic Jihad, a senior Al-Qaeda operative and a close associate of Osama bin Laden. It is also alleged that from 1996 until 2001, Khadr travelled throughout Afghanistan with his father, meeting senior Al-Qaeda members and visiting Al-Qaeda training camps and guest houses. Khadr is said to have received training in the use of arms and explosives and, on completion of his training, joined a team of Al-Qaeda operatives constructing and planting landmines targeted against US and coalition forces.[43]

Khadr was 15 years old when he allegedly threw a grenade that killed Sergeant Christopher Speer of the US military during a firefight between US Special Forces and a group of Al-Qaeda operatives. Khadr was the only survivor among the group of militants. He sustained three bullet

42 Happold Matthhew, "Child Prisoners in War," in Scheipers Sibylle (ed.). 2010, *Prisoners in War*, Oxford: Oxford University Press, pp. 237-250.

43 Omar Khadr was born on 19 September 1986 in Toronto, Canada. The son of Ahmed Sa'idKhadr, an alleged high-ranking member of the terrorist group Egyptian Islamic Jihad, Omar spent the first few years of his life in suburban Toronto with his maternal grandparents. In 1988, he moved from Toronto to Peshawar, Pakistan, where Ahmed worked for a charity known as Human Concern International, an organization through which he would allegedly funnel money to al Qaeda. Omar spent the majority of his youth in Pakistan. In 1996, Pakistani intelligence arrested Ahmed Khadr for his involvement in the 1995 Egyptian embassy bombing in Pakistan. By the age of 12, Omar had already undergone formal military training in bomb-making, assault-rifle marksmanship, and combat tactics. Rangaviz David, Dangerous Deference: The Supreme Court of Canada in *Canada v. Khadr,Harvard Civil Rights-Civil Liberties Law Review*, Vol. 46, 2011, p. 253-269.

injuries, but an American medic managed to save his life. Just 12 hours after sustaining life-threatening gunshot wounds, Khadr was interrogated while strapped to a stretcher. He stated that his interrogators threatened him with rape if he refused to cooperate. Khadr was later transferred to a hospital at the Bagram Air Base. In 2002, after his treatment, Khadr was transferred to Guantanamo Bay, Cuba. He had just turned 16 and was one of the youngest prisoners ever held at Guantanamo. He was shackled in painful positions and told that he would be sent to Egypt, Syria or Jordan for torture. He told his attorney that after one interrogation session during which he urinated on the floor, he was used as a "human mop".

The Canadian government initially opposed Khadr's transfer to Guantanamo and urged the US to take into account his juvenile status.[44] The US ignored Canada's request. Khadr was kept in confinement until November 2005 and was later charged under the newly created system of Guantanamo Military Commissions with conspiracy, murder by an unprivileged belligerent, and attempted murder by an unprivileged belligerent.[45] The commissions were based on the system of military courts-martial. However, human rights and legal groups — even the United States Supreme Court — criticized the commissions for the lack of due process and for criminalizing conduct retroactively. The commissions made no distinction between youths and adults, and their rules allowed for indefinite detention even after acquittal. These commissions were later struck down as being unconstitutional.[46]

After the Military Commission Act was signed, new charges were framed against Khadr. These included murder in violation of the law of war, attempted murder in violation of the law of war, conspiracy, and providing material support for terrorism and spying. The international community, including many American citizens strongly opposed Khadr's treatment at Guantanamo. The US military classified Khadr as an enemy combatant, a

44 Because Omar Khadr was Canadian, he had Canadian lawyers who raised legal challenges in the domestic courts there, to the extent that those courts were able to intervene in the US legal process. The lawyers drew on arguments regarding Omar's youth at the time of the events that resulted in his detention, and were remarkably successful in obtaining favorable decisions on Omar's behalf.

45 *The United States v Omar Khadr*, Case No 05-0008, United States Military Commission.

46 The original criminal proceedings brought against Khadr were discontinued as a result of the US Supreme Court's judgment in *Hamdan v. Rumsfeld* (2006). In this case, the Supreme Court ruled that the Bush administration's use of military commissions to try terrorist suspects violated the US Code of Military Justice and Geneva Conventions, and were not specifically authorized by any act of Congress.

perpetrator of war crimes, and not as a soldier (child) entitled to protection under the Geneva Convention III.[47] Khadr's attorneys argued that children can't be expected to understand the law of armed conflict. Therefore, they should not be prosecuted for their participation in armed conflict.[48]

In October 2010, Khadr entered a guilty plea under the US law. According to the plea agreement, he pleaded guilty to five counts of war crimes and was sentenced to eight years in prison with the possibility of parole. This sentence was in addition to the eight years that he had already served at Guantánamo Bay. In September 2012, Khadr was transferred to Canada under terms of the International Transfer of Offenders Act.[49] Canadian prison authorities classified Khadr as a maximum-security prisoner, despite the fact that he had been considered a minimum-security inmate at Guantanamo and one who had never caused any problems. On 7 May 2015, Khadr was released on bail on conditions including that he would wear an electronic tracking bracelet and would reside with his lawyer.

Khadr's case is controversial in many respects and his prosecution has been widely criticized. The US government had given him the status of "unlawful enemy combatant". This was a new terminology used in an armed conflict and was coined by the US. Since the US had signed and ratified the OP to the CRC on the Involvement of Children in Armed Conflict and the

47 Omar spent two years at Guantanamo undergoing regular, routine and sometimes brutal interrogation without representation by counsel, and four years in all before he was charged by a military commission with war crimes. He was ultimately classified by the United States government as an "alien unprivileged enemy belligerent," susceptible to charges by military commission for his unlawful acts in combat.

48 The 2000 Optional Protocol to the Convention on the Rights of the Child on the Involvement of Children in Armed Conflict was formally ratified by the US on 23 December 2002. It increased the age of recruitment and direct participation of children from 15 to 18, bringing it in line with the broadest definition of a child in the CRC. The Protocol, in Article 6(3), provides that "States Parties shall take all feasible measures to ensure that persons within their jurisdiction recruited or used in hostilities contrary to the present Protocol are demobilized or otherwise released from service. States Parties shall, when necessary, accord to such persons all appropriate assistance for their physical and psychological recovery and their social reintegration." Article 7(1) further provides that "States Parties shall cooperate in the implementation of the present Protocol, including in the prevention of any activity contrary to the Protocol and in the rehabilitation and social reintegration of persons who are victims of acts contrary to this Protocol."

49 Arbour, Jane M., Canada v. Khadr: Reflections on the Use of International Law in the Repatriation Litigation, The *Supreme Court Law Review: Osgoode's Annual Constitutional Cases Conference*, (2010), 51 SCLR (2d), 51.

ILO Convention No. 182 concerning the elimination of the worst form of child labour, it was under obligation to rehabilitate a former child soldier. Several international law experts were of the opinion that Omar Khadr should not have been prosecuted. In prosecuting Omar Khadr, the US did not respect its international obligations in terms of respecting juvenile justice standards. Omar Khadr was the first child to stand trial for a war crime since the Nuremburg trials.

David Crane has aptly said: "Omar Khadr, a young Canadian, could have been a child in Sierra Leone. But he was in Afghanistan, in similar circumstances, not of his making or under his control, in an environment from which, as a child, there was no escape. Legally, morally, and politically the international community, including the US, has separated out children from the horrors of combat, to protect and nurture, to rehabilitate and support, and not to punish. No children found in combat should be held liable for their acts."[50]

Omar Khadr was a child soldier, indoctrinated with a radical strain of Islam by his family and surroundings. As a child soldier, he possessed a lower degree of moral culpability for his crimes. Because of this status, the United States should not have prosecuted him. At the age of 15, he was a product of his environment, and lacked the resources, the moral motivation, and the developmental capabilities to escape the circumstances that placed him on a battlefield in Afghanistan.[51]

Omar's appeal against his convictions was rejected recently. In a brief decision in January 2020, the US Court of Appeals for the District of Columbia Circuit denied Khadr's request to force the issue. The exact number of children detained by the US military at Guantanamo is not known. According to materials posted to Wikileaks, the most reliable count appears to be that compiled by journalist Andy Worthington, who documents 28 juvenile detainees at Guantanamo.[52] The US was legally

50 Crane David M., Prosecuting Children in Times of Conflict: The West African Experience, *Human Rights Brief*, Vol. 15, No.3, 2008, p. 15.

51 Christopher L. Dore, What to Do with Omar Khadr? Putting a Child Soldier on Trial: Questions of International Law, Juvenile Justice, and Moral Culpability, *J. Marshall L. Rev.*, Vol. 41, Issue 4, 2008, pp. 1281–1320.

52 Wilson Richard J., Omar Khadr: Domestic and International Litigation Strategies for a Child in Armed Conflict,Santa Clara University School of Law Symposium, February 2012, pp. 68.

obliged to rehabilitate former child soldiers in its custody, and give them assistance for their psychological recovery and social reintegration.[53]

Conclusion

In accordance with the GC III, a captured child combatant is entitled to POW status. In addition to Article 4 of the GC III, the AP I Article 44(1) provides that any combatant falling into the hands of the enemy is a POW. Since the status of POW is not dependent on age, a captured child combatant is entitled to such a status, even if a State has not ratified the AP I. Under Article 5 of the GC III, where doubt exists regarding an individual's POW status, that person should be treated as a POW until his status is determined formally. The GC III provides extensive protection to a POW and this is applicable in the case of a child soldier. However, it fails to provide any specific protection for a child soldier, though Article 16 states that age may be the criterion for privileged treatment. In contrast, Article 77 provides that children under 15 years of age who take direct part in hostilities and are captured shall continue to benefit from the special protection accorded under Article 77 regardless of whether they are POWs.[54] Further, in case child soldiers are arrested, detained or interned for reasons related to armed conflict, they shall be held in quarters separate from the accommodation for adults, except where they are accommodated with their families.

The recruitment and use of children in armed conflict is an inhumane practice. In the eyes of the law, child soldiers are victims of a crime and are therefore entitled to special attention and protection. It is a crime under numerous widely ratified regional and international treaties. The Security Council has also taken the issue seriously and this practice should come to an end. The President of the Security Council, at a meeting held on 12 February 2020, reiterated that it has primary responsibility for the maintenance of international peace and security in accordance with its Charter. He also said that the UN is committed to address the widespread impact of armed conflict on children, and the long-term consequences this has for durable peace, security and development. He stressed that all parties to armed conflict must comply strictly with the obligations applicable to them under international law for the protection of children

53 Charlie Savage, Sentenced for War Crimes, *The New York Times*, 1 November 2010.

54 Article 77(3), AP I.

in armed conflict, including those contained in the Geneva Conventions of 1949 and the Additional Protocols of 1977 as well as in the Convention on the Rights of the Child and its Optional Protocol on the involvement of Children in armed conflict.[55] Various governmental and non-governmental organizations are playing an important role in ending the participation of children in armed conflicts.

55 The President of the Security Council also requested to the parties to armed conflict to include, where appropriate, provisions for the protection of children related to gender- and age-sensitive disarmament, demobilization and reintegration (DDR) of children associated with armed forces or armed groups. United Nations, Security Council, Statement by the President of the Security Council, S/PRST/2020/3 dated 12 February 2020.

Chapter V

Women Prisoners of War

Like men, women who take part in armed conflict are protected by international humanitarian law (IHL) from the moment they fall into the power of the enemy. In World War I, very few women participated in capacities which made becoming a POW a foreseeable possibility. Accordingly, the 1929 Geneva Convention relative to the treatment of POWs contained only one article related to the special protection of women. Article 3 of the Convention stated that POWs were entitled to respect for their persons and honour and that women must be treated with all consideration due to their sex. The treaty provided that differences of treatment between prisoners were permissible only if such differences were based on military rank, the state of physical or mental health, professional abilities, or the sex of those who benefit from them.[1] Since the number of women who actually participated as combatants in the Second World War was insignificant,[2] the need for special protection for women under the laws of war was not felt. The four 1949 Geneva Conventions and the 1977 Additional Protocols established a system of equality in the sense that no adverse distinction can be drawn between individuals on the basis of sex. Women benefit from the general protections offered by the Geneva

1 Article 4, Convention Relative to the Treatment of Prisoners of War, Geneva, 27 July 1929.

2 In World War II, women participated in hostilities in greater numbers, although they did not commonly bear arms. By an exception, the Soviet women participated directly in the fighting in all services and units, as snipers, riflewomen, air pilots, bombardiers, artillerists, etc. It is estimated that about a million Soviet women took part in the fighting, 800,000 in the armed forces and 200,000 in resistance movements, constituting 8% of the total armed forces. Krill Francoise, The Protection of Women in International Humanitarian Law, *International Review of the Red Cross*, No. 249, December 1985, p. 249. Also see: Higonnet Margaret R. et. al., 1987, *Behind the Lines: Gender and the Two World Wars*, London: Yale University Press.

Conventions relating to combatants,[3] the wounded, sick, and shipwrecked,[4] and civilians and persons detained in connection with an armed conflict.[5] The protection afforded under IHL to women combatants taken POW in an international armed conflict has been covered in this chapter.[6]

Women in Armed Conflict

Women are subjected to mistreatment by all participants in armed conflict–by friendly as well as enemy forces, by civilian and military personnel, including United Nations peacekeeping forces, who are entrusted with the task of protecting women. The physical and psychological consequences of this widespread abuse have devastating consequences, not only for the women themselves, but the societies of which they are a part. To some extent, IHL recognizes that women are peculiarly vulnerable during times of armed conflict. It does so through the so-called regime of 'special' protection, which provides safeguards for women when pregnant, and as mothers, maternity cases, and sexual beings.[7]

US military women played a prominent role in Operation Desert Shield and Operation Desert Storm in Iraq and Kuwait. In this conflict, 16 combatant women were killed and two were taken prisoner, becoming the first female POWs since World War II. In addition, Major Rhonda Cornum, US Army flight surgeon, was captured when her helicopter was shot down during a search and rescue mission. During her captivity, she was sexually assaulted.[8] The treatment meted out to Rhonda and two other

3 Articles 14 and 16 of the GC III.

4 Article 12 of the GC I and II states that persons shall be treated humanely and cared for by the Parties to the conflict in whose power they may be, without any adverse distinction founded on sex, race, nationality, religion, political opinions, or any other similar criteria.

5 Articles 13 and 27(3) GC IV.

6 The focus of this chapter is on women as POW. It relates to 'sex' and not the 'gender' of a POW. The term 'sex' refers to biological and physical characteristics, whereas 'gender' refers to the roles, attitudes and values ascribed to them on the basis of their sex. Gender roles vary widely within and between cultures, and depend on the particular social, economic and political context.

7 Gardam Judith G. and Michelle J. Jarvis, 2001, *Women, Armed Conflict and International Law*, The Hague: Kluwer Law International, p. 7.

8 Major Cornum, a 37-year-old flight surgeon and biochemist had broken both arms, smashed her knee and had a bullet in her right shoulder as a result of the downing of her Army helicopter. Later she informed the Presidential commission on women in

women POWs became an issue in the debate over whether women military should be allowed into combat.[9] Those who favoured limiting the role of women, seized upon Major Cornum's experience, saying it proved that women are more vulnerable than men in combat situations. None of the male POWs in Iarq, for instance, reported having been sexually abused during captivity. However, this incident did not lead the US to limit the combat role of women in the armed forces. Following Operation Desert Storm, efforts to expand the assignment of women were renewed by civil rights and women's advocacy groups. In 1992, the US Department of Defence established a policy to ensure that no person who is best qualified is denied access on the basis of gender to an assignment that is open to both men and women, except limiting assignment of women in special operations forces.[10]

In India, however, the induction of women in the armed forces has been frowned upon by military stalwarts on the ground that a woman POW may become the target of misogynistic treatment and a potential victim of sexual assault. Without citing examples of such treatment being meted out to women during wars in the last five decades, these stalwarts have tried to scuttle moves to enhance the role of women and their permanent commission in the armed forces. Strangely, such people have always evaded discussion on the sexual harassment or exploitation of women within the armed forces. Experts on POWs and military personnel are of the opinion that rape and sexual abuse are among the many forms of mistreatment suffered by POWs, and that men as well as women are at risk. In any case, the last two decades have seen an increased participation of women in armed conflicts, both in terms of the number of women serving in armed forces and in the variety of roles they have assumed on and off the

---

the military that she was "violated manually -- vaginally and rectally." Elaine Sciolino, Female POW is Abused: Kindling Debate, *The New York Times*, 29 June 1992.

9 Eritrea also alleged before the Eritrea-Ethiopia Claims Commission that Ethiopian soldiers had assaulted and raped women prisoners of war during the 1998–2000 Eritrean-Ethiopian conflict. The Commission found that the Article 14 obligation to protect the persons and honour of women was specifically concerned with assaults based on the prisoner's gender and unrelated abuse did not necessarily constitute a violation of that provision; Prisoners of War, *Eritrea's Claim, Partial Award*, 2003, paras 139–142.

10 Kamarck Kristy N, Women in Combat: Issues for Congress, Congressional Research Service, 13 December 2016.

battlefield. Women are increasingly involved in close combat functions on the frontline, where there is a greater risk of capture.

Status of women POWs

Women taking part in international armed conflict are protected by IHL from the moment they fall into the power of the enemy. Article 12 of the GC I/ II offer "respect, protection, humane treatment and care" to wounded, sick, and shipwrecked combatants. Article 12 paragraph 4 of the GC I/ II stipulate that "women shall be treated with all consideration due to their sex". Article 14 GC III calls for respect for the physical and moral well-being of the POW, as well as respect for the POW's honour. As members of the armed forces of a party to a conflict, women combatants are entitled to the status of POW upon capture.[11] In case of any doubt about their status, they must be presumed to be POWs, until the question has been decided by a competent authority. IHL extends the right to the status of POW to women taking part in a *levee en masse*- the inhabitants of a non-occupied territory who spontaneously take up arms at the approach of the enemy, without having had time to organize themselves - if they carry their arms openly and respect the laws and customs of war. The same right is accorded to various other categories of women who are not combatants, such as: (i) persons authorized to follow the armed forces without being directly part of them, (ii) crews of the merchant marine and civil aviation; (iii) members of military personnel serving in civil defence organizations. However, women who are medical personnel of the armed forces are not entitled to POW status.

Article 14(1) of the GC III imposes an obligation on the detaining power to ensure that POWs in their custody are treated in a way that is respectful

11 The armed forces of a Party to a conflict are recognized as such if they are organized and placed under a command responsible to that Party for the conduct of its subordinates, even if that Party is represented by a government or an authority not recognized by an adverse Party. In addition, these armed forces must be subject to an internal disciplinary system which enforces compliance with the rules of international law applicable in armed conflicts. In particular, this compliance requires combatants to distinguish themselves from civilians, by a uniform or other distinctive sign, visible and recognizable at a distance, or, at least, they must carry their arms openly while taking part in an attack. Violation by a combatant of the rules applicable in armed conflict is punishable but he is not deprived of his right to the status of prisoner of war in case of capture. Krill, Francoise, The Protection of Women in International Humanitarian Law, *International Review of the Red Cross*, Vol. 25, No. 249, December 1985, pp. 337–363.

of their persons and their honour. However, 'respect for person and honour' is not defined. According to common understanding, 'respect for [someone's] person' signifies 'esteem for or a sense of the worth or excellence of a person' and 'due regard for the feelings and rights of others'. Respect for a person's honour, while to some extent overlapping with respect for their person, more specifically entails due regard for the sense of value that every person has of themselves. Honour is a personal concept that may also be linked to a person's reputation, age and standing in their community or peer group. The respect for the person and honour of a POW would be dependent on a wide range of factors, including their cultural, social or religious background, gender and age. A minimum of respect is required towards any person, however, and the specific context can only expand, never diminish this respect. The obligation of respectful treatment is related to the more explicit prohibitions that can be found in the GC III, such as the prohibition of acts of violence against or insulting treatment of prisoners and the prohibition of outrages upon personal dignity, in particular humiliating and degrading treatment.

The GC III states that female POWs must be treated at least as favourably as male POWs, irrespective of what might be the practices of the detaining power. Article 16 of the GC III reads: "Taking into consideration the provisions of the present Convention relating to rank and sex, and subject to any privileged treatment which may be accorded to them by reason of their state of health, age or professional qualifications, all POWs shall be treated alike by the Detaining Power, without any adverse distinction based on race, nationality, religious belief or political opinions, or any other distinction founded on similar criteria." Additionally, by Article 88 of the GC III, a woman POW may not be "awarded or sentenced to a punishment more severe, or treated whilst undergoing punishment more severely, than a male member of the armed forces of the Detaining Power dealt with for a similar offence."

Special Protections for Women

The 1949 Geneva Conventions and both the 1977 Protocols provide that due "regard" or "consideration on account of their sex" must be given to women and that they must be accorded special respect and protection. These provisions are described as having the purpose of preserving the modesty and honour of women. For example, in the context of Article 14 of the GC III, the phrase, "women shall be treated with all the regard due to their sex ...", has been described in the following terms: It is difficult to give any general definition of the 'regard' due to women. Certain points should, however, be borne in mind;...these points are the following: (i) weakness --this will have a bearing on working conditions ... and possibly on food; (ii) honour and modesty --the main intention is to defend women POWs against rape, forced prostitution and any form of indecent assault; and (iii) pregnancy and childbirth --if there are mothers with infants among the prisoners, they should be granted early repatriation ... women who have given birth should be repatriated with their child, while pregnant women should either enjoy special treatment, or, if their state of health permits, should also be repatriated.[12]

The second paragraph of Article 14 requires that due regard be given to the specific needs of women and forbids any discriminatory treatment of them. The number of women joining armed forces and taking on active combat roles has been steadily rising since the adoption of the GC III. The special protection of women POWs and the call for treatment at least as favourable as that of men during captivity is therefore of greater importance today.[13]

The specific mention of the protection of women in Article 14(2) is not to be understood as implying that women have less resilience, agency or capacity within the armed forces, but rather as an acknowledgement that women have a distinct set of needs and may face particular physical and psychological risks. Article 14(2) requires Parties to the conflict to take into account the distinct needs and risks that women prisoners of war face during their internment, for example in relation to privacy, safety and medical care.

While both men and women may suffer sexual assault and other ill-treatment during captivity, sexual violence has distinct effects on women's physical and mental health and psychosocial well-being. In particular, they

12 Picket jeans S., (ed.), 1960, *Commentary: III Geneva Convention Relative to the Treatment of Prisoner of War*, Geneva: ICRC, p. 147.

13 The addition in 1949 of the sentence that women 'shall in all cases benefit by treatment as favourable as that granted to men' was intended to acknowledge that 'the position of women was not the same in all countries' and that experiences during the Second World War had shown that 'it was urgently necessary to safeguard the position of women in the hands of Detaining Powers where their status was lower than that of men'. The discussion during the 1949 Diplomatic Conference indicates that the drafters wished to stress that any discriminatory treatment of women POWs is forbidden irrespective of women's legal standing in the country of the Detaining Power.

face the additional risk of pregnancy, which may have adverse physical and psychological consequences, ranging from medical complications during pregnancy or labour to stigmatization and ostracism while pregnant or raising a child from rape. The protection and care owed to women POWs under Article 14(2) requires that the Detaining Power take proactive measures to prevent such incidents from occurring and to ensure that women who are victims of sexual violence have access to appropriate, gender-specific health care.

The duty to treat women with all regard due to their sex requires the Detaining Power to provide medical services with expertise in dealing with both male and female patients in POW camps. If women are pregnant or have just given birth when they fall into the hands of the enemy, or become pregnant during captivity, specific medical attention must be provided. Parties are obliged to ensure that the medical services available to female POWs are adequately equipped to address women's gynaecological and reproductive health issues.

In addition to the specific arrangements required to ensure the physical safety and relevant medical care of female prisoners, the duty to treat women 'with all regard due to their sex' affects all aspects of the organization of a camp and the overall conditions of internment. The duty must therefore be taken into account with regard to the clothing that is supplied to women, to the recreational activities provided, and to the work that is assigned to them.

The third paragraph of Article 14 addresses the civil capacity of POWs. Civil capacity signifies the recognition of a person as a full member of society who is able to take part in legal and business transactions and is a fundamental part of a person's dignity. While being detained as a POW during an armed conflict obviously affects this ability, Article 14(3) provides that restricting the civil capacity of POWs to act as natural legal persons and to exercise the rights such capacity confers must not go beyond those directly required by the captivity. Some of the specific protections afforded to women POWs are as follows.

Quarters: To protect women from indecent assault and to ensure that they are treated with all the regard due to their sex, the GC III obliges Detaining States to provide separate accommodation to women POWs. These provisions are contained in Articles 25, 29, and 97 require that specific accommodation (separate dormitories) be arranged for women POWs. This provision can be interpreted as women POWs having separate quarters, being supervised by women, and being searched by women. Rule 119 of Customary IHL, which deals with accommodation for women deprived of their liberty, links the physical separation of men and women to the requirement to take into account women's needs and to prevent them from becoming victims of sexual violence.

Women POWs undergoing disciplinary punishment by confinement or punishment following a judicial sentence must be provided separate quarters (i.e. sleeping quarters and conveniences) and be under the supervision of female staff.[14] In addition, under Article 75, paragraph 5 of AP I and Rule 119 of Customary IHL, there is a general obligation to provide such treatment to all women deprived of their liberty for reasons related to an armed conflict. The Standard Minimum Rules for the Treatment of Prisoners also provides that women should be kept in separate quarters and be under the immediate supervision of women.[15] The provisions under GC III relating to quartering can be interpreted to include separate quarters for women POWs with an obligation on the Detaining Power to ensure that women detainees are under the authority of a woman and that body search of women POWs is conducted by women in a manner consistent with human dignity.

In recent decades, the use of closed-circuit television monitoring systems in places of detention, including where POWs are held, has increased exponentially. Limited, well-regulated and well-managed video surveillance in POW camps should not in principle be considered as prohibited under Article 14(1) and may be an appropriate measure of surveillance in certain places and at certain times to prevent or deter escape attempts. It may also have humanitarian advantages, by discouraging abuses by guards, and may also help to prevent suicide or violence among POWs. However, the placement of cameras in toilets or bathrooms, generating a full view of women POWs would be inappropriate and violative of their dignity and honour.

---

14 Article 97 paragraph 4 and Article 108 of GC III.

15 Rule 8 and 53, the Economic and Social Council (ECOSOC), Standard Minimum Rules for the Treatment of Prisoners, Res 663 C (XXIV) and 2076 (LXII) of 31 July 1957 and 13 May 1977.

Sanitation: The right to adequate sanitation, is based on Articles 11 and 12 of the International Covenant on Economic, Social and Cultural Rights and is considered fundamental to human dignity and privacy. It is considered a human right that is essential for the full enjoyment of life and all human rights.[16] The Geneva Conventions enjoin States to provide prisoners with adequate sanitation facilities for POWs. Article 29 of the GC III requires States to ensure that sanitary measures are taken to keep the camps in a clean and healthy condition. POWs must be provided with water and soap for their personal hygiene, with facilities and installations for that purpose (e.g. baths and showers), and with enough time to wash. In addition, conveniences must comply with the rules of hygiene and be kept clean. In situations where POWs are undergoing punishment, Article 97 calls upon the Detaining Power to ensure that the same standards of sanitation are maintained. Though these provisions do not refer specifically to women, they could be interpreted to mean that the Detaining Power must attend to the special health and sanitary needs (e.g., relating to menstruation) of women POWs. In view of the Article 14 of the GC III, there must be special facilities to cater to women's privacy, safety and needs, and women must be allowed appropriate time to wash and clean, especially during menstruation.[17]

Health and medical care: The Detaining Power is under obligation to provide free medical care and medicines to all detainees. As women have certain health issues that are different from those of men, the Detaining Power needs to provide specific services to women POWs which may include medical check-ups and screening for cervical and breast cancer.[18]

16 UNGA Res 64/292 of 3 August 2010, para 1.

17 Article 29, para 2 of the GC III states: "Prisoners of war shall have for their use, day and night, conveniences which conform to the rules of hygiene and are maintained in a constant state of cleanliness. In any camps in which women prisoners of war are accommodated, separate conveniences shall be provided for them."

18 There are many health-related needs for women such as screening for cervical cancer, breast cancer (which could be life-saving), anaemia, and appropriate care during pregnancy, that entitle them to specific protection and assistance. Male medical staff should, wherever possible, be accompanied by female staff when carrying out examinations of women. Such examinations should not be observed by non-medical prison personnel for reasons of preserving the confidentiality of medical examinations. Abusive medical examinations (e.g. unnecessary intimate examinations of women POWs in front of male guards) should be prevented at all times. Charlotte Lindsey-Curtet, et, al., 2004, *Addressing the Needs of Women*, Geneva: International Committee of the Red Cross, p. 115, 132.

The Detaining Power is obliged to provide women with safe and regular access to clean toilets and shower facilities, with sufficient and suitable sanitary products, and means to dispose of them, and with clothing to deal with personal hygiene in dignity and privacy.[19]

Food and Work: The quality, quantity, and variety of the daily food ration distributed in POW camps must be in accordance with the particular needs of individuals, climatic conditions and the amount of work executed by them. Article 26 of the GC III, obliges the Detaining Power to ensure that internees are in a good state of health to prevent the development of nutritional deficiencies. This necessitates an individual appraisal, where the sex of the person is likely to play a part.[20] A women POW who is pregnant, for instance, would have additional nutritional requirements. The Detaining Power may be required to adjust the quality and quantity of food rations for women to avoid the risk of anaemia and mineral deficiencies. The Detaining Power has the right to compel POWs to work. However, Article 49 of the GC III explains that the type and amount of work to be carried out by POWs depend on a variety of factors, including sex. Interpreted in the light of Article 16 of the GC III, this means that women's physical strength and specificities must be taken into account when assigning work to them.[21]

---

19 Article 27 of the GC III states, "Clothing, underwear and footwear shall be supplied to POWs in sufficient quantities by the Detaining Power, which shall make allowance for the climate of the region where the prisoners are detained. Uniforms of enemy armed forces captured by the Detaining Power should, if suitable for the climate, be made available to clothe POWs. The regular replacement and repair of the above articles shall be assured by the Detaining Power. In addition, prisoners of war who work shall receive appropriate clothing, wherever the nature of the work demands."

20 Article 26 of the GC III provides, "The basic daily food rations shall be sufficient in quantity, quality and variety to keep POWs in good health and to prevent loss of weight or the development of nutritional deficiencies. Account shall also be taken of the habitual diet of the prisoners. The Detaining Power shall supply POWs who work with such additional rations as are necessary for the labour on which they are employed."

21 With regard to POWs performing labour, two articles of the Third Convention deal with liability for injuries resulting from occupational accidents. Articles 54(2) and 68 provide for compensation by the Power on which prisoners depend and require the Detaining Power to provide prisoners of war concerned with a medical certificate enabling them, if need be, to submit a claim for compensation to the Power on which they depend following repatriation.

The British Manual provides that women POWs are to be considered for work in the same manner as male POWs. However, they are only to be employed in supervising male POW who, prior to their capture, they could have commanded in the field. Where female POW are used to supervise male POWs, due attention is to be paid to religious and cultural sensitivities concerning the subordination of males. Also, pregnant female POWs are not to be employed on any work that might, directly or indirectly endanger their health or that of their unborn child.[22]

Punishment: Women POWs must not be sentenced to a punishment more severe, nor treated more severely while undergoing punishment than a woman member of the armed forces of the Detaining Power dealt with for a similar offence. A woman POW may in no case be sentenced or treated more severely while undergoing punishment than a male member of the armed forces of the Detaining Power dealt with for the same offence.[23] Women POWs, who are pregnant or having dependant infants shall have their cases considered with the utmost priority. To the maximum extent feasible, the detaining power must endeavour to avoid the pronouncement of the death penalty on pregnant women or mothers who having dependant infants, for an offence related to the armed conflict. The death penalty for such offences must not be executed on such women.[24]

A number of military manuals elaborate on the different facets of respect for POWs' honour. They prohibit, for example, the disclosure of strictly personal particulars; reporting that may affect the dignity or honour of POWs or that may lead to acts of violence, intimidation or insults against them or that may allow them to be identified individually; the marking of clothing in a humiliating or degrading way. More generally, the obligation to respect women prisoners' honour prohibits any conduct which cannot be reasonably justified by the requirements of proper and safe handling of the captives, including physical interference such as pushing and hustling or verbal assault.[25]

22 Prisoners of War Handling, JWP Publication 1-10, Annex 3G-1, Guidance for Employment of Prisoners of War, 2001.

23 Article 88, GC III.

24 Article 76(2) and (3) of the AP I.

25 For instance, see Netherlands' Military Manual, 2005, p. 85, paragraph 0711; Germany's Military Manual, 2013, p. 120, paragraph 811; and the United States' Law of War Manual, 2016, p. 569, paragraph 9.13.4.1.

Release: The clause, 'regard due to their sex' contained in Article 14 of the GC III could be interpreted to mean that the Detaining Power should arrange for early repatriation of female POWs who are pregnant and those who are mothers of young children. Such an interpretation is confirmed by Annex I, which reproduces the Model Agreement Concerning Direct Repatriation and Accommodation in Neutral Countries of Wounded and Sick Prisoners of War that relates to Article 110 of the GC III, and lists 'women POWs who are pregnant or mothers with infants and small children' among the individuals to be given priority in repatriation. These women benefit from special protection, along with the sick and wounded and children, as they are deemed to be at higher risk in internment and POW camps.

The wars in Iraq and Afghanistan marked the first era in which women rose to significant leadership roles in the American military. The treatment meted out to the American women POWs in Iraq shows that women combatants are in a much more vulnerable position than their male counterparts during a conflict. To some extent, IHL recognizes the vulnerability of women combatants and has provisions to protect the honour and modesty of women POWs. Otherwise, under IHL, it is assumed that the needs of women combatants are identical to those of male combatants. In the light of the fact that the participation of women in the armed forces has increased the world over in the last two decades, women POWs need to be specially protected from attacks on their honour, including any kind of ill-treatment.[26]

The International Committee of the Red Cross (ICRC) serves as a fact finder with respect to possible violations of IHL. It attempts to protect POWs, civilians caught in war zones, and wounded or sick military members. Both the ICRC and the international community - through the International Criminal Court - should insist on strict adherence to the Geneva Convention III in relation to men and women POWs alike.[27]

26 Ill-treatment includes any form of torture, or cruel, inhuman or degrading treatment. The ill-treatment of women in detention often includes such acts as rape and other forms of sexual violence, forced termination of pregnancy or sterilization, strip searches in the presence of men, abusive and degrading insults, forced separation from or disappearance of children, abusive medical examinations or body searches, solitary confinement, non-provision of sanitary material during interrogation, prohibition of family visits and forced prostitution.

27 Lilach Rosenberg-Friedman, Captivity and Gender: The Experience of Female

Conclusion

Article 13 of the GC III requires that POWs "must at all times be humanely treated. Any unlawful act or omission by the Detaining Power causing death or seriously endangering the health of a prisoner of war in its custody is prohibited, and will be regarded as a serious breach of the present Convention." The GC III speaks relatively little about women - primarily because, at the time it was drafted, women were not involved on the battlefield to the same extent as men.[28] Today, the law against rape and sexual violence in armed conflict is much stronger. Rape was specifically codified as a recognizable and independent crime within the statutes of the International Criminal Tribunals for the Former Yugoslavia (ICTY) and for Rwanda (ICTR). The ICTY and ICTR cases have reinforced the legal basis for arguing that rape and sexual violence are both individual crimes against humanity and violations of the laws and customs of war. Finally, the new statute of the International Criminal Court also recognizes rape as a crime against humanity when it occurs in the context of an armed conflict.

International human rights and refugee law also protect women's personal safety. Human rights law enshrines the right to life and the prohibition of torture, cruel, inhuman and degrading treatment or punishment. No derogation from these rights is permissible, even in times of public emergency. States are under a duty not to infringe these rights themselves and to protect them from infringement by others. In an international armed conflict, the physical and psychological integrity and dignity of women must be protected. The four Geneva Conventions of 1949 (in particular the Third Convention) and the 1977 Additional Protocol I and other bodies of law afford this protection to women. This part of the law must be respected, disseminated and enforced in times of peace as well as war. Humanitarian organizations must do their utmost to remind parties to an armed conflict of their obligations under IHL.

Prisoners of War during Israel's War of Independence, *Nashim: A Journal of Jewish Women's Studies & Gender Issues*, No. 33, Fall 2018, pp. 64-89.

28 Anita Ramasastry, What Happens When GI Jane Is Captured? Women Prisoners of War and the Geneva Conventions, 02 April 2003, available at: https://supreme.findlaw.com/legal-commentary/what-happens-when-gi-jane-is-captured.html.

Chapter VI

The Role of ICRC

On 24 June 1859, Henry Dunant, a young banker from Geneva, witnessed the aftermath of a bloody battle between the armies of France and Sardinia and the Austrian forces near the northern Italian village of Solferino. In ten hours of fierce fighting, more than 6000 soldiers were killed and some 40,000 wounded. Horrified by the suffering of the wounded soldiers left on the battlefield, Dunant wrote a book, *A Memory of Solferino*. He ended the book with a question, "Would it not be possible, in time of peace and quiet, to form relief societies for the purpose of having care given to the wounded in wartime by zealous, devoted and thoroughly qualified volunteers?" This simple question was the inspiration for the founding of the Red Cross, later the International Committee of the Red Cross (ICRC).

The ICRC is an impartial, neutral and independent organisation.[1] Its humanitarian mission is to protect the lives and dignity of victims of armed conflict and other situations of violence and to provide them with assistance. It is part of the International Red Cross and Red Crescent Movement.[2]As the guardian of IHL, the ICRC takes measures to ensure

1 The ICRC's mission statement: "The International Committee of the Red Cross (ICRC) is an impartial, neutral and independent organization whose exclusively humanitarian mission is to protect the lives and dignity of victims of armed conflict and other situations of violence, and to provide them with assistance. The ICRC also endeavours to prevent suffering by promoting and strengthening humanitarian law and universal humanitarian principles. Established in 1863, the ICRC is at the origin of the Geneva Conventions and the International Red Cross and Red Crescent Movement. It directs and coordinates the international activities conducted by the Movement in armed conflicts and other situations of violence." Available at: https://www.icrc.org/en/who-are-we/mandate.

2 Besides the ICRC, the Movement comprises the National Societies and their International Federation. There are around 190 National Societies in the world,

respect for, promote, reaffirm and develop this body of law. In order to carry out its activities in international armed conflicts, the ICRC has been granted an explicit right to regular access to prisoners of war (POW) under the Third Geneva Convention and to civilians protected by the Fourth Geneva Convention.

The ICRC is obliged to offer its services in the event of armed conflict for three reasons: (i) the Geneva Conventions refer specifically to it: the right to be notified of the identity of prisoners of war and civilian internees; the right for its delegates to visit them and speak in private with the captives of their choice; the right to have its special position in relief operations recognised at all times; (ii) the principle of impartiality obliges it to work without discrimination for all victims of armed conflict; and (iii) the Statutes of the International Red Cross and Red Crescent Movement dictate the ICRC's duty to carry out the tasks assigned to it by humanitarian law.[3]

The objective of the ICRC's activities for the protection of POWs and other people deprived of their freedom is to ensure that their physical and mental integrity is fully respected and that their living conditions and treatment are in line with IHL and other fundamental rules and internationally recognised standards. Visits to places of detention are carried out by the ICRC in accordance with strict conditions. These are: (a) ICRC delegates must be provided with full and unimpeded access to all detainees falling within its field of interest and to all premises and facilities used by and for them; (ii) delegates must be able to hold private interviews with the detainees of their choice; (iii)delegates must be able to repeat their visits; (iv) detainees falling within the ICRC's field of interest must be notified individually to the ICRC, or the ICRC must be able to draw up lists of their names to enable the individual follow-up of such people. In the case of POWs, the ICRC also organises the exchange of family news, tracing disappeared soldiers, reuniting and repatriating POWs.

carrying out humanitarian services for the benefit of the community. The ICRC considers the National Society its primary local partner in each country, sharing the same Fundamental Principles and working in partnership with it while at the same time contributing to further enhancing its emergency preparedness and response capacities. Partnership with National Societies is a valuable asset towards obtaining the best possible access to beneficiaries and delivering a relevant humanitarian response, and is one of the key features of the ICRC's cooperation within the Movement.

3 Bugnion Francois, 2003, *The International Committee of the Red Cross and the Protection of War Victims*, ICRC and Macmillan Education, p. xxxiii.

Status of the ICRC

The ICRC has "a status of its own" (*sui generis*). As a private association under Swiss law, the ICRC is not an intergovernmental organisation. However, in contrast to non-governmental organisations, the ICRC's recognised international legal personality enables it to sign agreements with States to provide its personnel, premises and correspondence with diplomatic protection. Although the ICRC's headquarters and employees in Geneva remain subject to Swiss law, its agreement with Switzerland duly takes into account the organisation's international mandate. The *sui generis* character of the ICRC is recognised by the fact that it was granted observer status by the UN General Assembly Resolution 45/6 of 16 October 1990.

Historical

In order to preserve the lives, security, dignity and physical and mental well-being of people adversely affected by armed conflict and other violence, the ICRC has adopted a protection approach that aims to ensure that the authorities and other stakeholders involved fulfil their obligations and uphold the rights of individuals protected by law. It also tries to prevent and stop violations of IHL and of other bodies of law protecting people in such situations. The beneficiaries include, *inter alia*, resident and displaced civilians, vulnerable migrants, people deprived of their freedom which includes POWs, security detainees, internees and other people at risk of being subject to ill-treatment. As a neutral, impartial and independent humanitarian organisation, the ICRC seeks to ensure that all the parties to a conflict and all authorities provide individuals and groups with the full respect and protection that are due to them under IHL.[4]

The activities of the Red Cross received significant response in wars which took place during 1864–1913: the Schleswig–Holstein conflict (1864); the Austro–Prussian War (1866); the Franco–Prussian War (1870–71); the war in the Balkans and the Caucasus (1875–78); the Serbo–Bulgarian War (1885); the Boer War (1899–1902); and the Balkan Wars (1912–13).[5] During the Franco–Prussian War, the International Committee established an international agency in Basel to provide aid to wounded soldiers. The Basel Agency set up an information bureau in respect of wounded and

4 For more details see: ICRC Annual Report 2017.

5 Bugnion Francois, 2003, *The International Committee of the Red Cross and the Protection of War Victims*, ICRC and Macmillan Education, p. 30

sick prisoners. Lists of names were obtained and published and enquiries were sent to Central Committees and governments in an effort to answer the numerous requests it received for information about missing soldiers. Article 6 of the Geneva Convention (1864) stipulated that wounded prisoners "who, after their recovery, are recognised as being unfit for further service, shall be repatriated". The International Committee and the Basel Agency attempted to put this rule into practice. With their sustained efforts, some 2600 wounded and disabled prisoners were repatriated through Switzerland. The Agency covered the cost of transport within Switzerland as well as accommodation and hospital expenses, mainly in Basel and Geneva. The relief supplied consisted mainly of dressings, medicines, surgical instruments, clothes and food; small amounts of other items were also sent, such as tobacco, soap and wine.[6]

The internment in Switzerland of French soldiers, in the height of winter and under appalling conditions, prompted the creation of a third body: the Central Relief Agency for members of the armed forces interned in Switzerland. This Agency carried out activities similar to those of its sister agency for POWs, but solely for soldiers interned on Swiss territory. In brief, the International Committee established basic operational procedures in the following fields: delivery of relief supplies; sending of delegates into the field; transmission of mail; opening of an information bureau and publication of lists of wounded soldiers and POWs; repatriation of the wounded POWs; and representations to ensure the application of the Geneva Convention.[7]

During most of the wars listed above, the International Committee was successful in promoting the application of the Geneva Convention and providing some form of assistance to the victims of conflicts. The ICRC went beyond its own mandate and provided humanitarian assistance in the Austro-Prussian War, the Russo–Turkish War (1877–78), the Hispano–American War (1898) and the Boer War. No appeals to Red Cross solidarity were made during the Russo–Japanese War (1904–05) or in the many colonial expeditions which marked European imperialism in the second half of the nineteenth century. Though the 1864 Geneva Convention (revised in 1906) had no provision for dealing with complaints

6 Bugnion Francois, 2003, *The International Committee of the Red Cross and the Protection of War Victims*, ICRC and Macmillan Education, p. 33-34.

7 Ibid, p. 35-36.

of alleged violations of its provisions, the Committee regularly published the complaints it received from governments or national societies of belligerent states without commenting on the alleged facts, but sometimes giving its own interpretation of the law applicable to the case in question. It also publicised the answers it received from the accused governments.

Establishment of Information Bureau: The question of establishing and forwarding lists of wounded, sick and dead soldiers, as well as lists of POWs, was of primary concern to the Red Cross since its foundation. In 1869, the Berlin Conference adopted a resolution calling for the creation of an international relief and information agency. However, such an agency had no formal basis in law. A belligerent state was under no obligation to provide the names of wounded enemy troops, nor of the prisoners of war it was holding. In many cases, they would have been incapable of providing such information, as the prisoners were not registered. The Hague Conference of 1899 took the first step towards solving the problem:

> A bureau for information relative to POWs be instituted on the commencement of hostilities in each of the belligerent States, and, when necessary, in the neutral countries on whose territory belligerents have been received.
>
> This bureau is intended to answer all enquiries about POWs, and will be furnished by the various services concerned with all the necessary information to enable it to keep an individual return for each POW. It will be kept informed of internments and changes, as well as of admissions into hospital and deaths.
>
> It is also the duty of the information bureau to receive and collect all objects of personal use, valuables, letters, etc., found on the battlefields or left by prisoners who have died in hospital or ambulance, and to transmit them to those interested.

This article 14 Annex to Convention required the creation of national information bureaux, on the lines of those created by Prussia in the 1866 and 1870 campaigns. It did not compel a belligerent to pass on the information assembled by its national bureau to the adversary. The Geneva conference proposed:

> As soon as possible, each belligerent shall forward to the authorities of their country or army the marks or military papers of identification

> found upon the bodies of the dead, together with a list of names of the sick and wounded taken into charge by him.
>
> Belligerents will keep each other mutually advised of internments and transfers, together with admissions to hospitals and deaths which occur among the sick and wounded in their hands. They will collect all objects of personal use, valuables, letters, etc., which are found upon the field of battle, or have been left by the sick or wounded who have died in sanitary formations or other establishments, for transmission to persons in interest through the authorities of their own country.

The 1907 Hague Conference adopted the same provisions concerning the wounded, sick and shipwrecked of naval forces, but with regard to POWs it merely rounded off the previous regulation, stipulating that the individual record cards established for each prisoner be sent to the opponent after the conclusion of peace.

The Geneva and Hague Conventions thus laid down two distinct sets of rules: one, applicable to the wounded, sick, shipwrecked and dead, making it obligatory to forward information during hostilities; the other, applicable to able-bodied POWs, creating the framework for forwarding information, but not making it compulsory to do so before hostilities had ceased. The Red Cross clarified that with regard to the wounded and sick, it was willing and able to do so and had already provided for a special body to that effect – the International Agency. The ICRC had the task of seeing that the Agency was set up when required. However, as regard POWs, the ICRC was of the opinion that forwarding of lists of able-bodied POWs was the role of the relief societies.

Relief Societies: The 1906 Geneva Convention placed the personnel of voluntary aid societies, duly recognised and authorised by their governments on an equal footing with members of the military medical services, upon condition that the said personnel shall be subject to military laws and regulations. Thus they were granted the same immunities as available to their colleagues in the medical services of the armed forces. The Regulations annexed to the Hague Convention respecting the Laws and Customs of War on Land also provided for intervention by relief societies:

> Relief societies for POWs, which are properly constituted in accordance with the laws of their country and with the object of serving as the channel for charitable effort shall receive from the

> belligerents, for themselves and their duly accredited agents, every facility for the efficient performance of their humane task within the bounds imposed by military necessities and administrative regulations. Agents of these societies may be admitted to the places of internment for the purpose of distributing relief, as also to the halting places of repatriated prisoners, if furnished with a personal permit by the military authorities, and on giving an undertaking in writing to comply with all measures of order and police which the latter may issue.[8]

The new Geneva Convention, as well as those of The Hague, recognised voluntary and officially recognised relief societies to work on behalf of the wounded, shipwrecked and POWs.

The First World War

In terms of scope and duration, the huge numbers of people drawn into the fighting and the means used to seek victory, the Great War was an upheaval without precedent. From the humanitarian point of view, the consequences were incalculable: millions of men perished in the inferno of the trenches, while hospitals overflowed with the wounded, amputees and victims of gas. Millions more struggled to survive in the grim conditions of POW camps, and at the same time civilians were deported, interned and taken hostage. Whole towns were left without supplies, production and transport were paralysed and crops destroyed, leaving countless people prey to hunger, cold and epidemics.[9] The International Committee created the International Prisoners-of-War Agency. The ICRC's position as a neutral intermediary between the warring parties was confirmed and strengthened.

When the war broke out, the legal instruments were binding on the belligerents.[10] However, certain shortcomings were observed in the

8 Article 15, Regulations respecting the Laws and Customs of War on Land, Annex to the Hague Convention (IV) of 18 October 1907, (the text is the same in both the 1899 and 1907 Conventions).

9 Bugnion Francois, 2003, *The International Committee of the Red Cross and the Protection of War Victims*, ICRC and Macmillan Education, p. 81.

10 These were: (i) the Geneva Convention for the Amelioration of the Condition of the Wounded and Sick in Armies in the Field, of 6 July 1906; (ii) the Hague Convention (X) for the Adaptation to Maritime Warfare of the Principles of the Geneva Convention, of 18 October 1907; and (iii) the Hague Convention (IV) respecting the Laws and

legal systems: (a) The Hague Regulations concerning POWs laid down general principles rather than rules which could be immediately applied. It was impossible, when implementing these principles, to avoid divergent interpretations, leading to serious discrepancies in the treatment of prisoners. (b) Apart from some general rules regarding occupied territories, the Hague Regulations contained nothing to protect the civilian population against arbitrary treatment by the enemy. The Regulations were completely silent on the problem of civilians who happened to be on enemy territory when hostilities broke out. (c) Neither the 1906 Geneva Convention, nor the Hague Conventions of 1907, allowed for supervision, in any form. Similarly, no provision was made for an intermediary to facilitate the exchange of communications between belligerents. Treaty law was, therefore, inadequate to guarantee protection to victims of war. To fill the gap, the belligerents tried to define and extend the legal protection of POWs through a series of bilateral agreements in 1917 and 1918. Unfortunately, these accords took effect too late to prevent abuse of prisoners. The 1906 and 1907 Conventions failed to give the International Committee any useful basis for its work, since they did not provide for any direct action by it and did not even mention the Committee.[11]

The ICRC made serious efforts in September 1914 to obtain a list of French soldiers held in Germany followed by lists of German and Austrian soldiers held in France and Britain. The International Committee received lists from all the belligerents, with the exception of Russia and Italy (which sent them to Vienna directly, without going through the Agency in Geneva). Following this the parties to the conflict agreed to exchange lists of prisoners through the good offices of the Protecting Powers. Lists of prisoners received by the Agency were always sent immediately to their respective country's National Society. There were three types of lists: those of able-bodied prisoners; those of wounded or sick prisoners, with an indication of their medical condition; and those of prisoners who had died, with information on where they had been buried.[12] The originals of the lists

Customs of War on Land, of 18 October 1907.

11 Bugnion Francois, 2003, *The International Committee of the Red Cross and the Protection of War Victims*, ICRC and Macmillan Education, p. 82-83.

12 In all, 398,336 pages giving lists of prisoners were received from official sources and passed on to the National Societies concerned. Since each page carried information on twenty to twenty-five prisoners, 25 more than eight million items of information were registered by the Geneva Agency. Ibid, p. 86..

sent to the Agency were stored and used as a basis for card-indexes. All items of information concerning the identity of a prisoner were copied onto a card, which also showed the source of this information. The cards were filed according to nationality and, within that grouping, in alphabetical–phonetical order. Requests for information about missing soldiers were recorded on cards of a different colour and filed in the relevant national indexes according to the same principles.[13]

The Agency carried out two kinds of enquiries: (i) concerning prisoners whose whereabouts were known by contacting the camp commandant, the head doctor of a hospital or the prisoner himself to obtain the information needed; and (ii) concerning missing persons who could not be traced through the Agency's files, the evidence of all members of the same regiment who had been captured during the same battle. This approach allowed the Agency to gather about 90,000 reports concerning French soldiers alone, from fellow-prisoners interned in Germany. Most of the information obtained in this way consisted of confirmations of death. The tracing service was also responsible for obtaining and forwarding various documents, such as death certificates, wills, and powers of attorney. The Agency thus managed to pass on more than a million items of information to prisoners' families in the First World War.

Visits to POW Camps: Even though the ICRC had no legal basis for making visits to detention camps, by the end of December 1914, its delegates visited France, Germany and Britain to ascertain the conditions of POWs and civilian internees in camps. This marked the opening of a new sphere of activity for the ICRC. The main concern of the ICRC was to gather information about the fate of the large number of prisoners captured during the fighting in East Prussia, Belgium and France. The detaining powers had made no arrangements for the shelter, clothing, food and medical supplies of the detainees. At the onset of winter, most of them had only the summer uniforms in which they were captured in August/ September 1914. The condition of the civilian internees was equally bad. Visits to prison camps by neutral and impartial delegates had two main objectives: first, to urge the belligerents to make improvements

13 In this way, the enquiry card was placed together with the index card on which the particulars of the missing person were recorded, thus establishing a link between them. The information was then verified against the original document and communicated to the enquirer. By this method alone, the Agency was able to provide more than 560,000 replies to French families.

in the prisoners' conditions; and second, to provide objective reports on the prisoners' conditions to governments and the prisoners' families.[14] The visits by neutral observers to prison camps on both sides in the war also aimed at achieving certain parity in the way POWs were treated. It would ensure a degree of 'reciprocal benefit' in favour of POWs.

During the visits, the delegates held general discussions with the authorities (war ministry, interior ministry, etc.) responsible for POWs/ civilian internee camps as well as with the officials of Red Cross Society. They ascertained the rules and regulations of detention and drew up a list of the camps they wished to visit. Thereafter, they inspected all the facilities, including the sleeping accommodation, workshops, refectory, kitchen, infirmary, washrooms, lavatories, disciplinary cells, food and parcel stores, and exercise areas. The delegates were thus able to gain a complete idea of the material conditions in each camp. Although the reports were usually written in general terms, certain specific remarks – such as comparing the calorie content of food rations in the different camps, or listing the death and sickness rates –shows that the visits were carried out with scientific precision. The delegates also tried to hold discussions with groups of detainees and interact with them freely. The ICRC stated several times that it would not carry out any new visits unless it received assurances that its delegates could converse in private with the prisoners of their choice. This was seen as an essential condition for visits.

Visits to places of detention and private discussions with the prisoners enabled the ICRC delegates to build up a precise, complete and detailed picture of the conditions in the camps. At the end of a visit, the delegates met the camp commandant and apprised him of their observations and suggestions and conveyed any requests or complaints from the prisoners. After the visit, major issues were raised with the relevant ministries and in the case of any particularly serious incidents, the delegates asked for an enquiry into the matter.

---

14 Statement issued by the ICRC in this regard: ".... these visits, carrying the greatest guarantees of independence and impartiality, are intended to reassure families by informing them of the real situation – too often distorted by a tendentious Press – and to bring about, where possible, a salutary lessening of tension between the opposing governments ..." Bugnion Francois, 2003, *The International Committee of the Red Cross and the Protection of War Victims*, ICRC and Macmillan Education, p. 93.

The delegates' final report usually consisted of three parts: a general section outlining the factors common to all the camps visited; a section describing the particular conditions at each camp; and the delegates' conclusions regarding the improvements which they felt should be made in the treatment and conditions of the prisoners. The reports were sent to the ICRC, which then published them as official documents. The reports were circulated as widely as possible, including to news agencies and to all the subscribers of the *Bulletin International*; they were also sold at bookshops, with some series being reprinted.

During the war and in the immediate post-war period, 54 missions were undertaken in Austria–Hungary, Britain, Bulgaria, Czechoslovakia, France, Germany, Greece, Italy, Poland, Romania, Russia, Serbia, Turkey, the Ukraine, Burma, India, Japan, Siberia, Algeria, Egypt, Morocco and Tunisia. The delegates conducted 524 visits to places of detention,

Relief Operations

Article 15 of the Hague Regulations authorised the activities of relief societies for POWs. The ICRC was compelled to take up this additional responsibility as no relief society was functioning during that time. Its role was to arrange the transport and distribution of relief supplies entrusted to it, acting as a relay between each National Society and prisoners of the same nationality. The ICRC dealt with two kinds of relief supplies: individual parcels, addressed to specific prisoners, and collective consignments. A number of relief operations were carried out by the ICRC, using its own resources, to help the civilian population and POWs, including a challenging relief operation in Siberia and organise their repatriation.

Repatriation of POWs

The ICRC initiated the repatriation of POWs in 1914. This continued until 1921. There were two distinct categories of prisoners: those to be repatriated during the war; and those to be repatriated at the end of the war.

Repatriations during the War: Article 12 of the Geneva Convention of 1906 required that military medical personnel, as well as members of relief societies be repatriated as soon as their services were no longer indispensable for the care of the wounded. Article 2 of the Convention allowed the detaining powers to send home wounded or sick POWs. The mass internment of enemy aliens was a major issue in the First World War. Although their status was not specifically defined in law, the basic distinction that had to be made was between combatants and non-combatants. Thus, it was justified to intern men of an age to serve in the army, but women, children, the sick and the elderly had to be repatriated. The prolonged detention experienced by soldiers captured at the beginning of the war gave rise to various medical problems (neurasthenia, anorexia, muscular atrophy, and the like) that was referred to as 'barbed-wire syndrome'.[15] This led to a marked impairment of the prisoners' physical and mental faculties. The ICRC was of the view that these POWs were no longer capable of rejoining the ranks, and should be sent home. After agreements were reached between the warring countries, the ICRC provided supplies and medical care during the repatriation journey of medical and invalid personnel. It was successful in repatriating several hundred thousand people before the war ended.

Repatriations at the end of the war: When the Central Powers called for a ceasefire, between seven and eight million prisoners were being held by the warring countries. Most of them were in captivity in Europe, but many had been transferred to North Africa, the Middle East, India, Central Asia and Siberia.[16] Three separate operations were undertaken by the ICRC for the repatriation of: (i) Allied prisoners held on the territory of the former Central Powers; (ii) former Central Power prisoners held by the Allied and Associated Powers; and (Iii) Russian prisoners held in Europe and former Central Power prisoners held in the Soviet Union.

The ceasefire agreements signed in 1918 between the Allied and Associated Powers and Bulgaria, the Ottoman Empire, Austria–Hungary and Germany, called for the immediate and unilateral repatriation of all POWs belonging to the victorious nations. This was carried out during the winter

15 The Swiss physician Adolf Lukas Vischer described a psychiatric syndrome among POWs, the 'barbed-wire disease' that follows a long-term incarceration and which involved boredom, confusion, clouding of consciousness and amnesia. A.J. Brock, Boredom and Barbed-wire Disease, *Br Med J*, Vol. 1, May 1940, p. 744.

16 There were immense problems in repatriating such a huge number of people as new borders had disrupted communications, vast areas of land had been devastated and coal was virtually not available. These practical difficulties were compounded by the civil war which had broken out in several parts of the former Russian Empire, Germany was facing revolutionary upheaval and the Austro-Hungarian Empire was falling apart.

of 1918–19 under the supervision of an Allied Commission and the ICRC was not involved in it.

The repatriation of POWs belonging to the former Central Powers was deferred until after the signing of a peace treaty. The treaty with Germany was signed at Versailles on 28 June 1919; those with Austria, Bulgaria, Hungary and Turkey were signed between September 1919 and August 1920. Articles 214 and 215 of the Treaty of Versailles made the repatriation conditional on the agreement coming into force. So more than six months after the cessation of hostilities, the repatriation of prisoners was postponed indefinitely. Concerned about the human cost of this continuing delay, the ICRC approached to the Allied Supreme Council on 22 August 1919 and urged for the rapid repatriation of POWs held by the Entente powers. On 28 August the Council authorised the release of German prisoners. Over the following months Britain, the United States, Italy and Serbia repatriated those held by them. France, on the other hand, waited until the Treaty of Versailles came into effect before doing likewise. Finally, in the spring of 1920, the League of Nations took charge of the repatriation of POWs and appointed Norwegian explorer Nansen to complete the repatriation process in cooperation with the ICRC.

The situation of prisoners captured on the eastern front was far more complex due to the political turmoil in central and Eastern Europe and in the former Russian Empire. The Treaty of Brest-Litovsk of 3 March 1918, between the Central Powers and Russia's new Soviet government opened the way for the immediate repatriation of all nationals of the signatory states. However, because of the Russian civil war only a very small number of prisoners were actually sent home. In the winter of 1918–19, a large number of POWs took advantage of the chaos reigning in Germany, in the collapsing Austro-Hungarian Empire and in Russia and made unsuccessful attempts to make their way home.[17]The ICRC then began putting together a plan to feed and evacuate Russian prisoners held in central Europe. It was of the view that the prisoners should be sent back to their native districts or elsewhere if they so wished, and that their repatriation should not be

17 These POWs were in appalling conditions. They were weakened by years of captivity and hardships, infested with vermin, their clothes and shoes in tatters, forced to steal food for their survival, ignorant of the new borders and often of their own new nationality, many of them died on the way, victims of exhaustion, sickness and deprivation; others ended up by returning to the camps from which they had escaped. This uncontrolled flow of people caused the epidemics of influenza and typhus.

delayed for political reasons. The ICRC organised transit camps and by the end of the operation, some 425,000 Russian, German, Austrian and Hungarian prisoners returned home under the auspices of the ICRC.

Breaches of IHL: Article 28 of the Geneva Convention of 1906 obliged the signatories to take national measures to repress and punish breaches of the Convention. Article 3 of the Fourth Hague Convention of 18 October 1907, respecting the Laws and Customs of War on Land, stated that a belligerent had to pay compensation for breaches committed by its armed forces, thereby laying down the principle of what had to be done at an international level in the event of violations of the Convention. However, this principle was unlikely to be applied during hostilities. The International Committee followed its former practice. When a National Society or government sent it a complaint, the ICRC passed it on to the alleged wrongdoer and asked for an enquiry to be held. The inquiry report, explanation or apology received from the government was then sent to the plaintiff. The ICRC gave three reasons justifying its procedure of passing on complaints: (a) The complaints were a reminder in themselves of the existence of treaty rules and of the desire of governments to abide by them and to claim the benefit of them. (b) The transmission of protests gave the accused belligerent an opportunity of providing an explanation, of refuting the complaint or of apologising. (c) An internal enquiry among subordinates would serve as a reminder of the international rules in force and would draw the attention of the troops to the need to comply with them.[18]

The ICRC became a vital organisation in protecting POWs during the First World War. Its complete independence guaranteed it exceptional freedom of action, allowing it to take a wide variety of initiatives and maintain relations with any authority, recognised or not, which was holding POWs. In many cases these initiatives were crucial. In forwarding lists of prisoners, mail and relief supplies and in carrying out visits to prison camps, the ICRC performed pioneering work. In the repatriation of prisoners, it sought to

18 The ICRC was forced to admit that the enquiries were not always carried out as thoroughly and in such good faith as might be hoped. In some cases governments found that the simplest response was to make counter-accusations, rather than hold enquiries whose results could have been damaging; at other times complaints were shelved and forgotten, despite reminders from the ICRC. Bugnion Francois, 2003, *The International Committee of the Red Cross and the Protection of War Victims*, ICRC and Macmillan Education, p. 106.

create common ground between governments which did not recognise one another and which refused to communicate directly. Overall, these efforts were applauded and earned the ICRC immense respect and authority.

The ICRC played a role independent of the parties to the conflict and had no interest other than securing humanitarian protection for the victims of war. Taking stock, the ICRC set itself three major objectives: the revision of the Geneva Convention; the drafting of a convention protecting POWs; and the drafting of a convention protecting civilians in the hands of an enemy. On the eve of the Second World War, there were two new Conventions, signed on 27 July 1929: the Geneva Convention for the Amelioration of the Condition of the Wounded and Sick in Armies in the Field; and the Convention Relative to the Treatment of Prisoners of War. Even though the 1929 Diplomatic Conference had not given the ICRC any specific rights of which it could avail itself, it had recognised its role in the protection of POWs and mandated the Committee to create a central information agency. Thus, the ICRC had a firm foundation for its work when dealing with countries that were party to the POW Convention.

Protection of POWs: 1919–1939

During the period 1919–1939, the ICRC carried out protection and assistance operations in the following international conflicts: the Greco-Turkish War (1919–23); the occupation of the Ruhr (1923–25); Estonia (1920): The armistice of November 1918 did not signal the closure of the International Prisoner of War Agency, which continued its activities as part of major prisoner repatriation operations. During the four years that followed the end of the war, the ICRC organised the repatriation of 425,000 prisoners; the Manchurian Incident (1931–33); the Chaco War (1932–25); the Italo-Ethiopian War (1935–36); and the Sino-Japanese conflict (1937-39). In some of these, the ICRC responded in three ways: visiting detainees; providing emergency assistance; and repatriating POWs. During the Chaco War between Bolivia and Paraguay, the ICRC was content to use an operational approach that had been successfully tried and tested during the First World War. It did not seek to broaden its activities by taking new initiatives. During the war, both the countries authorised the ICRC to visit their POWs on two occasions. Interestingly, neither country had signed the 1929 Geneva Convention on POWs. During the Sino-Japanese conflict, the Committee could not execute its functions satisfactorily since the ICRC's means were tragically inadequate.[19]

The Second World War

The First World War was confined to Europe, but the Second World War (1939–45) was a 'world war' in every sense. Although the decisive battles were fought in Europe, from the Pyrenees to the Urals, the campaigning armies left a trail of devastation through North and East Africa, Asia – from Japan to the borders of India – and the Pacific islands. The countries taking an active part in the war accounted for more than two-thirds of the world's total population.[20]Germany had more than 12 million men under arms, the Soviet Union more than 20 million. For the first time in modern history, the number of civilian casualties surpassed the number of servicemen killed or wounded. The main cities and towns of Germany and Japan were bombed repeatedly by formations of more than a thousand aircraft; whole districts were flattened in a single raid. The attacks culminated in the atomic explosions which wiped out Hiroshima and Nagasaki.

During the War, wounded and sick soldiers were protected by the relevant 1929 Geneva Convention, to which almost every country was party. Under Article 2 of the Convention, wounded and sick soldiers captured by the enemy had to be treated as POWs, except as regards the medical treatment to which they were entitled. The 1929 Convention Relative to the Treatment of Prisoners of War protected the soldiers taken prisoner through a detailed set of rules, and gave the ICRC a legal basis for its work.[21] However, two of the principal belligerents, the Soviet Union and Japan, were not party to it. Since a treaty applies only between the contracting parties, all the countries at war with the USSR or Japan were free of any obligations under the Prisoners-of-War Code towards these two countries. As a result, the Convention was in force only between the Allies and Germany and Italy.

19 Bugnion Francois, 2003, *The International Committee of the Red Cross and the Protection of War Victims*, ICRC and Macmillan Education, p.161.

20 Bugnion Francois, 2003, *The International Committee of the Red Cross and the Protection of War Victims*, ICRC and Macmillan Education, p.167.

21 The POW Convention gave the ICRC only the right to propose the opening of a central agency of information regarding prisoners of war (Article 79), and to offer its services for the protection of prisoners. Article 88 stated: "The foregoing provisions do not constitute any obstacle to the humanitarian work which the International Red Cross Committee may perform for the protection of prisoners of war with the consent of the belligerents concerned."

On Europe's Eastern Front and in the Far East, the belligerents were not bound by it.[22] This did not mean that the warring nations were free of all obligations towards POWs. Articles 4 to 20 of the 1907 Hague Regulations and the provisions of customary law remained in force.

During the Second World War, ICRC operations expanded tremendously. They were marked by outstanding achievements, but also by bitter failures. Throughout the War, the ICRC remained the main driving force for providing relief to POWs. An extensive logistics system was put in place by it to deliver aid to POWs. The Central Agency for Prisoners of War, with the help of the services of over 3000 volunteers, was able to restore a vital link between prisoners and their families.[23] The ICRC delegates travelled the world over to assist prisoners and to monitor the conditions in which they were held captive.[24] The ICRC set up a vast relief operation that became the largest civil transport undertaking during that period. The Central POW Agency's card index contained almost 36 million cards. The Agency received more than 59 million items of mail and dispatched some 61 million. From 1 September 1939 to 31 December 1948, ICRC delegates carried out more than 12,750 visits to places of internment. And despite the blockade and disruption of transport, the ICRC transported and distributed 470,000 tonnes of relief for POWs and civilian internees. In

22 In 1945 the Allies refused POW status for German and Japanese soldiers who fell into their hands after the capitulation of their respective countries, claiming that their situation was not covered by the 1929 Convention. Instead, they were classed as "Surrendered Enemy Personnel" (SEP). The ICRC protested against this measure, considering that its legality was questionable and that it created a dangerous precedent likely to undermine the moral authority and binding nature of the POW Convention. Nonetheless, the Allies' decision did not seriously limit its scope for action: the ICRC helped the SEP in much the same way as it assisted prisoners captured earlier, and continued to do so until they were repatriated. Bugnion Francois, 2003, *The International Committee of the Red Cross and the Protection of War Victims*, ICRC and Macmillan Education, p. 194

23 In September 1939 the ICRC opened the Central Prisoners-of-War Agency in Geneva, to perform three main tasks: (i) to centralize all information on prisoners of war (notification of capture, transfer, death, etc.); (ii) to act as an intermediary between the belligerents for the transmission of such information; and (iii) to reply, on the basis of the data assembled in its card-indexes or of research carried out, to requests from public or private organizations and from private persons, and in general try to restore contact between the prisoners and their families.

24 The differing legal provisions applied to the POWs led to the following categories of prisoners: (i) prisoners protected by the Geneva Convention; (ii) prisoners captured on the Eastern Front; (iii) prisoners captured in the Far East; and (iv) combatants who were denied prisoner-of-war status.

addition, the Joint Commission handed out 165,000 tonnes of relief, while more than 750,000 tonnes of food and other supplies were distributed in Greece.

The ICRC was awarded the Nobel Peace Prize for the second time in December 1944. However, it came under attack as soon as the fighting ceased. In the countries of the Far East, particularly in China, the ICRC had no means of carrying out relief operations on any significant scale for the population suffering the effects of the war. Its delegates could do no more than provide limited assistance for POWs and interned civilians. The ICRC was held responsible for the tragic fate of the Soviet POWs, over half of whom died in captivity. It was also blamed for not denouncing racial persecutions and the hell of the concentration camps, the full horror of which the world discovered after the collapse of Nazi Germany.[25] This was one of the greatest stains on the history of the ICRC as it failed to come to the aid of the victims of Nazi concentration camps and death camps.[26]

After World War II

After the Second World War, the ICRC worked for the revision of the Geneva Conventions of 1929, the shortcomings of which had been shown up by the war.[27] On 12 August 1949, a Diplomatic Conference adopted

25 The ICRC and its delegates managed to save tens of thousands of lives through their diplomatic approaches and ingenuity in the field, neither they nor any other organization were able to preserve entire communities from deportation and ruthless murder.

26 Despite the very great services it had rendered throughout the Second World War, the ICRC became the target of accusations as soon as the fighting abated. Bugnion Francois, Contribution to History: From the end of the Second World War to the dawn of the third millennium--The activities of the International Committee of the Red Cross during the Cold War and its aftermath: 1945-1995, *International Review of the Red Cross*, No. 305, 1995, p. 207-224.

27 In a memorandum of 15 February 1945, the ICRC had announced that it was starting consultations to that effect. In undertaking this revision, the ICRC had three main objectives: (i) to extend the protection of the Geneva Conventions to civilians who fall in the power of the enemy; (ii) to protect the victims of civil wars; and (iii) to add to the new Conventions a monitoring mechanism in which it would itself take part. The ICRC convened the National Red Cross Societies in 1946, and then a meeting of government experts in 1947. The drafts prepared on the basis of the discussions were approved by the Seventeenth International Conference of the Red Cross meeting in Stockholm in August 1948, then by a Diplomatic Conference, which met in Geneva from April to August 1949. Bugnion Francois, From the end of the Second World War to the dawn of the third millennium: The activities of the International Committee of

four Geneva Conventions for the protection of the wounded and sick in armed forces in the field; the wounded, sick and shipwrecked members of armed forces at sea; prisoners of war; and civilian persons. These four Conventions instituted supervisory mechanisms by specifying the role of Protecting Powers responsible for safeguarding the interests of the Parties to the conflict. In addition, special provisions recognised the role of the ICRC and confirmed its right of initiative. The ICRC has been successful in protecting prisoners in armed conflict which have taken place after the Second World War.

The 1948 Arab-Israeli War: In June 1948, the ICRC obtained access to approximately 400 Israeli POWs in Trans-Jordan, Egypt and Syria and visited some 2000 Arab POWs in Israel. During the First Indochina War of 1952, the ICRC had no access to prisoners captured by the Democratic Republic of Vietnam. However, it was able to visit North Vietnamese POWs. In 1955, the ICRC was authorised to make occasional visits to prisons in Algeria, and to conduct private interviews with prisoners. France did not recognise Algerian nationalists as POWs, which meant that they risked severe penalties simply for being involved in the fighting. During the final years of the Algerian war, the ICRC managed to ensure that all fighters captured carrying weapons and wearing a uniform would be treated as prisoners of war, and therefore would be entitled to ICRC visits.[28]

The Cold War gave rise to a series of setbacks. The ICRC was unable to provide assistance to French prisoners captured during the Indochina war, to prisoners of the United Nations forces captured in Korea, and to American prisoners held by the Vietnamese forces. Nor was it able to help the civilian populations cruelly affected by war and bombings.

The 1962 Indo–China War: The ICRC played an important role in the repatriation of Indian POWs in the 1962 Indo–China War. With both India and China being signatories to the Geneva Conventions of 1949, the ICRC had the mandate to protect POWs in the war but China refused to acknowledge this, stating that there was no formal declaration of war between the two countries. China informed the ICRC that India could

the Red Cross during the Cold War and its aftermath: 1945-1995, *International Review of the Red Cross*, No. 305, 1995, pp. 207-224.

28 From our Archives: protecting prisoners and detainees; https://www.icrc.org/en/document/150-years-humanitarian-action-protecting-prisoners-and-detainees.

directly deal with Beijing. The war started in October 1962 and despite the best efforts of the ICRC, it could not get access to the nearly 2000 prisoners taken by China.[29] The Chinese never allowed any access to the POW camps and instead publicised pictures of how well Indian soldiers were being looked after.[30] With the tireless efforts of the Indian Red Cross, the ICRC and the Chinese Red Cross Society (CRCS), all Indian POWs in China returned.

The 1965 Indo–Pak War: During the wars between India and Pakistan in 1965 and 1971, the ICRC's position and its role as a neutral intermediary were generally recognised. During the 1965 conflict, the ICRC was allowed to visit POWs and civilian detainees, assist in repatriation and provide relief to the affected population, in coordination with the Indian Red Cross Society. The ICRC was able to transmit the lists of POWs captured on both sides or to register them itself. Its delegates were able to meet POWs and civilian detainees at their places of detention and to talk in private with prisoners of their choosing. They were asked to assist with the repatriation of the wounded during the hostilities, and with the repatriation of prisoners at the end of active hostilities. The Central Tracing Agency set up family message services for relatives separated by war and organised countless family reunifications. The ICRC also set up extensive operations to provide food and medical care for war casualties, prisoners and civilian

29 The exact number of India POWs who were detained in China is not available. It has been reported elsewhere that for 3,968 Indian POWs in China, the experience was harrowing. The record of the debriefing of the POWs when they returned to India has never been made public. All POWs recounted that one of the worst aspects of their captivity in Tibet was the constant attempt at brainwashing by Chinese Communist propaganda. In order to break their morale, some Indian officers were sent to solitary confinement for weeks.Arpi Claude, Exclusive! How China released Indian troops after the 1962 War, 6 December 2019, available at: https://www rediff.com/news/special/how-china-released-indian-troops-after-the-1962-war/20191206.htm.

30 Very primitive medical facilities were available to Indian POWs in China. The author, an Indian POW in China writes, "After the full operation team had assembled, I was bodily lifted on to the improvised table. A sort of napkin soaked in rice water was placed over my face, presumably to prevent me from witnessing the going on. Four of the heftiest nursing attendants then caught hold of my leg and arms, and held me pinned down to the table for the entire duration of the operation (without administering any anesthesia). Surgical procedure was more agonizing than I could ever imagine. The sensation of a knife cutting through the live tissues of my finger was so all-encompassing, that it momentarily overcame the painful feeling I had been experiencing at the slightest touch of my injured wrist." Bakshi Lt Col K.N., 1989, *I was a Prisoner of War in China*, New Delhi: Lancer Publishers and Distributors, p. 80.

populations, while coordinating the National Red Cross and Red Crescent Societies' international relief activities for war victims.

1971 Indo–Pak War: During the 1971 liberation of Bangladesh and Indo-Pak War, the ICRC provided protection and assistance to POWs, civilian internees and civilian minorities on both sides. For this purpose, it had set up permanent delegations in Islamabad, New Delhi and Dhaka.[31]One of the primary duties of the ICRC delegates was to obtain lists of POWs and secure permission to visit them and bring them family mail. At that time, most Pakistani POWs (76,000) and civilian detainees (17,000) were in Bangladesh. From their internment in Bangladesh, at the end of December 1971, until their transfer to India, on 15 January 1972, permission was granted for visits by ICRC delegates, who went to the Dhaka, Chittagong and Sylhet transit camps. A large number of Pakistani civilians, especially destitute women and children, sought refuge in the Dhaka camp. The ICRC delegates supplied them with such essentials as clothing, blankets, soap, pots, and powdered milk. A medical team also examined and treated the sick.

At the request of Pakistani POWs and civilian detainees, the ICRC delegates launched an operation to trace persons reported missing or who were dispersed in the country. With the assistance of the Indian armed forces and local volunteers, several hundred persons were thus found and reunited with their families before being transferred to India. The ICRC took active part in the transfer of wounded POWs and sick civilians by air when it was felt that their state of health would not stand up to the long journey by train and boat. The ICRC delegates inquired into detention conditions. They delivered mail and parcels prepared for the POWs by their families or Red Cross Societies of the parties to the conflict.

On 4 February 1972, the Indian Government authorised the ICRC to visit Pakistani POWs and civilian detainees. Visits were made to 50 camps and

31 By the end of 1972, the Islamabad delegation comprised seven persons (the head of delegation, three visiting delegates, one Agency delegate, one administrator and one radio operator); the New Delhi delegation 14 (the head of delegation, nine visiting delegates, one Agency delegate, two secretaries and one radio operator), and the Dacca delegation 28 (the head of delegation, fourteen visiting delegates, one female nurse, one Agency delegate, three secretaries, one accountant, one administrator and six radio operators). These figures do not include local staff. From 1 December 1971 to 18 April 1972, the ICRC coordinated its joint relief action with the League of Red Cross Societies in Bangladesh. ICRC Annual Report 1972, p. 46-47.

20 hospitals. By the end of 1972, ICRC delegates had made more than 270 visits to places of detention, and had, on an average, visited most of them four times. During the visits, the delegates inquired more particularly about the wounded, the sick and civilians. They organised a relief operation for civilians in which multivitamins and food supplements were distributed among several thousand persons, mostly the old and children.

The Government of Pakistan authorised the ICRC delegates to visit Indian POWs from 4 January 1972. The 657 prisoners were held in two camps at Rawalpindi and Lyallpur, while the wounded were in six army hospitals. On 2 August, the Lyallpur camp was closed down and all able-bodied POWs were transferred to the Rawalpindi camp. From 4 January to 1 December, when the general repatriation of Indian POWs took place, the ICRC delegates made 34 visits to places of detention. The ICRC delegates also inquired about some 270 Indian civilians who had been captured by Pakistani armed forces and interned in the Harrapa camp. They visited them twice, in July and August 1972.

Repatriation of POWs: Under Article 118 of the Third Geneva Convention,[32] the ICRC made repeated approaches to the governments with a view to securing the repatriation of prisoners. In March 1972, prolonged captivity began to create growing tension among the Pakistani POWs. There were riots and some attempts to escape, particularly during March, October and November 1972; wherein 10 POWs were killed, and few others were wounded. The ICRC delegates immediately visited the POW camps. The statements made by the prisoners and the camp authorities responsible for supervision were included in the reports sent to the detaining power and the prisoners' own government.

The Government of Pakistan, to whom representations were also made under Article 118, on 1 December, repatriated all Indian POWs (617) save one who had just undergone surgery and who was subsequently

32 Article 118 of the Third Geneva Convention dealing with release and repatriation of POWs provides, "Prisoners of war shall be released and repatriated without delay after the cessation of active hostilities. In the absence of stipulations to the above effect in any agreement concluded between the Parties to the conflict with a view to the cessation of hostilities, or failing any such agreement, each of the Detaining Powers shall itself establish and execute without delay a plan of repatriation in conformity with the principle laid down in the foregoing paragraph. In either case, the measures adopted shall be brought to the knowledge of the POW."

transferred to India.[33] Simultaneously, the Indian Government repatriated 542 Pakistani soldiers captured on the western front. The twofold operation was carried out at the Wagah frontier post, in the presence of ICRC delegates. This ended ICRC activities on behalf of Indian POWs in Pakistan, while the ICRC pursued its activities on behalf of some 94,000 Pakistani POWs and civilian detainees in India. As in the case of POWs, the ICRC approached the governments concerned regarding the release and repatriation of civilian detainees.[34]

On 16 September, in the presence of ICRC delegates, the Government of Pakistan repatriated 273 Indian civilians at the Wagah border. On 18 and 19 September, the Indian Government, in turn, repatriated nearly 700 Pakistani civilians detained by the Indian armed forces on the western front. Neither the Indian nor the Pakistani Government agreed to grant members of crews of the merchant marine who had been captured the status of POW to which they were entitled under Article 4 of the Third Convention. In India, the ICRC delegates were permitted only one visit to members of a Pakistan crew, in February 1972. In Pakistan, ICRC delegates were to begin visits to Indian seamen early in 1973.

Pending general repatriation at the end of hostilities, the ICRC laid special stress on seriously wounded and seriously sick POWs. In a total of six airlift operations, 550 POWs and 41 civilians of Pakistan and 40 Indian POWs were repatriated. A large number of soldiers of Bengali origin who had served in the Pakistani armed forces were disarmed and assembled in 15 repatriation centres in Pakistan. These centres too were visited by the ICRC

33 It is believed by many in India that 54 POWs were never returned by Pakistan. The families of missing POWs have approached both the United Nations and the International Committee for the Red Cross in their five decade campaign, but neither body was able to offer assistance. James Maclaren, The Last Secret of the 1971 India-Pakistan War, *The Diplomat*, 14 December 2018, available at: https://thediplomat.com/2018/12/the-last-secret-of-the-1971-india-pakistan-war/. For more recent account of the issue see: Dogra ChanderSuta, 2020, *Missing in Action: The Prisoners who never came back*, India: HarperCollins Publishers, pp. 340.

34 The ICRC drew the Indian Government's attention to the matter on 23 March 1972. In a reply dated 25 April, the detaining power stated that the Pakistani soldiers had surrendered to the Joint Command of Bangladesh and India and that decision as to repatriation therefore rested with those two countries. On 25 May, the ICRC again communicated with the Indian Government. It pointed out that the existence of a joint command constituted an understanding between India and Bangladesh which concerned those two countries alone and could have no effect on India's obligation to repatriate the POWs.

delegates. On 28 August 1973, India and Pakistan signed an agreement in Delhi to repatriate Pakistani POWs and civilian military personnel. A tripartite agreement between India, Pakistan and Bangladesh resolved all contentious issues related to the 1971 war and paved the way for the return of Pakistani POWs as well as war criminals.[35] By February 1974, all Pakistani POWs who had been held by India were repatriated to Pakistan.[36]

The Central Tracing Agency forwarded 5 million letters addressed by Indian and Pakistani POWs to their families, while 1.5 million family messages were exchanged between the civilian populations of Pakistan and Bangladesh. The Agency also received 6000 inquiries regarding missing civilians and servicemen; 3000 of them elicited a favourable reply. In order to effectively fulfil its various duties, including the registration of POWs and civilian detainees, the Central Tracing Agency had to increase its Geneva staff by 10. It detached experts for the tracing bureaux opened in Islamabad, New Delhi and Dhaka.[37]

Sino-Vietnamese Conflict, 1979: During the Sino-Vietnamese conflict of February 1979 — between two Communist States — that the ICRC's role as a neutral intermediary was again recognised. The ICRC was given access both to Vietnamese prisoners detained by China and to Chinese prisoners captured by Vietnamese forces, and it helped in their repatriation from both sides.

35 In March 2012, the government of Bangladesh has paid tribute to the work of the ICRC during and following the 1971 war. The *Friends of Liberation War Honour* was given to 75 foreign individuals and organizations from across the world for their support during and in the aftermath of the conflict. The ICRC carried out a humanitarian operation in Bangladesh from 1971 to 1975 to alleviate the suffering of the victims of the conflict that had displaced millions. The war of 1971 had left 120,000 Bengalis stranded in Pakistan, mainly military personnel and civil servants from former East Pakistan, and their families; thousands of Pakistani civilian internees and prisoners of war remained in Bangladesh. On 28 August 1973, the governments of India, Pakistan and Bangladesh concluded an agreement in New Delhi arranging for the repatriation of Bengalis in Pakistan and Pakistanis interned in Bangladesh. The ICRC was asked to register people who were eligible for repatriation to Pakistan and Bangladesh. It facilitated the return home of 118,070 Bengalis to Bangladesh and 117,727 people to Pakistan, an operation taking several years.

36 Mustafa Ghulam and Gill Qasim Shahzad, The Issue of Prisoners of War, 1971 and Recognition of Bangladesh, *International Journal of Business and Social Research* (IJBSR), Volume 4, No. 3, March 2014, pp. 114-118.

37 ICRC, Annual Report 1972, p. 57.

Kargil Conflict: In May 1999, Pakistan and India intensified the exchange of fire along the line of control in Jammu and Kashmir after several high positions were illegally occupied by Pakistani army personnel (in the guise of militants) in the Kargil area.[38] Heavy fighting continued through August, resulting in the deaths of hundreds of combatants and non-combatants and the displacement of tens of thousands of people within Pakistan Occupied Kashmir. The ICRC monitored the humanitarian situation of those affected by the fighting, distributing material assistance such as winter clothing, toiletries and school materials to displaced families. It fulfilled its role of neutral intermediary in the repatriation of POWs released by both sides, and in the return of the mortal remains of soldiers to Pakistan.[39]

Iran–Iraq War: The Iran–Iraq war, which started in 1980 and lasted eight years, was one of the longest international armed conflicts of the 20th century. On 23 September 1980, shortly after the outbreak of hostilities, the ICRC appealed to both sides to honour their obligations under the Geneva Conventions of 1949.[40] In 1983, it observed that despite certain genuine difficulties, the Iraqi authorities were still endeavouring to implement the Geneva Conventions, while the leaders of the Islamic Republic of Iran were committing breaches of the Conventions, forcing the ICRC to suspend its visits to the POW camps.[41] In view of the grave and repeated breaches of IHL committed by both parties to the conflict, the ICRC appealed on 13 February 1984 to all the States party to the Geneva Conventions. The ICRC deplored the escalation of the methods of combat used by the belligerents, which constituted grave violations of IHL. Following Iran's acceptance of UN Resolution 598 on 18 July 1988 (Iraq had accepted the resolution in 1987), the ICRC submitted concrete proposals to both parties for the comprehensive repatriation of all POWs, but only a few isolated repatriations could be carried out.

---

38 A careful assessment of Pakistan Army casualties in Operation VIJAY has been carried out, based on a multiplicity of inputs. It has been established that, 737 Pakistani soldiers (including 45 officers, 68 Special Service Group (SSG) soldiers and 13 ISI personnel), died in about two months of operations that ensued in the Kargil Sector. Besides, two POWs were taken in the Yaldor Sector. Naik Inayat Ali of 5 Northern Light Infantry was captured at Pt 4812, inside the Batalik Sector, on 03 Jul 99. On 15 Jul 99, Sepoy Humar Shah also of 5 Northern Light Infantry was taken prisoner at the Padma Go heights, again in the Batalik Sector.

39 ICRC Annual Report 1999.

40 ICRC Annual Report 1980.

41 ICRC Annual report 1983.

During the war and up until 1990, the ICRC was involved in carrying out various humanitarian activities, including visiting places of detention, helping with the exchange of Red Cross messages containing brief family news, repatriation of POWs and handing over of mortal remains. The Iranian Red Crescent Society (IRCS) was also involved in some humanitarian operations. The ICRC, together with its Movement partners, was involved in 17 phases of repatriation of Iraqi POWs and 18 phases of repatriation of Iranian POWs, in which 717 Iraqi POWs and 718 Iranian POWs were repatriated. During the war, the ICRC was invited by the parties to the conflict to be involved in the repatriation of seriously wounded as well as seriously sick prisoners and of civilians. The first operation of this kind took place on 16 June 1981. A tripartite committee on missing persons brought together Iran, Iraq and the ICRC. The ICRC acted as a neutral intermediary, supporting the process of finding out what happened to the missing persons by attending handovers of remains, training Iranian and Iraqi forensic personnel and supplying specialised equipment for the recovery and identification process. The remains were repatriated to their respective countries on 22 January 2015 during a ceremony at the Shalamcha border crossing near Basra (Iraq), attended by military and civilian officials from both countries in the presence of ICRC staff.

The Ethio-Somali War 1977: The Ogaden War, or the Ethio-Somali war was a Somali military offensive between July 1977 and July 1978 over the disputed Ethiopian region of Ogaden. Almost 4000 people, most of whom had been detained in Ethiopia and Somalia for almost 11 years, were released and repatriated in 1988. The ICRC had tried for years to persuade the two governments to repatriate all POWs, with priority being given to the seriously wounded and sick, in accordance with Articles 109, 110 and 118 of the GC III. The offer was accepted by both parties and the ICRC was authorised to visit the places of detention to interview each of the detainees and register for repatriation.

Conflict in Bosnia-Herzegovina: The armed conflict in Bosnia-Herzegovina (1992–1995) presented the ICRC with one of its most complicated programmes ever.[42] The ICRC established its first long-term

42 The break-up of the Socialist Federal Republic of Yugoslavia began in June 1991 when Slovenia proclaimed independence, followed by a similar declaration by Croatia. While Slovenia achieved statehood without bloodshed, skirmishes broke out between Croatia's Serb minority and the majority ethnic Croat population. The ensuing war in Croatia was to last four years. In April 1992, a second, more bloody conflict broke out

presence in the former Yugoslavia just after the outbreak of war in Croatia in 1991. In addition, UNHCR led humanitarian assistance in the region. In May 1992, the ICRC withdrew temporarily from Sarajevo following the fatal shooting of one of its delegates. The humanitarian operation received huge funding, allowing the ICRC and UNHCR to deliver massive quantities of aid to the region. The ICRC's programme was its largest and represented about half of its 1993 budget. By the end of the war, the ICRC had visited over 54,000 detainees in 520 places, exchanged 18 million Red Cross messages, reunited over 4500 families, distributed over 100,000 metric tons of food, and spent over 47 million Swiss francs on medical and surgical assistance. Through its reports on the situation on the ground, the ICRC regularly denounced forcible displacement, and violations of human rights and IHL.[43] Humanitarian personnel in Bosnia–Herzegovina were exposed to unacceptable levels of risk which had never been experienced in the past. The ICRC staff was given pre-assignment training in handling threats such as shelling, sniping and landmines.[44] The ICRC maintained its traditional stand of not being associated with military participants and operated without escorts throughout the war.

On 16 and 17 June 2000, following agreements between the authorities of the Democratic Republic of the Congo, Rwanda, Zimbabwe and Namibia, the ICRC repatriated 177 former POWs of Rwandan, Zimbabwean and

---

in Bosnia-Herzegovina when it, too, declared independence — pitting Bosnia's three main constituent communities, ethnic Serbs, Croats and Muslims, against each other. The war resulted in massive displacement. In less than three months, the number of Bosnian refugees and internally displaced persons reached 2.6 million. Young Kirsten, UNHCR and ICRC in the former Yugoslavia: Bosnia-Herzegovina, *International Review of the Red Cross*, Vol. 83, No. 842, September 2001, p.782.

43 The ICRC and UNHCR built up a substantial body of written reports documenting violations of IHL and human rights law which could be used for criminal hearings by the International Criminal Tribunal for the former Yugoslavia (ICTY). The ICRC, however, did not share this information with the ICTY by taking the position that this would jeopardize its operational ability to gain access to war victims, which is based on confidentiality. Young Kirsten, UNHCR and ICRC in the former Yugoslavia: Bosnia-Herzegovina, *International Review of the Red Cross*, Vol. 83, No. 842, September 2001, p.786.

44 ICRC as well UNHCR staff were threatened and intimidated, their vehicles regularly hijacked and stolen, and they were often the target of deliberate attack. Bullet-proof vests and armoured vehicles were used to an extent never seen before in any major humanitarian operation. Young Kirsten, UNHCR and ICRC in the former Yugoslavia: Bosnia-Herzegovina, *International Review of the Red Cross*, Vol. 83, No. 842, September 2001, p. 792.

Namibian nationality who had been detained by the various belligerents in the Congo. The ICRC acted at the request of the parties to the conflict in its capacity as a neutral intermediary, and carried out the operation in accordance with its mandate. The POWs had all been registered and regularly visited by the ICRC during the period of their captivity.

A six-point peace agreement was mediated by the European Union following the 2008 armed conflict between Georgia and Russian. All prisoners held by Georgia were exchanged for the 159 Georgian civilians and 39 POWs held by the Russian authority. The ICRC was afforded unimpeded access to Georgian detention facilities. It also visited facilities maintained by the Ministries of Defence and Justice on a number of occasions, inspecting the conditions of not only POWs, but also of the detained members of separatist illegal armed formations.[45]

The ICRC has also worked to alleviate the humanitarian consequences of the Nagorno–Karabakh conflict. In February and December 2017, at the request of the authorities, the ICRC acted as a neutral intermediary to facilitate the transfer of the remains of soldiers across the international border between Armenia and Azerbaijan.[46] Today, the Tracing Agency's work is backed by an increasingly sophisticated global tracing system that endeavours to take advantage of the communications revolution to deal with new challenges.

Violation of International Norms: The ICRC is mandated by the High Contracting Parties to the Geneva Conventions to monitor the full application of and respect for the GC III and IV in relation to the treatment of persons deprived of their liberty. It reminds the High Contracting Parties concerned, maintaining confidentiality, of their humanitarian obligations under the four Geneva Conventions, Additional Protocol I, the customary law and universally acknowledged principles of humanity. During the Ethiopia–Eritrea War, all efforts by the ICRC to visit Ethiopian POWs held by Eritrea were refused by Eritrea until August 2000, just after Eritrea acceded to the 1949 Geneva Conventions. Ethiopia alleged the following violations of the GC III in Eritrea's POW camps: physical and mental abuse; lack of adequate medical care; unhealthy camp conditions;

45 Available at: https://ihl-in-action.icrc.org/case-study/georgiarussia-release-prisoners-war.

46 ICRC Annual Reports 2017 and 2018.

failure to maintain the well-being of POWs; impermissible forced labour; improper handling of deaths; lack of complaint procedures; prohibition of communication with the exterior; failure to post camp regulations; and inhumane conditions during transfer from the camps. Ethiopia also alleged that Eritrean troops regularly beat and frequently killed Ethiopians upon capture and immediately afterwards.[47]

The ICRC visited places of detention in Iraq in 2003. In its "Report on the Treatment by the Coalition Forces of Prisoners of War and other protected persons in Iraq", the ICRC drew the attention of the Coalition Forces (CF) to a number of serious violations of IHL.[48]During its private interviews with persons deprived of their liberty, the ICRC team recorded allegations relating to the treatment by the CF of protected persons during their capture, arrest, transfer, internment and interrogation. The main violations included:

- Brutality against protected persons upon capture and initial custody, sometimes causing death or serious injury;
- Absence of notification of arrest of persons deprived of their liberty to their families causing distress among persons deprived of their liberty and their families;
- Physical or psychological coercion during interrogation to secure information;
- Prolonged solitary confinement in cells devoid of daylight;
- Excessive and disproportionate use of force against persons deprived of their liberty resulting in death or injury during their period of internment.
- Other serious problems related to the conduct of CF personnel included: (i) seizure and confiscation of private belongings of persons deprived of their liberty; (ii) exposure of persons deprived of their liberty to dangerous tasks; and (iii) holding persons

47 Sassoli Marco, Bouvier Antoine A. and Quintin Anne, 2011, *How Does Law Protect in War?* Volume II, Geneva: ICRC, p. 1380-81.

48 The Wall Street Journal of 7 May 2007 had published extensive excerpts from a confidential document entitled "Report of the ICRC on the Treatment of the Coalition Forces of Prisoners of War and other persons in Iraq during arrest in Iraq, Internment and Interrogation" of January 2004.

deprived of their liberty in dangerous places where they were not protected from shelling.

Consequently, the ICRC asked the CF authorities:

- To respect, at all times, the human dignity, physical integrity and cultural sensitivity of persons held under their control;
- To set up a system of notifications of arrest to ensure quick and accurate transmission of information to the families of persons deprived of their liberty;
- To prevent all forms of ill-treatment, moral or physical coercion of persons deprived of their liberty in relation to interrogation;
- To set up an internment regime which ensure the respect of the psychological integrity and human dignity of persons deprived of their liberty;
- To ensure that all persons deprived of their liberty are allowed sufficient time in the sunlight every day, and to move and exercise outside;
- To define and apply regulations and sanctions compatible with IHL to ensure that persons deprived of their liberty are fully informed upon arrival of such regulations and sanctions;
- To thoroughly investigate violations of IHL in order to determine responsibilities and prosecute those found responsible for violations;
- To ensure that battle group units arresting individuals and staff in charge of internment facilities receive adequate training enabling them to operate in a proper manner and fulfil their responsibilities as arresting authority without resorting to ill-treatment or making excessive use of force.

Access to the benefits of humanitarian activities is subject to the consent of the Parties to a conflict. However, international law in general and IHL in particular, has evolved and a Party to an armed conflict is not completely at liberty to decide how it responds to an offer of services made by an impartial humanitarian organisation to undertake humanitarian activities. In case a party is unable or unwilling to address the humanitarian needs of such persons, international law requires it to respond positively to an offer by an impartial humanitarian organisation to do so in its place. Under GC III, the primary responsibility for meeting the humanitarian needs of persons affected by an international armed conflict lies with the Power detaining them. The activities of impartial humanitarian organisations should only complement, where necessary, the Detaining Power's efforts to address those needs itself.

The GC III confirms the right of the ICRC to visit POWs during international armed conflicts and receive all relevant information pertaining to them. The five main conditions governing ICRC visits are: (i) access to all detainees within the ICRC's field of interest; (ii) access to all premises and facilities used by and for detainees; (iii) authorisation to repeat the visits; (iv) opportunity to speak freely and in private (without witnesses) with detainees of the ICRC's choice; and (v) assurance that the authorities will give the ICRC a list of the detainees within its field of interest or authorise it to compile such a list during the visit.

In the last 150 years of its existence, the ICRC has undertaken up extensive operations world over to provide food and medical care for war casualties, prisoners and civilian populations, while coordinating the National Red Cross and Red Crescent Societies' international relief activities for war victims. While Henry Dunant was one of two laureates for the first Nobel Peace Prize in 1901, the ICRC itself has been awarded this honour twice: in 1917, 1944 and; with the International Federation of Red Cross and Red Crescent Societies, in 1963. This makes the ICRC unique: no recipient has been awarded the Peace Prize as often as this organisation.

Chapter VII

POWs in the 21st Century

The means and methods of warfare have been undergoing a rapid transformation. The conventional techniques of warfare are being replaced by new tactics and tools incorporating artificial intelligence such as unmanned aerial vehicles (UAV)[1] and lethal autonomous weapons systems (LAWS).[2] The militaries of various countries, in particular the US, the UK, France, Israel, Russia, South Korea and China, are working to increase the autonomy of weapon systems. A few countries are trying to develop 'super-soldiers' by enhancing their cognitive faculties. In fact, future warfare may resemble what is now seen in science fiction movies.[3] This chapter takes a look at the status of POWs and other related issues in the changing scenario.

1 Most unmanned aerial vehicles (UAV) or drones are flown by a pilot at a remote site possibly thousands of miles away, but some advanced drones are fully automated and fly without human control. Nearly 40 counties in the world have armed drones in their military.

2 Fully autonomous lethal weapons can select and engage targets without meaningful human control. Due in large part to their lack of human control, these systems, also known as lethal autonomous weapons systems (LAWS) or "killer robots," raise a host of legal and ethical concerns. These weapon systems present significant hurdles to compliance with international humanitarian law's fundamental rules of distinction and proportionality.

3 A US Army research report says that future wars will be conducted with robots, genetically engineered 'super humans', and other types of cyborgs - and we can expect this around the year 2050. *The battlefield of the future will be populated by fewer humans, but these humans would be physically and mentally augmented with enhanced capabilities that improve their ability to sense their environment, make sense of their environment, and interact with one another, as well as with 'unenhanced humans', automated processes, and machines of various kinds.* Kott Alexander, David Albert, Amy Zalman, Paulo Shakarian, Fernando Maymi, Cliff Wang, and Gang Qu, 2015, *Visualizing the Tactical Ground Battlefield in the Year 2050: Workshop Report*, the US Army Research Laboratory.

For nearly 70 years the Geneva Conventions have been a key instrument in the protection of POWs and others who are affected by international armed conflicts. However, the third Geneva Convention is facing certain challenges in recent armed conflicts. In the war against terrorism, for example, some States have created a new category of enemy soldiers called "unprivileged enemy combatants" and justified non-adherence to the provisions of the GC III. These States have ignored the common article 3 to the Geneva Conventions, which requires that noncombatants captured during an armed conflict, must be treated in a humane manner.

Special Operations and POWs

Military commandos or special operations forces (SOFs) have been constituted in a number of States to conduct short-duration offensive operations in a hostile and sensitive territory to seize or destroy designated enemy targets. In a conventional military operation, wounded and other military persons who are *hors de combat* are evacuated and protected under the regime of the GC III. However, during special operations they are left unattended and do not get any protection as POWs under the GC III. The main reason is that unlike conventional military units, SOF teams have very limited or no resources to hold POWs or to evacuate them. To cite one instance, in 2003, during Operation Iraqi Freedom, American SOF teams were tasked with conducting commando raids to destroy Iraqi Scud launch sites. The mission required the SOF teams to be heavily armed yet highly mobile. The United States Central Command (CENTCOM) planners anticipated that they would not be in a position to take custody of defeated Iraqis because they lacked the manpower and logistical resources to fulfil duties under the GC III to protect, evacuate, and provide medical care, food, and clothing to the defeated soldiers. The planners, therefore, assumed that the teams would leave wounded or defeated enemy soldiers and quickly proceed to destroy the next site.[4]

One of the basic obligations under the four Geneva Conventions is to provide the wounded and sick with the medical care and attention required by their condition to the fullest extent practicable and with the least possible delay. The obligations of a commander leading a military operation under the GC I (Articles 12 to 15) are to ensure that after an engagement, the

4 Bart Gregory Raymond, Special Operations Commando Raids and Enemy*Hors de Combat*, *The Army Lawyer*, July 2007, pp. 33-44.

members of his team take all possible measures to search for and collect the wounded and sick, to protect them against pillage and ill-treatment, to provide them with adequate care, and to search for the dead and prevent their being despoiled. Members of the enemy armed forces (as well as other persons mentioned in Article 13) who are wounded or sick must be respected and protected in all circumstances and treated humanely. Any attempts upon their lives, or violence to their persons is strictly prohibited; in particular, they must not be murdered or exterminated. Further, the wounded and sick of the enemy forces are POWs, and the provisions of international law concerning POWs apply to them. The victorious forces have a duty to capture defeated soldiers and render them POWs.[5]

Article 13 of the GC III recognizes that POWs are no longer combatants and includes prohibitions against murder, mutilation, torture, corporal punishment, sensory deprivation, collective punishment, humiliation and medical experimentation. A captor may not use force or coercion to interrogate POWs, who are obligated only to reveal their name, rank, service number, and date of birth. In brief, the commander of a SOF team, as all commanders, is obligated to keep POWs in protective custody and must remove them from the battlefield to camps that are located far from the zone of combat operations.[6]

According to Charles Staab (2016), the SOF undertakes clandestine operations in the grey area between overt military operations and covert operations.[7] Members of SOF teams may also adopt certain measures that fall under the definition of 'perfidy', which is prohibited under Article 37 of AP I.[8]

5 Article 44(1) of the 1977 AP I states that any combatant "who falls into the power of an adverse Party shall be a POW." Article 44 (2), further clarifies that all combatants are obliged to comply with the rules of international law applicable in armed conflict. Violations of these rules shall not deprive a combatant of his right to be a combatant or, if he falls into the power of an adverse Party, of his right to be a prisoner of war.

6 Bart Gregory Raymond, Special Operations Commando Raids and Enemy*Hors de Combat*, *The Army Lawyer*, July 2007, pp. 33-44.

7 Staab Charles, Uncloaking the Dagger: Does Adherence to the Geneva Conventions Betray Special Operations Forces? *Small Wars Journals*, 22 December 2016.

8 Article 37 of the 1977 AP I explicitly prohibits perfidy defining it as "acts inviting the confidence of an adversary to lead him to believe that he is entitled to, or is obliged to accord, protection under the rules of international law applicable in armed conflict, with intent to betray that confidence."

A combatant is lawfully subject to lethal force, however, the right to kill and injure in war is not unlimited. IHL supports the following maxim: if enemy combatants can be put out of action by capture, they should not be injured; if they can be put out of action by injury, they should not be killed; and if they can be put out of action by light injury, grave injury should be avoided.[9] The ICRC in its Interpretive Guidance on the Notion of Direct Participation in Hostilities under International Humanitarian Law states, "The kind and degree of force which is permissible against persons not entitled to protection against direct attack must not exceed what is actually necessary to accomplish a legitimate military purpose in the prevailing circumstances."[10] The POW status and right contained under the GC III are fundamental rights to all lawful combatants and should not be denied regardless of the nature of the military operation. Thus, SOF teams should treat defeated enemy forces as POWs.

Super Soldiers as POWs

The idea of creating an army of enhanced or super soldiers is not new. During the American Civil War (1775-1783) vaccinations were used to enhance the immune system of American soldiers. Now, research organizations in some countries have begun developing technology to enhance human strength and endurance to produce soldiers who will out-perform traditional soldiers.[11] The branches of science and technology involved in these projects include neuroscience, biotechnology, nanotechnology, robotics, and artificial intelligence.[12] The US Army has

---

9 Goodman Ryan, The Power to Kill or Capture Enemy Combatants, *The European Journal of International Law*, Vol. 24, No. 3, 2013, pp. 819-853.

10 Interpretive Guidance on the Notion of Direct Participation in Hostilities under International Humanitarian Law, Geneva: ICRC, 2009, p. 77.

11 Human enhancement is defined as the process of endowing an individual with an ability that goes beyond the typical level or statistically normal range of functioning for humans generally (or the personal unenhanced capabilities of a particular individual), where the ability is either integrated into the body or is so closely worn or connected that it confers an advantage similar to an internal or organic enhancement that transforms the person. Human enhancement technologies can be broadly divided into three overlapping categories: biochemical, cybernetic (or brain-machine interfaces) and prosthetic. Heather A. Harrison Dinniss and Jann K Kleffner, Soldier 2.0: Military Human Enhancement and International Law, *International Law Studies*, Vol. 92, 2016, pp. 423-482.

12 It has been visualized in a report that the principal army unit of the United States operating in 2050 will be mixed human-robot teams. To enable humans to partner

already started creating enhanced military technology to give soldiers superhuman strength.[13]

Under IHL, wounded or captured enemy soldiers are entitled to protection as POWs. In the event of a super soldier being captured, the detaining power may face problems related to providing medical treatment and food, as well as questioning, internment and detention.

An injured super soldier who has been taken POW may require specific medical treatment and medication of which the medical authorities of the detaining power may not be aware. Military medical officers have been held responsible for the death or seriously endangering the health of a POW through medical procedures, which were later considered unnecessary.[14] A medical officer may, therefore, be unwilling to provide medical treatment to an injured super soldier. Internment or detention of a super soldier can also severely affect his physical and mental health. In such events any unintentional act or omission by the detaining power may lead to serious illness or death of a super soldier which would be treated as a serious breach of the GC III.

effectively with robots, human team members will be enhanced in a variety of ways. These super-humans will feature exoskeletons, possess a variety of implants, and have seamless access to sensing and cognitive enhancements. They may also be the result of genetic engineering. The net result will be that they will have enhanced physical capabilities, senses, and cognitive powers. The presence of super-humans on the battlefield in the 2050 timeframe is highly likely because the various components needed to enable this development already exist and are undergoing rapid evolution. Kott Alexander, David Alberts, Amy Zalman, Paulo Shakarian, Fernando Maymi, Cliff Wang, and Gang Qu, Visualizing the Tactical Ground Battlefield in the Year 2050: Workshop Report, US Army Research Laboratory, June 2015.

13 Several research organizations are developing exoskeletons to increase human strength and endurance — including the ability to carry payloads of 200 pounds and to sustain a run at seven to 10 miles per hour (11 to 16 kph). These include Lockheed Martin's HULC, Raytheon's XOS, UC Berkeley's BLEEX, and other projects. Peak Soldier Performance programme of the United States' *Defence Advanced Research Projects Agency* (DARPA) seeks to boost human endurance, both physical and cognitive, thus, turning a human war-fighter into a fighting robot.

14 International courts and tribunals have taken the view that "causing serious bodily or mental harm ... does not necessarily mean that the harm is permanent and irremediable", but it "must go beyond temporary unhappiness, embarrassment or humiliation. It must be harm that results in a grave and long-term disadvantage to a person's ability to lead a normal and constructive life". ICTR, *Akayesu* Trial Judgment, 1998, paragraph 502.

Article 15 of the GC III obliges the detaining power to provide free of charge for the maintenance of POWs and for the medical attention required by their state of health. This obligation represents one of the most important aspects of the protection afforded to POWs under the GC III. The opening words of Article 15, "The Power detaining prisoners of war shall be bound...", make it clear that the obligation is incumbent on the Detaining Power and that it is unconditional. The lack of medical expertise/ specific medication or economic pressure may create a complicated situation for a Detaining Power when it takes a super soldier as prisoner. In such circumstances the only options available to the Detaining Power would be to accept assistance from other States or from an impartial humanitarian organization, transferring the super soldier or releasing and repatriating them. Such options may not be in the military interest of the Detaining Power.

Under Article 17 of the GC III, the Detaining Power has the right to determine the identity, status and rank of captured persons in order to accord them the treatment to which they are entitled. Article 17 authorizes the Detaining Power to disarm and search a POW immediately after his capture. It is generally in the prisoners' interest to establish their identity, status and rank as soon as possible and provide sufficient information to establish their status as members of the enemy armed forces.

However, the Detaining Power may wish to obtain additional information on the prisoners themselves, the Power on which they depend and the circumstances that preceded their capture. This information may be of interest from a military point of view, particularly for intelligence purposes in the case of a super soldier prisoner. The possibility of exerting more psychological pressure, not amounting to torture, on a super soldier cannot be ruled out since Article 17 does not prohibit the Detaining Power from seeking any particular kind of information. It prohibits only the methods mentioned. An overzealous military interrogator may exceed the limit, if he finds that that POW is not cooperating since prisoners are usually questioned shortly after capture, sometimes on the battlefield and amid some confusion. Article 17 does not prohibit the detaining power from interrogating super-soldier POWs with a view to ascertaining the truth in relation to an alleged crime. An interrogator may use interrogation techniques that are not unlawful under Articles 13 and 17 or any other applicable rules.[15]

Autonomous Weapons and Geneva Conventions

Drones and Lethal autonomous weapon systems (LAWS) are posing serious challenges to the laws of war.[16] Once LAWS have been put on operational mode by a remote human operator, subsequent manoeuvre, detection and release of lethal force is based on decisions arrived at through the use of artificial intelligence. For instance, the SGR-Al is an autonomous sentry robot that scans the demilitarized zone (DMZ) dividing North Korea and South Korea. It is capable of identifying targets, issuing commands to surrender, observing signs of surrender, and responding appropriately. It can attack a target without direct human control when it has been set to operate automatically. It identifies a person/object that enters the DMZ as an enemy merely by virtue of that person/object having entered the prohibited zone.

In an armed conflict, the IHL rules of distinction, proportionality and precautions in attack require a party to the conflict to identify targets that are lawful (i.e. combatants, civilians participating directly in hostilities, and military objectives) and persons and objects that must be protected from attack (e.g. civilians).[17] It has been argued at various forums that LAWS will

15 The GC III does not provide a definitive list of permissible and prohibited interrogation techniques. However, certain types of interrogation techniques are clearly prohibited. For example, attempts to gain information from an unwilling POW through the deliberate denial of required medical treatment or through the use of mind-altering chemicals (such as a 'truth serum'), drugs and physiological or psychological devices (such as hypnosis), which impair or deprive prisoners of their free will without being in their interest (as would be, for example, bona fide medical treatment), are also prohibited for their coercive nature and, when employed by a Detaining Power, would be deemed violations of Article 13 (humane treatment of prisoners) and Article 17. Paragraph 1828, Updated Commentary on the Third Geneva Convention, 2019, available at: https://www.icrc.org/en/document/updated-commentary-third-geneva-convention.

16 The US Department of Defence (Autonomy in Weapons Systems, directive No. 3000.09 dated 21 November 2012) describes an autonomous weapons system as a "weapons system that, once activated, can select and engage targets without further intervention by a human operator". There is a strong possibility that China, Israel, Russia, the United States, and other nations will deploy increasingly autonomous robotic weapons in the years ahead.

17 Boulanin Vincent, et.al., Limits in Autonomy in Weapon Systems: Identifying Practical Elements of Human Control, SIPRI, June 2020, pp. 39.

not be able to follow these rules.[18] However, this discussion is confined to likely violations of the Geneva Conventions by LAWS.

Article 48 of AP I states that in order to ensure respect for and protection of the civilian population and civilian objects, the Parties to a conflict shall at all times distinguish between the civilian population and combatants and between civilian objects and military objectives.[19] A major IHL issue is that LAWS cannot discriminate between combatants and non-combatants or other persons likely to be present at the place of conflict. The list includes combatants who are unwilling to fight or are wounded or sick, aircrew members, war correspondents, military doctors, religious personnel, civilian drivers and porters. LAWS lack adequate sensing mechanisms to differentiate between civilians and combatants.[20]In a battlefield full of uncertainties and unknown situations, LAWS would lack the 'common sense' used by an experienced soldier for taking various decisions. Would it, for example, be able to distinguish between a soldier holding his weapon high and crossing an obstacle from a soldier holding his weapon in raised arms with a wish to surrender. A human combatant has to take positive steps to understand a situation; develop his/her own mental model of offence or defence; and then recommend or demand engagement, a process that is extremely difficult to incorporate in LAWS.

According to Sparrow (2015), an important shortcoming of LAWS is to recognize surrender by a soldier.[21] A fundamental requirement of IHL is that combatants should not attack an enemy who has clearly indicated the desire to surrender. It is possible that LAWS might not be able to detect a change in the intent or ability of their targets. As a result, they might keep engaging soldiers even though they now signal their wish to surrender or

18 Mind the Gap: The Lack of Accountability for Killer Robots, Human Rights Watch and IHRC, April 2015.

19 The term 'military objectives' are defines in Article 52, para 2 and 3 as: ... those objects which by their nature, location, purpose or use make an effective contribution to military action and whose total or partial destruction, capture or neutralization, in the circumstances ruling at the time, offers a definite military advantage. In case of doubt whether an object which is normally dedicated to civilian purposes, such as a place of worship, a house or other dwelling or a school, is being used to make an effective contribution to military action, it shall be presumed not to be so used.

20 Sharkey Noel E., The Evitability of Autonomous Robot Warfare, *International Review of the Red Cross*, Vol. 94, No. 886, Summer 2012, p. 787-799.

21 Sparrow Robert, Twenty Seconds to Comply: Autonomous Weapon Systems and the Recognition of Surrender, *International Law Studies*, Vol. 91, 2015, p. 299-728.

those who have become incapable of resisting. According to the Geneva Conventions, it is a war crime to kill soldiers who wish to surrender or who no longer have the means to resist.[22]

The use of LAWS is also associated with the risk of creating a serious accountability gap. During an armed conflict, soldiers are capable of making decisions and reflecting on their own autonomy. They can be held responsible for any action they choose to undertake. They can be prosecuted for violating the principles and laws of IHL which dictate that an individual is to be held legally responsible for grave breaches of the Geneva Conventions. LAWS, on the other hand, lack the capacity for moral autonomy, and thus cannot be held responsible. It would be legally challenging to hold a military commander, an operator, or an AI specialist responsible for the unlawful actions of LAWS.

Torturing Prisoners of War

The Geneva Conventions of 1949 expressly provide that a POW may be questioned by his captors to establish his identity during the vetting process. Article 17 of the GC III states that every POW is bound to give only his surname, first name and rank, date of birth, and army, regimental, personal or serial number, or failing this, equivalent information.[23] If a prisoner wilfully fails to abide by this rule, he may render himself liable to a restriction of the privileges accorded to his rank or status. However, a POW who refuses to answer may not be threatened, insulted, or exposed to unpleasant or disadvantageous treatment of any kind. In case a wounded POW is unable to identify himself to his captors on the battlefield as a

22 For instance in Syria, Pakistan, Afghanistan and elsewhere, the remotely controlled drones are being used by the US to fire missiles on the designated enemies. The US army is rarely stepping foot on the battlefield. Thus, the possibility of taking a prisoner of war is ruled out. How can a wounded enemy soldier surrender to a drone?

23 Article 17 of the GC III: Each Party to a conflict is required to furnish the persons under its jurisdiction who are liable to become POW, with an identity card showing the owner's surname, first names, rank, army, regimental, personal or serial number or equivalent information, and date of birth. The identity card may, furthermore, bear the signature or the fingerprints, or both, of the owner, and may bear, as well, any other information the Party to the conflict may wish to add concerning persons belonging to its armed forces. As far as possible the card shall measure 6.5 x 10 cm. and shall be issued in duplicate. The identity card shall be shown by the POW upon demand, but may in no case be taken away from him.

result of his wounds, he is to be handed over to medical personnel for necessary treatment.[24]

Captured combatants are a good source of strategic and tactical military information. The higher the rank of a combatant prior to capture, the more important he will be as a source of potential information for his captors. Even lower-ranking soldiers may carry valuable information about the enemy's position, numbers, movements and routes, whereas higher-ranking prisoners may have more information about actual tactics and future strategies.[25] Therefore the possibility of using coercive methods against POWs or their ill-treatment by captors cannot be ruled out.

Torture and ill-treatment are prohibited at all times and all circumstances under international law. The term torture has been defined as: "Any act by which severe pain or suffering, whether physical or mental, is intentionally inflicted on a person for such purposes as obtaining from him or a third person information or a confession, punishing him for an act he or a third person has committed or is suspected of having committed, or intimidating or coercing him or a third person, or for any reason based on discrimination of any kind, when such pain or suffering is inflicted by or at the instigation of, or with the consent or acquiescence of a public official

24 POWs who are unable to state their identity owing to their physical or mental condition, for example because of wounds or exhaustion, must be handed over to the medical service. The purpose of this provision is to ensure that such prisoners receive the necessary medical assistance to the fullest extent practicable and with the least possible delay and that any questioning complies with the restrictions specific to their situation. The identity of such prisoners must be established by all possible means, subject to the prohibition of torture and coercion. In particular, such prisoners may be identified through their identity cards or their identity discs or by fellow prisoners. Recourse may also be had to other methods, such as the transmission of digital or analog photographs or biometric identification procedures such as fingerprints or retinal scanning. Any identification procedure used must be consistent with the requirements of Article 13. For example, if POWs are photographed for identification purposes, the photographs must be handled and used in a way that does not violate the prohibition of exposure to public curiosity contained in Article 13(2). A DNA sample may be taken and analyzed only with the prisoner's informed consent, except where an overriding public interest dictates otherwise, such as to identify persons who are unable to state their identity, and other methods of identification are not adequate. Paragrpahs 1832 and 1833, Updated Commentary on the Third Geneva Convention, 2019, available at: https://www.icrc.org/en/document/updated-commentary-third-geneva-convention.

25 Geib Robin, Name, rank, date of birth, serial number and the right to remain silent, *International Committee of the Red Cross*, Volume 87, Number 860, December 2005, pp. 721-735.

or other person acting in an official capacity. It does not include pain or suffering arising only from, inherent in or incidental to lawful sanctions."[26] Article 1 of the Convention Against Torture thus codifies four necessary elements for an action to constitute torture: (i) infliction of severe pain or suffering, whether physical or mental; (ii) with intent; (iii) for a purpose prohibited by the Convention; and (iv) by a public official or with an official's involvement or acquiescence.[27]

"Torture or inhuman treatment" is considered as grave breaches of all four Geneva Conventions and two Additional Protocols of 1977. Grave breaches are a species of war crime under Article 8 of the Rome Statute of the International Criminal Court (ICC). They are subject to jurisdiction by any state party "regardless of their nationality". Rule 90 of the customary international humanitarian law states that torture, cruel or inhuman treatment and outrages on personal dignity, in particular humiliation and degrading treatment, are prohibited.[28]

However, after the attacks of 11 September 2001, the United States Office of Legal Counsel at the Department of Justice issued "torture memos",[29]which authorized the CIA and the US military to use "enhanced interrogation techniques" in questioning suspected terrorists. A large number of detainees at Bagram, Guantanamo Bay, Abu Ghraib and at some secret locations (black sites),[30] were subjected to hooding; sleep adjustment (e.g., reversing sleep cycles); false flag (convincing the detainee that individuals from a country other than the US were interrogating him); threat of transfer (threatening to transfer the subject to a third country that the subject is likely to fear would subject him to torture or death); isolation

26 Article 1, The UN Convention Against Torture was adopted by the UN General Assembly in December 1984, the Convention entered into force in June 1987.

27 Hathway Oona A., Aileen Nowlan and Julia Spiegel, Torture Reasoning: The Intent to Torture under International and Domestic Law, *Virginia Journal of International Law*, Vol. 52, No.4, 2012, pp. 791-837.

28 Marie Henckaerts and Louise Doswald-Beck (eds.), 2005, *Customary International Humanitarian Law*, Vol. I, Cambridge and International Committee of the Red Cross, p. 315.

29 Memorandum from Jay S. Bybee, Assistant Attorney General, to Alberto R. Gonzales, Counsel to the President, on Standards of Conduct for Interrogation under 18 USC (2340-2340A), dated 1 August 2002.

30 The American intelligence agency, CIA instead of establishing American-style prisons abroad, created a series of "black sites" where detainees were treated (in few other undisclosed countries) far more harshly than would be allowed in the United States.

for up to 30 days; forced grooming (consider the effect of forced shaving on a devout Muslim); use of stress positions such as prolonged standing; sleep deprivation; removal of clothing; increasing anxiety by the use of aversions (e.g. presence of dogs); deprivation of light/auditory stimuli, etc. Some detainees were shackled in painful positions, locked in boxes the size of a coffin, kept awake for over 100 hours at a time, and forced to inhale water in a process known as water-boarding. Interrogators sometimes went far beyond what Washington had authorized, sodomizing detainees with blunt objects, threatening to sexually abuse their family members, and, on at least one occasion, freezing a suspect to death by chaining him to an ice-cold floor overnight.[31] The administration of President George W. Bush took the position that aggressive interrogation techniques were both necessary and permissible in the fight against al-Qaeda and other terrorists.[32]A number of the techniques approved by the US Government for possible use by interrogators could be classified as torture and/or cruel or inhuman treatment.[33]

It has been reported that in the post-9/11 environment, traditional standards of conduct were substituted by coercive interrogation techniques

31 Johnson Douglas A., Alberto Mora and Averell Schmidt, The Strategic Costs of Torture: How "Enhanced Interrogation" Hurt America, *Foreign Affairs*, September/October 2016.

32 After the September 2001 attacks, President Bush expanded the authority of the CIA, permitting it to capture, detain and use deadly force against al-Qaeda operatives around the world. In February 2002, he issued an order stating that members of al-Qaeda, the Taliban, and associated forces are unlawful enemy combatants who are not entitled to protections under the GC III. Executive Order: Interpretation of the Geneva Conventions Common Article 3 as Applied to a Programme of Detention and Interrogation Operated by the Central Intelligence Agency, 20 July 2007.

33 The US Marine Corps Major General James N. Mattis told the men and women of the US Army interrogators in Afghanistan: "You are helping us to kill the enemy. Let's not make any mistakes about this. Let's not try to sugarcoat it. You are assisting my marines to kill evil. To bayonet it, to shoot it with machine guns, to cut its eyes out and shit in the sockets. And you can take pride in that. You can take pride in knowing that you had a hand in gouging out the eyes and cutting out the tongue of evil." General Mattis, cited in Mackey, Chris and Miller, Greg, *The Interrogators: Inside the Secret War Against Al Qaeda*, New York and Boston: Little Brown, 2004, p. 153. This talk of 'gouging out eyes' and 'cutting out tongues' was directed at personnel charged with handling enemy POWs. It is hardly surprising that it subsequently came to light that US troops abused and occasionally even killed prisoners in both Afghanistan and Iraq. Robinson Paul, 2006, *Military Honour and the Conduct of War: from Ancient Greece to Iraq*, London and New York: Routledge, p. 182.

similar to Communist methodologies.[34] There was widespread criticism of the US military and the government when graphic imagery of interrogation and abuses in the detention camps at Guantanamo Bay and Abu Ghraib became public. In 2009, President Barack Obama admitted that certain interrogation techniques amounted to torture and issued Executive Order 13491 banning the use of torture by military authorities.

The term interrogation can be misleading for both professionals and the layperson.[35] Unfortunately, there have been far too many instances in which interrogation has been a guise for torture, and such heinous behaviour still remains a tool of intimidation under far too many political regimes.[36] It is essential that tactical or combat interrogation of POWs be carried out by highly skilled interrogators who can effectively glean information from sources in a time-compressed environment. Interrogation can be divided into three general categories: (i) interrogation to obtain military information; (ii) interrogation in order to convert; and (iii) interrogation in order to break the will.[37]

Military interrogators often claim that limited physical and psychological pressure does not necessarily meet the generally accepted definitions of torture. The Committee Against Torture, in its concluding remarks on the periodic report of Israel determined that the following methods of

34 Kleinman Steven M., The Promise of Interrogation v. the Problem of Torture, *Valparaiso University Law Review*, Vol. 43, No. 4, 2009, pp. 1577-1590.

35 Interrogation is the process of questioning a source to obtain the maximum amount of usable information. The goal of any interrogation is to obtain reliable information in a lawful manner, in a minimum amount of time, and to satisfy the intelligence requirements of any echelon of command. An interrogation involves the interaction of two personalities – the source and interrogator and may differ because of individual characteristics and capabilities of the participants.

36 According to the US Army Manual, the US policy expressly prohibits acts of violence or intimidation, including physical or mental torture, threats, insults, or exposure to inhumane treatment as a means of or aid to interrogation. The Manual further states, "such illegal acts are not authorized and will not be condoned by the US Army. Acts in violation of these prohibitions are criminal acts punishable under the Uniform Code of Military Justice. Experience indicates that the use of prohibited techniques is not necessary to gain cooperation of interrogation source." Intelligence Interrogation, Headquarters, Department of Army, Washington DC, Field Manual 34-52, 28 September 1992, page 1-6 to 1-9.

37 Paul Fein, We Have Ways ... The Law and Morality of the Interrogation of Prisoners of War, unpublished Ph.D. dissertation, Georgetown University, 30 November 1994, p.112-136.

interrogation constituted torture as defined by Article 1 of the Convention Against Torture, particularly when used in combination: (i) restraining in very painful conditions, (ii) hooding under special conditions, (iii) exposure to loud music for prolonged periods, (iv) sleep deprivation for prolonged periods,(v) threats, including death threats, (vi) violent shaking, and (vii) using cold air to chill. The Committee also held that these methods constituted cruel, inhuman, or degrading treatment.[38]

Torture and ill-treatment are totally prohibited under international law. The world community must accept that every individual has the legal right not to be subjected to torture or cruel, inhuman or degrading treatment or punishment. The States must ensure that acts involving torture or cruel, inhuman or other inhumane treatment are "crimes" under their national laws. They must also ensure that all agencies of the government are subject to that law.

The Missing

Combatants as well as civilians are often reported missing in armed conflicts. At times this leads to a serious dispute, for example, the disappearance of two Israeli soldiers from the border between Israel and Lebanon sparked the 2006 war. Uncertainty about the fate of a relative is a harsh reality for families of missing combatants in situations of armed conflict. Their anxiety continues for years after the fighting ends and peace returns.[39] Under IHL, the task of collecting and identifying the remains of soldiers, informing their families and keeping their memory alive falls on the belligerents.[40] The governments and military authorities have a duty

38 The Committee Against Torture, Eighteenth session, Israel Special Report, 9 May 1997. The Israel Government neither confirmed nor denied the content of the report.

39 For an account of those Indian military personnel still reported missing after the 1971 Indo-Pak War, see: Dogra Chander Suta, 2020, *Missing in Action: The Prisoners who never came back*, NOIDA: Harper Collins Publishers, pp. 339.

40 Standards in international law: 1. Parties to an armed conflict must take all possible measures to search for and collect the dead, without delay and without distinction. 2. Parties to an armed conflict must treat the dead with respect and dignity and must prevent their remains from being pillaged, mutilated or despoiled. 3. Parties to an armed conflict must take measures to identify the dead before disposing of their remains. 4. In armed conflicts, the dead must be disposed of in a respectful manner and their graves respected. 5. In armed conflicts, persons whose remains cannot be handed over to their families should be buried individually; collective graves must be the exception, and all graves must be marked. 6. Parties to an armed conflict must take all possible measures to provide information to the appropriate authorities or to

to prevent disappearances. However, every country may not invest much in this task. The ICRC, with the use of modern technology, has played an important role in this regard.

A "missing person" is anyone unaccounted for as a result of an armed conflict.[41] Soldiers can become missing persons in many situations: (i) They may be killed when they are captured or they may die in custody, or be held incommunicado or in a secret location. (ii) After an engagement, the bodies of the dead soldiers may be abandoned, buried in haste or even destroyed. (iii) Members of armed forces may go missing in action because they have not been issued with any means of identifying themselves, such as identity discs. (iv) Evidence confirming death is not always preserved and handled appropriately during exhumations and post mortem procedures.[42]

The ICRC works with States to establish legal systems and frameworks aimed at preventing people from going missing and at helping missing persons and their families. In early 2000, the ICRC began developing expertise in forensic science for humanitarian purposes. The UK and Argentina recently requested the ICRC to identify the remains of soldiers killed during the 1982 Falkland War. In 2018, the ICRC has launched a new Missing Persons Project aimed at developing international standards in this field.

Identifying members of armed forces is a key means of preventing them from going missing as a result of armed conflict. Identity tags help to establish the fate of people captured, wounded or killed in action. Armed forces must maintain a repository of biological samples (blood and saliva) of all their members. This could be used identify the remains of soldiers killed during armed conflicts.

the family on the identities, locations and causes of death of those who have died. 7. Parties to an international armed conflict must endeavour to facilitate the return of remains and personal effects to the home country of the deceased at the request of the authorities or the next-of-kin. The Missing: ICRC Progress Report, Geneva: ICRC, 2006, p. 14.

41 The ICRC has defined "missing persons" as all those whose whereabouts are unknown to their families or, based on reliable information, who are reported missing as a consequence of armed conflict, internal violence or internal disturbances. Accompanying the Families of Missing Persons: A Practical Handbook, Geneva: ICRC, 2013.

42 The Missing: ICRC Progress report, Geneva: ICRC, 2006, pp. 25.

The Role of the United Nations

The maintenance of peace, and the prevention of armed conflict are vital concerns of the United Nations (UN). Respect for human rights at all times and in all places is a fundamental principle of the Organization. The UN and its organs have played an important role in promoting peace around the world and taken various steps to ensure compliance of its forces with IHL.

The UN participated as an observer in the Diplomatic Conference of 1949 at which the Geneva Conventions were adopted, but the Geneva Conventions themselves do not refer to the UN, except in an article common to the Geneva Conventions concerning the registration of the Conventions with the Secretariat of the UN and the notification to the Secretariat of all ratifications, accessions, and denunciations with respect to those Conventions.[43] The UN is not a party to the GC III and therefore not bound by the provisions of the Convention. In 1972, the Office of Legal Affairs of the UN Secretariat stated that the UN cannot accede to the Geneva Conventions.[44]

One of the purposes of the UN, as stated in Article 1(3) is to achieve international cooperation in solving international problems of

43 Article 143 of the GCIII, concerning registration with United Nations provides, "The Swiss Federal Council shall register the present Convention with the Secretariat of the United Nations. The Swiss Federal Council shall also inform the Secretariat of the United Nations of all ratifications, accessions and denunciations received by it with respect to the present Convention."

44 "The question of the application of the Geneva Conventions to United Nations peacekeeping operations is one of long standing, having been raised at least since the days of the Congo operation. The question was raised again at the Conference, this time in the form of a suggestion to insert in the draft Additional Protocol to the Conventions a clause providing for accession by the UN. The ICRC has been of the opinion that the UN should formally undertake by accession to apply the Conventions each time Forces of the UN are engaged in operations. We have always maintained, however, that the UN is not substantively in a position to become a party to the 1949 Conventions, which contain many obligations that can only be discharged by the exercise of juridical and administrative powers which the Organization does not possess, such as the authority to exercise criminal jurisdiction over members of the Forces, or administrative competence relating to territorial sovereignty. Thus the UN is unable to fulfil obligations which for their execution require the exercise of powers not granted to the Organization, and therefore cannot accede to the Conventions." Legal opinions of the Secretariat of the United Nations: Question of the possible accession of Intergovernmental Organizations to the Geneva Conventions for the Protection of War Victims, *United Nations Juridical Yearbook*, 1972, p. 153.

humanitarian character, and in promoting and encouraging respect for human rights. Today, there is no doubt that international humanitarian law has become one of the most important areas of international law that guide the work of the UN. UN peacekeeping operations are deployed on the basis of a mandate from the Security Council. IHL is relevant to peacekeeping operations because these missions are often deployed in post-conflict environments where violence may be ongoing or conflict could reignite. Additionally, in post-conflict environments there are often large civilian populations that have been targeted by the warring parties, prisoners of war and other vulnerable groups to whom the Geneva Conventions or other humanitarian law would apply in the event of further hostilities. UN peacekeepers must have a clear understanding of the principles and rules of international humanitarian law and observe them in situations where they apply.[45]

The 1994 Convention on the Safety of United Nations and Associated Personnel provided protection to captured or detained UN personnel who "shall be treated in accordance with universally recognized standards of human rights and the principles and spirit of the Geneva Conventions of 1949", which would include the GC III.

Finally, in August 1999, the Secretary-General's Bulletin on the "Observance by UN Forces of IHL" set out the fundamental principles and rules of international law that may be applicable to peacekeepers. Section 4 of the Bulletin provides that in case of violations of IHL, military members of peacekeeping forces are subject to prosecution in their national courts. Section 7 states that persons not, or no longer, taking part in military operations, including civilians, members of armed forces who have laid down their weapons and persons placed *hors de combat* by reason of sickness, wounds or detention, shall, in all circumstances, be treated humanely and without any adverse distinction based on race, sex, religious convictions or any other ground. They shall be accorded full respect for their person, honour and religious and other convictions.[46] Section 8 of the Bulletin dealing with the treatment of detained persons provides:

45 United Nations Peacekeeping Operations: Principles and Guidelines, United Nations, 20008, p. 15.

46 The Bulletin (ST/SGB/1999/13) entered into force on 12 August 1999.

The UN force shall treat with humanity and respect for their dignity detained members of the armed forces and other persons who no longer take part in military operations by reason of detention. Without prejudice to their legal status, they shall be treated in accordance with the relevant provisions of the Third Geneva Convention of 1949, as may be applicable to them *mutatis mutandis*. In particular:

(a) Their capture and detention shall be notified without delay to the party on which they depend and to the Central Tracing Agency of the International Committee of the Red Cross, in particular in order to inform their families;
(b) They shall be held in secure and safe premises which provide all possible safeguards of hygiene and health, and shall not be detained in areas exposed to the dangers of the combat zone;
(c) They shall be entitled to receive food and clothing, hygiene and medical attention;
(d) They shall under no circumstances be subjected to any form of torture or ill-treatment;
(e) Women whose liberty has been restricted shall be held in quarters separated from men's quarters, and shall be under the immediate supervision of women;
(f) In cases where children who have not attained the age of sixteen years take a direct part in hostilities and are arrested, detained or interned by the UN force, they shall continue to benefit from special protection. In particular, they shall be held in quarters separate from the quarters of adults, except when accommodated with their families;
(g) ICRC's right to visit prisoners and detained persons shall be respected and guaranteed.

The protection of the wounded, the sick, and medical and relief personnel, as contained in Section 9 provides the following safeguards:

> 9.1 Members of the armed forces and other persons in the power of the UN force who are wounded or sick shall be respected and protected in all circumstances. They shall be treated humanely and receive the medical care and attention required by their condition, without adverse distinction. Only urgent medical reasons will authorize priority in the order of treatment to be administered.

9.2 Whenever circumstances permit, a suspension of fire shall be arranged, or other local arrangements made, to permit the search for and identification of the wounded, the sick and the dead left on the battlefield and allow for their collection, removal, exchange and transport.

9.3 The UN force shall not attack medical establishments or mobile medical units. These shall at all times be respected and protected, unless they are used, outside their humanitarian functions, to attack or otherwise commit harmful acts against the United Nations force.

9.4 The UN force shall in all circumstances respect and protect medical personnel exclusively engaged in the search for, transport or treatment of the wounded or sick, as well as religious personnel.

9.5 The UN force shall respect and protect transports of wounded and sick or medical equipment in the same way as mobile medical units.

9.6 The UN force shall not engage in reprisals against the wounded, the sick or the personnel, establishments and equipment protected under this section.

9.7 The UN force shall in all circumstances respect the Red Cross and Red Crescent emblems. These emblems may not be employed except to indicate or to protect medical units and medical establishments, personnel and material. Any misuse of the Red Cross or Red Crescent emblems is prohibited.

9.8 The UN force shall respect the right of the families to know about the fate of their sick, wounded and deceased relatives. To this end, the force shall facilitate the work of the ICRC Central Tracing Agency.

9.9 The UN force shall facilitate the work of relief operations which are humanitarian and impartial in character and conducted without any adverse distinction, and shall respect personnel, vehicles and premises involved in such operations.

The Role of the Security Council

The Security Council has, on several occasions, specifically recalled its primary responsibility under the Charter of the United Nations for the maintenance of international peace and security, and in this context, the need to promote respect for the rules and principles of IHL. The Council has mainly invoked the GC III in relation to situations under its consideration, such as the Middle East conflict in 1967 (Resolution 237/1967), the India–Pakistan war in 1971 (Resolution 307/1971), the Iran–Iraq conflict in the 1980s (Resolution 540/1983 and 598/1987),[47] the conflict in Bosnia and Herzegovina in the 1990s (S/25557), and the Eritrea–Ethiopia conflict (Resolution 1369/2001), to ensure the timely release and repatriation of POWs.

In 2019, the Security Council adopted the first ever resolution dealing specifically with persons reported missing in an armed conflict.[48]Adopting the resolution unanimously, the Council called upon parties to an armed conflict to take appropriate measures to prevent persons from going missing, to pay the utmost attention to cases of children reported missing, and to register and notify the personal details of persons deprived of their liberty, including POWs. The resolution urged parties to an armed conflict to collect, protect, and manage all relevant data and documents on missing persons; to search for, recover and identify the dead; to return the remains, wherever possible, to their relatives; and to refrain from the deliberate relocation of the remains from mass graves. It reiterated the Council's support to the ICRC in seeking access to information on persons reported missing; and called for peace agreements to include provisions to facilitate the search for missing persons. Incidentally, in 2018, more than 45,000 people were registered as missing by the ICRC's Central Tracing Agency. This figure, according to the ICRC, was only the tip of the iceberg.

---

47 Security Council Resolution 540 (1983) condemned all violations of IHL in First Gulf War (Iran/Iraq), in particular, the provisions of the Geneva Conventions of 1949 in all their aspects, and called for the immediate cessation of all military operations against civilian targets, including city and residential areas. UN Doc. S/RES/540 (31 October 1983).

48 Secuirty Council Resolution 2474 of 2019.

The Role of the General Assembly

The General Assembly has invoked the GC III in its resolutions in relation to a number of armed conflicts, such as the Middle East conflict in 1967 (Resolution 2252 (ES-V)), the Afghanistan conflict in the 1980s (Resolution 47/141), and the Gulf War in 1990–1991 (Resolution 46/135),[49] and sometimes in relation to those to which the Convention did not formally apply, such as the Second World War (Resolution 741/VIII) and the Korean War (Resolution 610/VII). Most of these resolutions were to ensure the timely release and repatriation of POWs and interned civilians.

The General Assembly resolution 610/VII affirmed that the release and repatriation of POWs shall be effected in accordance with the GC III, the established principles and practice of international law and the relevant provisions of the draft agreement. It also affirmed that force shall not be used against POWs to prevent or effect their return to their homeland and they shall be treated humanely in accordance with the specific provision of the GC III and with the general spirit of the Convention. According to the resolution, in order to facilitate their return, a repatriation commission shall be established. All POWs shall be released to the repatriation commission from military control and from the custody of the detaining side in agreed numbers and at agreed points in agreed demilitarized zones. The resolution also provided that if at the end of 120 days after the armistice agreement, there are POWs whose return to their homeland has not been effected under the procedure prescribed in the resolution, the responsibility for their care and maintenance and for their subsequent disposition shall be transferred to the United Nations, which in all matters relating to them shall act in accordance with international law.[50]

49 The resolution requested the Government of Iraq to provide information on all Kuwaiti persons and third-country nationals deported from Kuwait between 2 Aug. 1990 and 26 Feb. 1991 who may still be detained and, in accordance with its obligations under article 188 of the Geneva Convention relative to the Treatment of Prisoners of War of 12 Aug. 1949 and article 134 of the Geneva Convention relative to the Protection of Civilian Persons in Time of War of 12 August 1949, to release these persons without delay. The resolution also requested the Government of Iraq to search for the persons still missing and to cooperate with international humanitarian organizations, such as the ICRC in their search for and eventual repatriation of Kuwaiti and third-country national detainees and missing persons.

50 General Assembly resolution 610/VII, dated 3 December 1952.

The General Assembly has also recognized the applicability of the provisions of the GC III to combatants captured during struggles against colonial and alien domination and racist regimes. Resolutions have been issued in relation to specific contexts such as South Africa (Resolution 2369/XXIII), Southern Rhodesia (Resolution 2508/XXIV) and Namibia (Resolution 38/36), and also as a general principle (Resolution 3103/XXVIII). Resolution 3103/XXVIII proclaimed that armed struggles of people against colonial and alien domination and racist regimes are to be regarded as international armed conflicts in the sense of the 1949 Geneva Conventions. Further, combatants struggling against colonial and alien domination and racist regimes are to be accorded the status of POW and treated in accordance with the provisions of the GC III when they are captured.[51] These resolutions contributed to the inclusion in the AP I of Article 1 (4), which recognizes armed conflicts in the exercise of the right of self-determination as international armed conflicts.[52]

The Third Geneva Convention: Updated Commentary

In the 1950s, the ICRC published a set of commentaries on the Geneva Conventions, giving guidance on their implementation. But in keeping with the developments in law and practice since then, it commissioned a new set of commentaries which reflect the current interpretations of the Conventions. The updated commentary on the Third Geneva Convention related to the treatment of prisoners of war was issued in 2019.[53] The updated commentary sheds light on many issues, in particular on the obligations of the Parties to a conflict towards POWs. The updated Commentary has considered developments in branches of international law other than IHL, such as international criminal law and international human rights law.

The most essential protections afforded by the Third Geneva Convention (GC III) to POWs can be summarized as follows.[54]

51 Para 3 and 5, General Assembly resolution 3103/XXVIII, dated 12 December 1973.

52 Sandoz Yves, et. al., (ed.), 1987, Commentary on the Additional Protocol of 8 June 1977, Geneva: ICRC and MartinusNijhoff Publishers, p. 51-56.

53 Updated Commentary on the Third Geneva Convention, 2019, available at: https://www.icrc.org/en/document/updated-commentary-third-geneva-convention.

54 Droege Cordula, GC III Commentary: ten essential protections for prisoners of war, 23 July 2020, available at: https://blogs.icrc.org/law-and-policy/2020/07/23/gciii-commentary-prisoners-of-war/.

- GC III protects members of the armed forces and certain other categories of persons who fall into the power of the enemy during an international armed conflict. These persons, designated as POWs, are protected persons and cannot be punished for their participation in armed conflict. GC III embodies a balance between the requirements of humanity and military necessity.

- Humane treatment and protection at all times: POWs are protected against acts of violence and intimidation, insults and public curiosity, and against reprisals.[55] POWs may never be subjected to medical or scientific experimentation.

- Respect for persons and honour in all circumstances: POWs must be allowed to wear their badges of rank and nationality and their military decorations and be treated in accordance with their rank and age. Their working conditions must not be humiliating.

- Equality and non-adverse distinction: All POWs are entitled to the same respect and protection and must be treated equally.[56] Women POWs must be afforded 'treatment as favourable as that granted to men'.[57] Equal treatment does not mean identical treatment. POWs

55 Just a day after the victory from Pakistani occupation, a grotesque real-life drama was enacted at Dhaka Stadium on 17 December 1971. The actor was freedom fighter Kader Siddiqi, and the victims were two men alleged to be Razakars. They were bayoneted to death by Siddiqi in front of a cheering crowd of the Muktibahini or the liberation armed groups. ... The horrifying AP photo series "Death in Dacca" haunted the then government. And it was one of the reasons why all the prisoners of war (POW) of 1971 were immediately shifted to India for safety. Munshi M.B.I., 2012, *The India Doctrine (1947-2007): A Contemporary study on Indian Hegemony and Geo-Strategic Perspective on South Asia*, Labmert Academic Publishing, pp. 384.

56 After the Indian defeat in the war of 1962, China took in over 3,900 Indian POW. But among them, about 700 Gorkha POWs were singled out for different – 'perhaps better' – treatment, to be indoctrinated against their Indian officers, and told that Chinese and Nepalis are 'brothers'. China even made a direct offer to Nepal to take back Gorkha POWs, an offer Kathmandu declined. Jha Prashant, Post-1962, China treated Gorkha POW's better, indoctrinated them: Research, *Hindustan Times*, 01 December 2014.

57 Article 16 of the GC III requires that all POWs 'be treated alike'. This does not mean that all prisoners must receive identical treatment; on the contrary, to achieve equal treatment, non-adverse distinctions, i.e. distinctions that are justified by the substantively different situations and needs of protected persons, are allowed and sometimes required. To the extent that the situation and needs of women POWs are different from those of men POWs, they must in fact receive different treatment to ensure that women and men POWs are protected in equal measure.

in different situations/ needs may need to be treated differently in order to achieve equality of treatment.

- Questioning: The Detaining Power must properly identify POWs and accord them the treatment to which they are entitled. It is absolutely prohibited to subject POWs to any physical or mental torture, or to any other form of coercion for securing information.[58]

- Adequate medical attention: POWs must receive proper medical care as required by their state of health, including special treatment in case of serious disease or disability. Seriously wounded or sick POWs must be directly repatriated to their own country or transferred to a neutral country for treatment.

- Contact with the outside world: POWs must be allowed to keep in touch with their families. Modern means of communication such as video-conferencing and email should also be considered.

- The right of the ICRC to visit POWs must be honoured by the Detaining Power. The authorities must not impose any restriction on which places and POWs may be visited. The ICRC should provide additional support to the authorities through the Central Tracing Agency.

- POWs have the right to escape.[59] The use of weapons against POWs who attempt to escape must constitute an extreme measure and must be preceded by warning.

---

58 The GC III prohibits the use of coercion, but does not define the term. The US military's Field Manual 34-52, defines coercion as "actions designed to unlawfully induce another to compel an act against one's will." The use of Functional Magnetic Resonance Imaging (FMRI) in interrogation of POWs would violate IHL and, therefore, cannot be used against them. Thompson Sean Kevin, Legality of the Use of Psychiatric Neuroimaging in Intelligence Interrogation, *Cornell L. Rev.*, Vol. 90, 2005, pp. 1601-1637.

59 Typical of all POWs, the majority of their time is spent in thinking about means of escape. It is an honour for any prisoner to escape legitimately. A military officer from Pakistan who successfully escaped from an Indian POW camp in 1971 writes, "Whether he is a common citizen or an ordinary soldier, it is a matter of utmost disgrace for anyone to fall a POW into the hands of the enemy. Even when one is mortally wounded, one's last conscious action should be directed towards avoiding this possibility." Sehgal Ikram, 2012, *Escape from Oblivion: The Story of a Pakistani POW in India*, Oxford: OUP, p. xiii.

- Right to a fair trial: If accused of an offence, a POW must be tried before an independent and impartial court, affording all essential judicial guarantees.

- Prisoners killed or injured: Each death or serious injury of a POW must be investigated. It is the commander's duty to prevent and punish for violations of the Geneva Conventions committed by his subordinates.

- Missing persons: Both IHL and human rights law include detailed provisions regarding the duty of the State to report and investigate missing cases in an armed conflict.[60]

- Educational and recreational activities: The detaining authorities must encourage POWs to pursue intellectual, educational, and recreational activities. They must provide adequate premises and equipment with special attention to physical exercise and open-air activities.

- Release and repatriation: If a POW is seriously wounded or sick, he must be repatriated for medical reasons. After cessation of active hostilities, a POW must be repatriated without delay.

Derek Jinks has argued in his paper, "The Declining Significance of POW Status" that POW status carries no significant, unique protective consequences and the gap in protection for those classified as POWs and those not so classified (e.g., those designated "unlawful combatants") is closing.[61] There is no doubt that the traditional aspects of armed conflict are being replaced rapidly. Newer means of warfare, such as information warfare, use of autonomous weapons, and artificial intelligence, are blurring the lines between combatants and noncombatants. However, it must be understood that the right to use any means or method of warfare is not unlimited.[62]

60 During international armed conflict, Articles 32-34 of the 1977 AP I stipulate the rights of families to know the fate of their relatives and oblige to parties to conflict to "search for the persons who have been reported missing by an adverse party" and to "transmit all relevant information concerning such persons in order to facilitate such searches."

61 Derek Jinks, The Declining Significance of POW Status, University of Chicago Public Law & Legal Theory Working Paper No. 65, 2004, pp. 57.

62 Article 35 of the 1977 AP I provides a general normative framework. Article 35 states: "(2) It is prohibited to employ weapons, projectiles and material and methods of warfare

The Geneva Conventions have not become obsolete. The GC III provides a robust rights regime for POWs. There have been various occasions when the provisions of the Convention have been violated or POWs have been denied their rights by their captors. But these have arisen not because of shortcomings of the Convention, but the machinations of military commanders and their political masters.[63] What has gone missing in the last few decades is the old martial virtue of courage in the military leaders and their political masters. The Geneva Conventions do matter and will continue to be significant as long as there are soldiers in the battlefield.[64] However, the legal framework has to be buttressed with new rules in order to meet certain current challenges. Till then, the States have to comply with their treaty obligations. Article 127 of GC III states:

> The High Contracting Parties undertake, in time of peace as in time of war, to disseminate the text of the present Convention as widely as possible in their respective countries, and, in particular, to include the study thereof in their programmes of military and, if possible, civil instruction, so that the principles thereof may become known to all their armed forces and to the entire population.[65]Any military

of a nature to cause superfluous injury or unnecessary suffering. (3) It is prohibited to employ methods or means of warfare which are intended, or may be expected, to cause widespread, long-term and severe damage to the natural environment." These principles provide an overarching framework for Article 36 of AP I dealing with new weapons: "In the study, development, acquisition or adoption of a new weapon, means or method of warfare, a High Contracting Party is under an obligation to determine whether its employment would, in some or all circumstances, be prohibited by this Protocol or by any other rule of international law applicable to the High Contracting Party."

63 The US prison camp in Guantanamo Bay, Cuba, and other detention sites were not 'legal black holes', but were misuse of skills of lawyers in the cause of evil. Guantanamo and the Bush administration's detention policy more generally were built on legal opinions and memos. It was in fact the erroneous and morally corrupt interpretation of the law. Scheipers Sibylle, 2010, *Prisoners in War*, Oxford: OUP, p. 314-315.

64 Evangelista Matthew and Nina Tannenwald, (ed.), 2017, *Do the Geneva Conventions Matter?* Oxford: Oxford University Press, pp. 362.

65 Bringing the Geneva Conventions to the knowledge of the general population is a significant element for attaining full compliance with the Conventions. This is also relevant because the obligation of States Parties to suppress all violations of the Conventions and, in the case of grave breaches, to repress them under domestic criminal law, applies not only to violations committed by persons acting on behalf of a State, but also to violations by private persons. Thus, members of the general population may become subject to prosecution for grave breaches of the Geneva Conventions, and their knowledge of the Conventions is therefore important.

> or other authorities, who in time of war assume responsibilities in respect of POWs, must possess the text of the Convention and be specially instructed as to its provisions.

The implication of this provision is that through dissemination and instructions, the military and the general population must be made aware of the norms regulating armed conflict. The aim being that all nations must observe their obligations towards POWs at all times. Compliance with the Convention is not simply a matter of training officers and soldiers in IHL. Empirical evidence suggests that the intensity of training in humanitarian law and how it is taught makes a difference to battlefield conduct.[66]Many nations have proven that it is possible to provide adequate care and treatment for prisoners. The question is that are all States willing to provide adequate care and treatment for POWs? The civilian masters of the military as well as military commanders must always remember that they have a serious responsibility in protecting the rights of enemy soldiers taken as POWs.

66 In order to be effective and to induce behaviour compliant with the law, IHL must not be taught as an abstract and separate set of legal norms, but must be integrated into all regular military activity, training and instruction. Such integration should aim to inspire and influence the military culture and its underlying values, in order to ensure that legal considerations and principles of IHL are incorporated, as much as possible, into military doctrine and decision-making. The Roots of Behaviour in War, Geneva: ICRC, 2004.

Bibliography

Abraham Bryce, Bringing them all back home: Prisoner of war contact, recovery and reception units, 1944–45, *Australian War Memorial*, SVSS paper, 2015, pp. 33.

Alain Aeschlimann, Protection of detainees: ICRC action behind bars, *International Review of the Red Cross*, Volume 87, No. 857, March 2005, pp. 83-122.

Alexandra Kylie, Laws, War, and the People Caught in Between: The Legal Status of Guantanamo Bay Detainees during the Bush Administration and the Chance for Progressive Change Under the Obama Administration, *HOHONU*, Vol. 8, 2010, pp. 69-73.

Amanda McAllister, Cybernetic Enhancement of Soldiers: Conserving hors de combat Protections for Combatants under the Third Geneva Convention, *Jour of Law and Cyber Warfare*, Volume 7, No. 2, Fall 2019, pp. 67-100.

Archer Bernice, 2004, *The Internment of Western Civilians Under the Japanese 1941-1945*, London: Routledge Curzon, pp. 281.

Arnson Cynthia and Philippa Strum, Legal Standards and the Interrogation of Prisoners in the War on Terror, Woodrow Wilson International Centre for Scholars, Division of United States Studies Latin American Programme, Division of International Security Studies, 2007, pp. 71.

Bailey Jordyn, Arrival of the Fittest: German POWs in Ontario during the Second World War, Unpublished Thesis, University of Western Ontario, 2019, pp. 122.

Bakshi Lt Col K.N., 1989, *I was a Prisoner of War in China*, New Delhi: Lancer, pp. 75.

Banerjee S. S., The True Story of India's Decision to Release 93,000 Pakistani POWs After 1971 War, available at: https://thewire.in/history/the-untold-story-behind-indira-gandhis-decision-to-release-93000-pakistani-pows-after-the-bangladesh-war.

Bartov Omer (ed.), 2000, *The Holocaust: Origin, Implementation, Aftermath*, London: Routledge, pp. pp. 300.

Bass Gary J., Bargaining Away Justice: India, Pakistan, and the International Politics of Impunity for the Bangladesh Genocide, *International Security*, Vol. 41, No. 2 , Fall 2016, pp. 140–187.

Benard Cheryl, et al., 2011, *The Battle Behind the Wire: US Prisoner and Detainee Operations from World War II to Iraq*, RAND: National Defence Research University, pp. 102.

Blum Gabriella, The Dispensable Lives of Soldiers, *Journal of Legal Analysis*, Spring 2010, Vol. 2, No. 1, pp. 115-170.

Borhan Uddin Khan, Protection of Defenceless Persons in International Humanitarian Law, *The Dhaka University Studies*, Part-F Vol. XIII (1), June 2002, pp. 73-94.

Cao Jiahao, Memoirs of Wehrmacht Soldiers: From Survival to Victimhood, *Honours Papers*, 2020, pp. 76.

Captured Persons (CPERS), Joint Doctrine Publication 1-10. Ministry of Defence, UK, January 2015, pp. 437.

Case Concerning Trial of Pakistani Prisoners of War, *Pakistan v. India*, International Court of Justice, 1973, pp. 26.

Chang Karl S., Enemy Status and Military Detention in the War Against Al-Qaeda, *Texas International Law Journal*, Vol. 47(1), 2011, pp. 1-73.

Charmatz Jan P. and Wit Harold M., Repatriation of Prisoners of War and the 1949 Geneva Convention, *The Yale Law Journal*, Vol. 62, 1953, pp. 391-416.

Chaturvedi S.C., The Proposed Trial of Pakistani War Criminals, *Indian Journal of International Law*, Vol. 11, No. 4, October 1972, pp. 645–654.

Chesterman Simon and Lehnardt Chia (ed.), 2007, *From Mercenaries to Market: The rise and regulation of private military companies*, Oxford: Oxford University Press, pp. 287.

Chhina Rana, 2014, *Last Post: Indian War Memorials Around the World*, Centre for Armed Forces Historical Research, United Service Institution of India, Delhi, pp. 242.

Chopra Surabhi, The International Crimes Tribunal in Bangladesh: silencing fair comment, *Journal of Genocide Research*, Vol. 17, No. 2, 2015, pp. 211-220.

Commander's Guide to Biometrics in Afghanistan: Observations, Insight, and Lessons, Handbook, United States Publication No. 11-25, April 2011, pp. 89.

Communist Treatment of Prisoners of War, A Historical Survey, The Committee on the Judiciary, US Government, 1972, pp. 35.

Cox Andrew, Five Years as a Prisoner of War, *Canadian Military History*, Vol. 2, issue 1, 1993, pp. 115-122.

Craig A. Brannagan, The Copenhagen Process on the Handling of Detainees in International Military Operations: A Canadian Perspective on the Challenges and Goals of Humane Warfare, *Journal of Conflict & Sec. Laws*, Vol. 15, 2010, pp. 501-532.

Cronogue Graham, A new AUMF: Defining Combatant in the War on Terror, *Duke Journal of Comparative & International Law*, Vol. 22, 2012, pp. 377-406.

Custodis Johann, Employing the enemy: the contribution of German and Italian Prisoners of War to British agriculture during and after the Second World War, Agriculture History Review, Vol. 60, No. II, 2012, pp. 243-265.

Dalvi Brig J.P., 1969, Himalayan Blunder: The Curtain Raiser to the Sino-Indian War of 1962, Bombay: Thacker & Company Limited, pp. 506.

Davis, Gerald H., Prisoners of War in Twentieth-Century War Economics, *Journal of Contemporary History*, Vol. 12(4), 1997, pp. 623-34.

Deek Ashley S., Administrative Detention in Armed Conflict, Case W. Res. J. Int'l L., Vol. 40, Issue 3/4, 2009, pp. 403-436.

Dogra Chander Suta, 2020, *Missing in Action: The Prisoners, Who Never Came Back*, India: HarperCollins Publishers, pp. 339.

Detter Ingrid, The Law of War and Illegal Combatants, *The George Washington Law Review*, Vol. 75, 2007, pp. 1049-1104.

Dinnis Harrison Heather A., and Jann K. Kleffner, Soldier 2.0: Military Human Enhancement and International Law, *International Law Studies*, US Naval War College, Vol. 92, 2016, pp. 433-482.

Documents on Prisoners of War, 1979, *International Law Studies*, Vol. 60, pp. 892.

Dormann Knut, The legal situation of "unlawful/unprivileged combatants", *International Review of the Red Cross*, March 2003, Vol. 85, No. 849, pp. 45-74.

Dormann Knut, Detention in Non-International Armed Conflicts, *International Law Studies*, Vol. 88, pp. 347-366.

Douds G.J., The Men who never were: Indian Prisoners of WW I, *South Asia: Journal of South Asian Studies*, Vol. XXVII, No. 2, August 2004, pp. 183-216.

Elliott H Wayne, Hostages or Prisoners of War: War Crimes at Dinner, *Military Law Review*, Vol. 149, 1995, pp. 241-274.

Elsea Jennifer K., Treatment of "Battlefield Detainees" in the War on Terrorism, *CRS Report for Congress*, 23 January 2007, pp. 56.

Elsea Jennifer K., US Treatment of Prisoners in Iraq: Selected Legal Issues, *CRS Report for Congress*, 19 May 2005, pp. 28.

Elsea Jennifer K., Lawfulness of Interrogation Techniques under the Geneva Conventions, *CRS Report for Congress*, 8 September 2004, pp. 36.

Enforcing the Third Geneva Convention on the Humanitarian Treatment of Prisoners of War, *US Air Force Academy Journal of Legal Studies*, Vol. 7, 1997, pp. 459-467.

Esgain Albert J. and Waldemar A. Solf, The Geneva Convention Relative to the Treatment of Prisoners of War 1949: Its Principles, Innovations, and Deficiencies, *North Carolina Law Review*, Vol. 41, 1963, pp. 537-596.

Ethics Abandoned: Medical Professionalism and Detainee Abuse in the "War on Terror," A task Force Report funded by IMAP/OSF, USA, November 2013, pp. 268.

Evangelista Matthew and Nina Tannenwald, (ed.), 2017, *Do the Geneva Conventions Matter?* Oxford: Oxford University Press, pp. 362.

Finch Edward R., Forgotten Prisoners, *International Lawyer*, Vol. 5, No. 1, 1971, pp. 165-168.

Fischer Miles P., Applicability of the Geneva Conventions to "Armed Conflict" in the War on Terror, *Fordham International Law Journal*, Vol. 30, Issue 3, Article 4, 2006, pp. 509-534.

Fook Herbert C., 1924, *Prisoners of War*, Maryland: The J.W. Stowell Printing Co., pp. 450.

Forcese Craig, Prosecuting Kurt Meyer: The Abbaye d'Ardenne War Crimes Trial, 14 January 2020, pp. 39, available at: https://papers.ssrn.com/sol3/papers.cfm?abstract_id=3519427.

Frost Ryan, American prisoners of war in Vietnam tell their stories, Honours Thesis, University of Richmond, April 2005, pp. 56.

Garrett Richard, 1981, *POW*, London: David & Charles, pp. 240. .

Gagro Sandra Fabijanic, Defining and recognizing prisoners of war in contemporary armed conflicts, *International Journal of Social Sciences*, Vol. 3, No. 5, Special issue 2014, pp. 60-78.

Gebhardt James F., The Road to Abu Ghraib: US Army Detainee Doctrine and Experience, Global War on Terrorism Occasional Paper 6, Combat Studies Institute Press, Fort Leavenworth, Kansas, 2005, pp. 142.

Geiss Robin, Name, rank, date of birth, serial number and the right to remain silent, *International Review of the Red Cross*, Vol. 87, No. 860, December 2005, pp. 721-736.

Genovese Ann, Trish Luker and Kim Rubenstein (ed.), 2019, *The Court as Archives*, Australian National University Press, pp. 291.

George S Prugh, The Code of Conduct for the Armed Forces, *Columbia Law Review*, Vol. 56, No, 5, May 1956, pp 678-797.

Gilbert Adrian, 2006, *POW: Allied Prisoners in Europe 1939-1945*, John Murray, pp. 398.

Glod Stanley J. and Smith Lawrence J., Interrogation under the 1949 Prisoners of War Convention, *Military Law Review*, Vol. 21, July 1963, pp. 145–156.

Goodman Ryan, The Detention of Civilians in Armed Conflict, Editorial Comments, *The American Journal of International Law*, Vol. 103, 2009, pp. 48-73.

Goodman Ryan, Authorization versus Regulation of Detention in Non-International Armed Conflicts, *International Law Studies*, Vol. 91, 2015, pp. 155-170.

Graham David E., Repatriation of Prisoners of War During Hostilities - A Task Unsuited for the Private Citizenry, *International Lawyer*, Vol. 8, No. 4, 1974, pp. 832-868.

Guidelines for Investigating Deaths in Custody, Geneva: International Committee of the Red Cross, October 2003, pp. 36.

Hakimi, Monica, A Functional Approach to Targeting and Detention, *Mich L. Rev.* Vol. 110, No. 8, 2012, pp. 1365-1420.

Handbook on International Rules Governing Military Operations, Geneva: International Committee of the Red Cross, 2013, pp. 459.

Hartman Jacques, The Copenhagen Process: Principles and Guidelines, *Yearbook of International Humanitarian Law*, Vol. 16, 2013, pp. 1-31.

Holderness Clifford G. and Pontiff Jeffrey, Hierarchies and the Survival of POWs during WWII, 9 January 2012.

Horn Karen, Changing Attitudes among South African Prisoners of War towards their Italian Captors during World War II, 1942–1943, *Scientia Militaria*, Vol. 40, No, 3, 2012, pp. 200-221.

Hugo Grotius, 1625, *The Rights of War and Peace Including Law of Nature and of Nations, (1901 ed.)*, New York: M. Walter Dunne, pp. 315.

Hull Mark M., Military Law and Vigilant Justice in POW Camp during WW II, *Military Justice*, January-February 2020, pp. 100-107.

Hunger Strikes and the Practice of Force-Feeding, Physician for Human Rights, October 2013, pp. 6.

International Committee of the Red Cross, Reports on British Prison-camps in India and Burma, 1917, London: T Fisher Unwin Ltd., pp. 68.

Ishaq Nasser, Violating international legal obligations: Israel's treatment of Palestinian prisoners, Policy Department, Directorate-General for External Policies, European Parliament, March 2013, pp. 14.

Internment in Armed Conflict: Basic Rules and Challenges, International Committee of the Red Cross (ICRC), Opinion Paper, November 2014, pp. 14.

Jackson Ashley, 2006, The British Empire and the Second World War, London: Hambledon Continuum, pp. 604.

Jafa Dhirendra S., 2014, *Death wasn't Painful: Stories of India Fighter Pilots from the 1971 War*, New Delhi: Sage Publications India Pvt Ltd, pp. 247.

James Maclaren, The Last Secret of the 1971 India-Pakistan War, *The Diplomat*, 14 December 2018.

Jenks Chris and Eric Talbot Jensen, Indefinite Detention under the Laws of War, *Stanford Law and Policy Review*, Vol. 22, No. 1, 2011, pp. 41-91.

Jinks Derek, The Declining Significance of POW Status, *Harvard International Law Journal*, Vol. 45(2), June 2004, pp. 367-443.

Jinks Derek and David Sloss, Is President Bound by the Geneva Conventions, Chicago Public Law and Legal Theory Working Paper No. 61, July 2004, pp. 1-2.

Jonathan F. Vance, Men in Manacles: The Shackling of Prisoners of War, 1942–1943, *Journal of Military History*, Vol. 59, 1995, pp. 483–504.

Jones Edgar and Wessely Simon, British Prisoners-of-War: From Resilience to Psychological Vulnerability: Reality or Perception, *Twentieth Century British History*, Vol. 21, No. 2, 2010, pp. 163–183.

Joseph N. Pato and Lynette I. Millett (ed.), 2010, *Biometric Recognition: Challenges and Opportunities*, Washington DC: The National Academies Press, pp. 165.

Kant Vedica, 2014, *India and the First World War: If I die here, who will remember me?* New Delhi: Roli Books, pp. 255.

Koh Harold Hongju, Why Do Nations Obey International Law? *Yale Law Journal*, Vol. 106, No. 8, 1997, pp. 2599–2659.

Kowner Rotem (ed.), 2007, *The Impact of the Russo-Japanese War*, London: Routledge, pp. 348.

Kutner Luis, International Due Process for Prisoners Of War: The Need for a Special Tribunal of World Habeas Corpus, *U. Miami L. Rev.*, Vol. 21, No. 4, 1967, pp. 722-750.

Kyoichi Tachikawa, The Treatment of Prisoners of War by the Imperial Japanese Army and Navy Focusing on the Pacific War, *NIDS Security Reports*, pp. 45-90. S-28.

Law Reports of Trials of war Criminals, United Nations War Crimes Commission, Vol. XI, London: United Nations War Crimes Commission, 1949, pp. 123.

Lawson Konrad Mitchell, Wartime Atrocities and the Politics of Treason in the Ruins of the Japanese Empire, 1937-1953, Doctoral dissertation, Harvard University, pp. 404.

Lehmann Wady, Recollections Concerning Canadian War Crimes Investigations and Prosecutions, *Canadian Military History*, Volume 11, Number 4, Autumn 2002, pp. 71-80.

Lennon Chad, Detainees in the Global War on Terrorism Aboard Guantanamo Bay, *Turo Law Review*, Vol. 31, No. 4, 2015, pp. 1013-1042.

Levie Howard S., Prisoners of War Under 1977 Protocol I, *Akron Law Review*, Vol 23 (1), Summer 1989, pp. 55-72.

Levie H. S., Penal Sanctions for Maltreatment of Prisoners of War, *American Journal of International Law Series*, Vol. 56(2), pp. 433-468.

Levie Howard S., Prisoners of War in International Armed Conflict, *International Law Studies*, Vol. 59, 1977, pp. 529.

Linton Suzannah, Towards a Global Understanding of the Humane Treatment of Captured Enemy Fighters, *Frontiers of Law in China*, Vol. 12, No. 2, June 2017, pp. 217-277.

Lippold Matthias, Between Humanization and Humanitarization? Detention in Armed Conflicts and the European Convention on Human Rights, *Heidelberg Journal of International Law*, Vol. 76, 2016, pp. 53-96.

Mackenzie S. P., The Treatment of Prisoners of War in World War II, *The Journal of Modern History*, Vol. 66:3, 1994, pp. 487-520.

MacKenzie S.P., The Shackling Crisis: A Case-Study in the Dynamics of Prisoner-of-War Diplomacy in the Second World War, *The International History Review*, Vol. 17, No. 1, February 1995, pp. 78-98.

Madsen Chris, Victims of Circumstance: The Execution of German Deserters by Surrendered German Troops under Canadian Control in Amsterdam, May 1945, *Canadian Military History*, Vol. 2, No. 1, 1993, pp. 93-113.

Makepeace Clare, 2017, *Captives of War, British Prisoners of War in Europe in the Second World War*, Cambridge: Cambridge University Press, pp. 289.

Malpass Alan Patrick, British attitudes towards German prisoners of war and their treatment: 1939-48, Doctoral Thesis, Sheffield Hallam University Research Archive, 2016, pp. 221.

Mao Xiao, Are "Unlawful Combatants" Protected under International Humanitarian Law? *Amsterdam Law Forum*, Spring 2018, pp. 62-71.

Marquez-Grant Nicholas, et. al., Searching for the Missing Soldier: Identifying casualties from the First World War, *Metode Science Studies Journal*, University of Valencia., 2019, pp. 9.

May Larry, 2007, *War Crimes and Just War*, Cambridge: Cambridge University Press, pp. 343.

McDonald Neil and Sullivan Scott, Rational Interpretation in Irrational Times: The Third Geneva Convention and the "War on Terror," *Harvard International Law journal*, Vol. 44, 2003, pp. 301-315.

Mears Dwight S., Better Off as Prisoners of War: The Differential Standard of Protection for Military Internees in Switzerland during World War II, *Journal of the History of International Law* , Vol. 15, 2013, pp. 173–199.

Missing People, DNA Analysis and Identification of Human Remains: A guide to best practice in armed conflicts and other situations of armed violence, Geneva: International Committee of the Red Cross, 2009, pp. 49.

Mofidi, Manooher and Eckert, Amy E., Unlawful Combatants or Prisoners of War: The Law and Politics of Labels, *Cornell International Law Journal*, Vol. 36: Issue 1, 2003, pp. 60-92.

Montejo Victor, A study of prisoners of war in the twentieth century, Student Thesis, City University of New York (CUNY), pp. 50.

Moore Bob and Barbara Hately-Broad (ed.), 2005, Prisoners of War, Prisoners of Peace: Captivity, Homecoming and Memory in World War II, International Committee for the History of the Second World War, Oxford: BERG, pp. 270.

Moore, Bob, Enforced Diaspora: The Fate of Italian Prisoners of War during the Second World War, *War in History*, Vol. 22 (2), 2015, pp. 174 - 190.

Moore Bob and Kent Fedorowich, 2002, *The British Empire and its Italian Prisoners of War, 1940–1947*, New York: Palgrave Macmillan, pp. 329.

Morris Narrelle, "Accessing the Archives of the Australian War Crimes Trials after World War II," in Genovese Ann, Trish Luker and Kim Rubenstein (ed.), 2019, *The Court as Archives*, Australian National University Press, pp. 291, at pp. 145-166.

Moses A. Dirk, War Crimes/Genocide Trials for Pakistani Soldiers in Bangladesh, 1971–1974, pp. 258-279.

Murphy Mahon, Prisoners of War and Civilian Internees Captured by British and Dominion forces from the German Colonies during the

First World War, London School of Economics, Ph D Thesis, July 2014, pp. 230.

Mustafa Ghulam and Gill QasimShahzad, The Issue of Prisoners of War, 1971 and Recognition of Bangladesh, *International Jour of Business and Social Research*, Vol. 4, No. 3, March 2014, pp 114-118.

Myser Adrian T., The Archaeology of Reform at a German Prisoner of War Camp in a Canadian National Park during the Second World War (1943–1945), Ph D Thesis, Stanford University, May 2013, pp. 287.

Nachtigal Reinhard and Lena Radauer, Prisoners of War (Russian Empire), International Encyclopedia of the First World War, pp. 12.

Naqvi Yasmin, Doubtful Prisoner-of-war Status, *International Review of the Red Cross*, Vol. 84, No. 847, 2002, pp. 571-595.

Oswald Bruce 'Ossie' and Thomas Winkler, Copenhagen Process Principles and Guidelines on the Handling of Detainees in International Military Operations, *Insight*, Vol. 16, Issue 39, 26 December 2012, pp. 6.

Oswald Bruce 'Ossie', Some controversies of detention in multinational operations and the contributions of the Copenhagen Principles, *International Review of the Red Cross*, Vol. 95, No. 891/892, 2013, pp. 707–726.

Paschal Allen W., The Enemy in Colorado: German Prisoners of War, 1943-46, *The Colorado Magazine*, Vo. 56, No. 3 and 4, 1979, pp. 119-230.

Pato Joseph N. and Millett, Lynette I. (eds), *Biometric Recognition: Challenges and Opportunities*, National Research Council/National Academies Press, Washington, D.C., 2010.

Pearlman Adam R., Meaningful Review and Process Due: How Guantanamo Detention is Changing the Battlefield, *Harvard National Security Journal*, Vol. 6, 2015, pp. 255-298.

Pejic Jelena, Procedural principles and safeguards for internment/ administrative detention in armed conflict and other situations of violence, *International Review of the Red Cross*, Vol. 87, No. 858, June 2005, pp. 375-391.

Peter Raven-Hansen, Detaining Combatants by Law or by Order? The Rule of Lawmaking in the War on Terrorists, *Louisiana Law Review*, Vol. 64, 2004, pp. 831-850.

Petty Keith A., *Are You There, Geneva – It's Me, Guantanamo*, Case W. Res. J. Int'l L., Vol. 42, 2009, pp. 171-186.

Pirzada Sunniya Ahmad, My father, a prisoner of war in India, 16 May 2015, available at: https://www.aljazeera.com/indepth/features/2015/05/150513130813859.html.

Plaws Jacob, Bystanders, blackmailers, and perpetrators: Polish complicity during the Holocaust, Graduate Thesis and Dissertations, Iowa State University, 2011, pp. 90.

Poles Joseph H., From Koje-Do to Panmunjom: The Problem of Repatriation of Prisoners of War During the Korean Armistice Negotiations, Master's Thesis, Florida Atlantic University, May 1997, pp. 188.

Porter Thomas Earl, Hitler's Forgotten Genocides: The Fate of Soviet POWs, *Elon Law Review*, Vol. 5, 2013, pp. 359-388.

POW: The Fight Continues After the Battle, The Report of the Secretary of Defence's Advisory Committee on Prisoners of War, August 1955, pp. 82.

Rayle Crystal, Captives of Hell: The Treatment of Soviet Prisoners of War Captured by the Nazi Army 1941-1942, pp. 19, available at: https://his.uncg.edu/ghro/issues/issue_1/rayle_issue1.pdf.

Regan PM, Neglected Australians: POWs from Western From 1916 to 1918, Master's Thesis, University of New South Wales, Australia, 2005, pp. 229.

Report of the Inquiry into Recognition for Far East Prisoners of War who were Killed While Escaping or Following Recapture, Australian Government: Defence Honours and Awards Appeals Tribunal, 17 August 2017, pp. 247.

Riconda Harry P., 2003, *Prisoners of War in American Conflicts*, Oxford: The Scarecrow Press Inc., pp. 360.

Rock Adam, The American Way: The Influence of Race on the Treatment of Prisoners of War During World War Two, Thesis, University of Central Florida, 2014, pp. 97.

Roland Charles G., The Use of Medical Evidence in British Trials of Suspected Japanese War Criminals, *CBMH/BCHM*, Volume 27, No. 2, 2010, p. 385-402.

Rona Gabor, Is There a Way Out of the Non-International Armed Conflict Detention Dilemma? *International Law Studies*, Vol. 91, 2015, pp. 33-59.

Rose G. L., Detention of non-state actors engaged in hostilities: the future law – summary report, Australian Civil-Military Centre, 2012, pp. 18.

Rose Simon, Security detention in non-international armed conflicts - The view of the European Court of Human Rights, Thesis, Stockholm University, Spring 2016, pp. 101.

Roy Franziska, Indian Seamen in World War I Prison Camps in Germany, *South Asia Chronicle*, Vol. 5, 2015, pp. 63-91.

Roy Franziska, Heike Liebau and Ravi Ahuja (ed.), 2011, *When the War Began We Heard of Several Kings: South Asian Prisoners in World War I Germany*, New Delhi: Social Science Press, pp. 273.

Sadat Leila Nadya, A Presumption of Guilt: The Unlawful Enemy Combatant and the US War on Terror, *Denv J. Int'l L. & Pol'y*, Vol. 37(4), 2009, pp. 539-553.

Salunke S.P., 2014, *Pakistani POWs in India*, India (NOIDA): Vikas Publishing House Ltd Pvt Ltd., pp. 178.

Sari Aurel and Aughey Sean, Targeting and Detention in Non- International Armed Conflict: *Serdar Mohammed* and the Limits of Human Rights Convergence, 2015, *International Law Studies*, Vol. 91, 2015, pp. 61-118.

Scheipers Sibylle (ed.), 2010, *Prisoners in War*, Oxford: Oxford University Press, pp. 330.

Schmitt Michael N. and Green Lesie C., Prisoners of War and the Protecting Power, *American Journal of International Law*, Vol. 55, 1961, pp. 52.

Schmitt Michael N., 1998, Levie on the Law of War, *International Law Studies*, Vol. 70, 1998, pp. 515.

Schwarzkopf Matthew, The Second Mission: Canadian Survival in Hong Kong Prisoner-of-War Camps, 1941-1945, Master's Thesis, University of Ottawa, 2019, pp. 150.

Segal Julius, Hunter Edna J. and Segal Zelda, Universal Consequences of Captivity: Stress Reactions Among Divergent Populations of Prisoners of war and Their Families, Report No. 75-84, *Int. Soc. Sci. J.*, Vol. XXVIII, No. 3, 1976, pp. 593-612.

Segesser, Daniel Marc, The Punishment of War Crimes Committed against Prisoners of War, Deportees and Refugees during and after the First World War, *Immigrants & Minorities*, Vol. 26: 1-2 2008, pp. 134-56.

Shannon, Timothy J., French and Indian Cruelty? The Fate of the Oswego Prisoners of War: 1756-1758, *New York History*, Vol. 95, No. 3, Summer 2014, pp. 381-407.

Sinha Manoj Kumar, Hinduism and International humanitarian law, *International Review of the Red Cross*, Vol. 87, No. 858, June 2005, pp. 285-294.

Smiley Will, 2018, *From Slaves to Prisoners of War: Ottoman Empire, Russia, and International Law*, Oxford: Oxford University Press, pp. 267.

Sloan Alastair, India, Pakistan and the 1971 War POWs, *The Diplomat*, 01 August 2015.

Stark Tamas, Genocide or Genocidal Massacre? The Case of Hungarian Prisoners in Soviet Custody, *Human Rights Review*, April-June 2000, pp. 109-118.

State Responsibility for Non-State Actors that Detain in the Course of a NIAC, A Report of the Center for Global Legal Challenges, Centre for Global Legal Challenge, Yale Law School, 7 December 2015, p. 45.

Steuer, Kenneth, First World War Central Power Prison Camps, History Faculty Publications, Western Michigan University, 2013, pp. 40.

Sun Lu, Prisoners, Diplomats, and Saboteurs: An International History of the Diplomacy of Captivity During and Following the Korean War,

Ph D Dissertation, Graduate School of Vanderbilt University, 2017, pp. 199.

Surendra Chopra, Sino-Indian Border Conflict and the Treatment of Prisoners of War, *The Indian Journal of Political Science*, Vol. 29, No. 4, October-December 1968, pp. 369-385.

The Copenhagen Process on the Handling of Detainees in International Military Operations: Principles and Guidelines, 11 October 2007, pp. 25.

The US Department of Defence: Law of War Manual, June 2015 (updated December 2016). Officer of the General Counsel, Department of Defence, pp. 533-664.

Thomas Troy S., *Jihad's* Captives: Prisoners of War in Islam, Department of Defence, Washington DC, 2005, pp. 10.

Thompson, Sean Kevin, The Legality of the Use of Psychiatric Neuro-imaging in Intelligence Interrogation, *Cornell Law Review*, Vol. 90, September 2005, pp. 1601–1638.

Tilbury Alisha, "A Damaged Dangerous Act": New Zealand prisoners of war on the run in Europe during the Second World War, Master Thesis, Massey University, Albany, New Zealand, 2016, pp. 124.

Turns David, The Treatment of Detainees and the "Global War on Terror"; Selected Legal Issues, *International Law Series*, Vol. 84, pp. 199-221.

Urban Nicole, Handbook: Media professionals and armed conflict: Protection and responsibilities under International Humanitarian Law, British Red Cross, July 2017, pp. 129. USA: Human dignity denied: Torture and accountability in the 'war on terror', Amnesty International Report, AMR 51/145/2004 dated 27 October 2004, pp. 202.

Vance Jonathan (ed.), 2006, Encyclopedia of Prisoners of War, New York: Grey House Publishing Inc, pp. 754.

Vaughn Leisa, The German Hun in the Georgia Sun: German Prisoners of War in Georgia, Master's thesis, Georgia Southern University, 2016, pp. 125.

Watkin Kenneth, Warriors Without Rights? Combatants, Unprivileged Belligerents, and the Struggle Over Legitimacy, HPCR Occasional Paper Series, Harvard University, Winter 2005, pp. 75.

William E. S. Flory, 1942, *Prisoners of War: A Study in the Development of International Law* Washington, DC: American Council on Public Affairs, pp. 177.

Wylie Neville, Allied special forces and prisoner of war recovery operations in Europe, 1944-1945, *Journal of Military History*, Vol. 81 (2), 2017, pp. 469-489.

Wylie, N., and Crossland, J., The Korean War and the Post-war Prisoner of War Regime, 1945–1956, *War in History*, Vol. 23(4), pp. 439-456.

Wylie Neville, 2010, *Barbed Wire Diplomacy: Britain, Germany, and the Politics of Prisoners of war 1939-1945*, Oxford: Oxford University Press, pp. 312.

Wylie Neville and Lindsey Cameron, The Impact of World War I on the Law Governing the Treatment of Prisoners of War and the Making of a Humanitarian Subject, *The European Journal of International Law*, Vol. 29, No. 4, 2019, pp. 1327-1350.

Yoo John C., The Status of Soldiers and Terrorists under the Geneva Conventions, *Chinese J. Int'l L.*, Vol. 3, 2004, pp. 135-150.

Zamil Khalid M.Z., The Legal Status of Prisoners of War in Islamic Law: Assessment of its Compatibility with the 1949 Geneva Convention Relative to the Treatment of Prisoners of War, Ph D Thesis, University of Hull, August 2002, pp. 273.

Zillman Donald N., Prisoners in the Bangladesh War: Humanitarian Concerns and Political Demands, *International Lawyer*, Vol. 8, No.1, 1974, pp. 124-135.

Index

R

S

T

U

W

www.ingramcontent.com/pod-product-compliance
Lightning Source LLC
Chambersburg PA
CBHW051400240926
51852CB00002B/73
* 9 7 8 9 3 9 0 9 1 7 6 5 5 *